Behind the Curtain

Pamela Coutts

First published by Busybird Publishing 2020

Copyright © 2020 Pamela Coutts

ISBN
978-1-922465-22-1 (paperback)
978-1-922465-23-8 (ebook)

This work is copyright. Apart from any use permitted under the *Copyright Act 1968*, no part of this publication may be reproduced, stored in a retrieval system or transmitted in any form or by any means, electronic, mechanical, photocopying, recording or otherwise, without the prior written permission of Pamela Coutts.

Cover design: Busybird Publishing

Layout and typesetting: Busybird Publishing

Busybird Publishing
2/118 Para Road
Montmorency, Victoria
Australia 3094
www.busybird.com.au

In loving memory of my parents
Harold and Eileen Smith

Contents

The Early Years	1
Pitt-Draffen Dancing Academy	8
Pwllheli, Wales	13
The Windmill Theatre, London	18
Kensington Park Road	24
Bognor Regis, England	28
London Cabaret	36
The Audition	43
Amsterdam, Holland	49
Jersey, The Channel Isles	57
Scotland	62
Madrid, Spain	70
Spanish Tour	79
Monte Carlo	84
Paris Rehearsals	91
Barcelona, Spain	98
Returning to Madrid	103
Farewell Madrid	111
Home, Sweet Home	133
Lunel, France	142
Monty in Lunel	148
Geneva, Switzerland	154
Europe – Part One	163
Europe – Part Two	169
Europe – Part Three	174
Flying to Tokyo	182
Touring Japan	190
Asia	200
Returning to Europe	210
Kenya, Africa	219
Back to the Far East	228
Surviving in Hong Kong	237
Touring Solo	248
Burlesque in Melbourne	259
The Aftermath	267
Acknowledgments	272

The Early Years

Nothing in my family's ancestry suggested I'd become a dancer.

Life was tough in 1940s post-war England, living frugally in the market town of Kettering in the heart of the Midlands. The countryside was steeped in history, castle ruins, old manor houses and rolling hills. Edmund Street, where we lived, was narrow and bare without trees. Tight terraced houses and dark entries led to segregated backyards sporting long washing lines. Smoking chimney pots invited warmth. An odd dog roamed the streets and the Working Men's Windmill Club on the corner provided entertainment. The local fish and chip shop sold soggy chips for thruppence, with crispy batter pieces thrown on top.

Daddy cycled daily while hunting for a job, impossible to get in the lean years. He eventually succeeded working in a factory as a leather dresser, dying cow skins with toxic ingredients that stained his hands. Meanwhile, my mother worked full time in a shoe factory.

Renting an allotment at the edge of town, we had sacks of potatoes, peas and brussel sprouts brought home at weekends. Chickens in the backyard provided eggs and a roast meal for Christmas.

Family gatherings at my Aunt Rose's house were popular. Uncle Frank, who couldn't read a note of music, belted out jazz tunes on the piano, and everyone sang as a bird joined in the merriment, popping its head out of a clock every hour calling *'cuckoo, cuckoo.'*

In 1947 Daddy came home with a strange contraption. Bright lights flashed across a screen with people running across it. Daddy had bought the first nine inch television set in the street. Word spread amongst the neighbours like wild fire and they invited themselves in to see the new creation.

A beautiful lady appeared on the screen, gliding to soft music in a short, white dress. As she rose on her toes she appeared to grow taller and lose her feet. Margot Fonteyn was dancing as Aurora from *The Sleeping Beauty*.

'Daddy, Daddy!' I shrieked, my eyes glued to the screen. 'I know what I want to be! I want to be a fairy.'

Mummy would pull her hair out in despair with my constant pleas, tantrums and tugging at her skirt. 'Mummy, let me go to dancing class.' *Nag, nag, nag.*

My physique didn't quite meet ballet standards, though. I'd inherited Daddy's big hands and cumbersome large feet, with a glimpse of an instep and knobbly knees protruding from skinny, inward turned legs. Straight bodies, strong legs, high insteps and an inborn musicality were essential – but I was undeterred. At age four, everything is possible.

Cruel Mother Nature tormented us with bitter winters. Coal fires, cuddling hot water bottles, bottomless cups of boiled tea, scalding hot soup, snivelling noses and the dreaded flu! I suffered it all.

Cold permeated the thickest of clothing as breath turned into a misty haze. Icicles dangled from naked branches, with slush and snow on the roads as birds lay frozen in the gutters. The streets were colourless, with only white milk bottles dotting the grey pavements. Cycling to school, the cracked skin from my bare legs and frostbitten toes would ooze blood. Chilblains on my fingers became unbearable. I became sick easily.

Flu and the dreaded tonsillitis continued unabated until the doctor recommended an operation and dancing lessons to strengthen my weak legs. Patting my head, Mummy carried me to the hospital amongst squeals and howls of, 'Dance. Mummy. I want to be a dancer.' Sucking an ice cream to relieve a sore throat, I bounced up and down on the bed when she came to collect me. 'Dance. Mummy, you promised me,' I croaked as ice cream dribbled everywhere.

'Get well first darling,' she replied, kissing my forehead as she swept me into her arms.

'Please, please Mummy. Why can't we go now?'

'Next Saturday when you're well enough,' she replied softly. 'I promise you.'

She kept her promise. Next Saturday, wearing a new dress and clutching Mummy's hand tight we walked around the corner, past my primary school and the park into the unknown. The road continued up a long, steep hill lined with houses until we reached the town centre.

Frightened, I held Mummy's hand tighter as we saw huge buildings, cars, shops and big people. Turning into a large square we stopped outside a bank and passed the main doors, continuing to a smaller door on the left, with a sign on it saying 'Reg Civil Dancing School'. Mummy understood as I clambered up the wooden stairs, holding her hand tighter. I went rushing towards the music dragging Mummy along, eager to explore a new world.

Strange people came into view. Coats, scarfs and shoes were scattered everywhere. The front bay windows let the light in as a plump lady played the piano. A pole as high as my head stretched the length of the room and other kids were lounging on it. Pictures in black and white displayed dancers posing in fascinating costumes. Could I be one of them?

A lady with short, curly brown hair stood in the centre wearing large, dangling earrings and high heel shoes, with her feet turned outwards like a duck. She was instructing another little girl who looked like me to dance. The girl was an apparition of beauty. Her costume's bodice was white satin with wings attached to the back, and the short net skirt stuck out like they did in television shows. A sparkling tiara adorned her blonde curls as she waved a silver wand, casting a spell on me. Besotted, I listened as Duck Feet Lady instructed her to 'Step hop, step point, watch your arms and turn.' When the music finished, the girl curtsied and disappeared into a side room.

Duck Feet Lady approached us and Mummy introduced her to me as Miss Hale. I was so shy, I couldn't speak.

The lady clapped her hands and the kids screamed with delight, running around the floor. Mummy watched as I flung off my coat to join them, following the other girls and

Miss Hale's pleasant voice as she gave us instruction. We were birds, butterflies, bees and lambs, waving hands, pointing feet, hopping and clapped hands to the beat of the music.

After class, babbling parents surged like parrots towards Miss Hale to pay her before leaving with their budding ballerinas.

Mummy bought me some ballet slippers and would bring me to class on Saturday mornings. After a while, she grew tired of this onerous task and bribed my older brother with extra pocket money to take me instead. He hated it. Knowing how determined I was to go, though, Mummy decided I was old enough to take myself. Aged seven, I took my first steps towards a dancing career spanning two decades, leading me to far-away places and dancing for royalty.

One day Miss Hale told Mummy, 'She's going to be a lamb on stage in our Annual Display. You must make her costume.'

So Mummy set to work and made it on an old Singer sewing machine. Getting measured for the ugly costume with white ears and stubby tail was horrid. Fluffy material for the lamb's wool got scattered everywhere. Where was the sparkling fairy?

The day of the display finally came, and after endless classes of bobbing up and down, begging, and doing what lambs do, I felt confident.

The display was held at the Central Hall in the town centre. Mummy took me back stage. Passing older children dressed in colourful tutus by doting mums, she found our group, plastered my mouth with red lipstick and smothered my face in powder, making me sneeze.

On cue, Miss Hale led us to the stage as the pianist played our tune. Trotting onto the stage into glaring red and blue lights, I stared at a sea of cabbage faces and forgot what I was supposed to do as we ran around the stage. What do lambs do? They bah, sit and wait. I sat and peed in the ugly costume and waited. A strange woman picked me up and put me in Mummy's arms to take me home.

The next few years were uneventful until I was eight when Mummy made my first white tutu costume, and I was given a bicycle for Christmas. I'd go out exploring the town, buying ballet magazines with my pocket money and putting them into a scrap book.

Aged ten, Mummy introduced me to her friend who was interested in dancing. She belonged to a local Scottish band and introduced me to the dancing teacher. This warmed my feelings towards her and I learnt The Highland Fling and Sword Dance, spending memorable summer weekends performing at fetes and old people's homes.

Aged eleven, Mother, as I now called her, bought a house with a lovely garden on the other side of town. We'd escaped the poverty cycle and Father made me a ballet barre in my bedroom.

Ballet books became an obsession. Practising leg stretches and splits were painful. Pirouette turns made me dizzy and a pointed foot had to resemble half a cross. My ballet marks improved, but technique didn't exist.

Auditions were advertised for ballet pupils to apply for the Royal Ballet School in London. Miss Hale was blunt when I asked if I could try. 'You've got no physique or technique. You'll NEVER be a dancer.'

I rushed home crying and screaming inwardly. My whole world had crashed. Mother comforted me as I leapt onto her lap. Soothing and caring, she cuddled me while wiping away the tears. 'It's alright me duck. If you want to dance you will.'

My pathetic results at high school resulted in cooking scones becoming rocks. A pricked finger on the sewing machine rendered me a princess waiting to be awakened by a prince, and the woollen scarf I attempted to knit resembled Swiss cheese. Alone at lunch time playing records and dancing to my heart's delight, for a few precious moments I was a ballerina, a nymph and even an Egyptian Princess.

When I was thirteen Mother insisted I take tap classes. I found this disgusting, when ballet was in my heart. But Mother insisted, 'Me duck. Try it, me duck. Please try for me?' I gave it a go, and disbelief! I froze on the spot when they called my name for first place at the local Eisteddfod. I couldn't walk forward to accept the award. It was beyond my youthful dreams, but worse was to come. In tap exams I won the school shield twice, and Miss Hale looked at me with renewed interest.

One evening with a twinkle in his eyes Father declared, 'You're growing lemons.' Embarrassed, I retaliated by calling him 'Popsey' and didn't speak to him. The name stuck though as I was a teenager, and made us both laugh.

Late one night singing carols for pocket money to buy precious ballet books, I sang 'Ava Maria'. Tired, I was walking away when a housewife called out, 'Don't go. I love your voice. Come inside, I want to talk to you.'

Timid, I entered her living room where she had a piano. 'I want to give you free singing lessons once a week.' Gobsmacked, I rushed back to Mother, who was delighted I'd have a singing coach, which might stop me from being so talkative! She replied, 'Go back. I'll pay her two shillings a lesson.'

Nora trained me to breathe from the diaphragm, and after months of training she said, 'You're good enough to join the Amateur Kettering and District Theatrical Society. I'll arrange a singing and dancing audition for you.'

At the same time, Mother offered me an astonishing choice. 'Pass your exams and I'll send you to a dancing academy.' What an incentive – and in the summer term, I was top of the class.

Aged fourteen I was accepted into the Theatrical Society, where to my surprise Miss Denise Pitt-Draffen from Northampton was choreographing an amateur revival of the 1940's musical *Maritza*. The Pitt-Draffen Dancing Academy had entered pupils in every category in the Kettering Eisteddfod. They swept the board, winning gold medals and silver cups for outstanding solo and group performances. Their technique was flawless. Pointed toes, graceful arms and reaching out to the audience with their hearts beating in unison, they were stunning. Graceful in dark grey tutus with maroon headbands tied neatly around slick hair buns resembling cygnets, they never returned as they were lacking competition.

Ms Pitt-Draffen swept into the hall, dressed in a white blouse and grey skirt. In her mid-thirties with puffed up blonde curls enhancing an intelligent face, her eyes darted everywhere, noting every detail of the smorgasbord of young dancers in front of her. Spirited and enthusiastic, her routines were simple and effective. I adored her work and followed every direction she gave, struggling to point feet at all times, extend the leg further and hold my head in the right direction, praying she'd notice me. She did. After the last rehearsal I was overwhelmed when she asked if my parents could take me to Northampton to rehearse in her studio with her own dancers to perform for one night at the Kettering Wicksteed Park Pavilion. At her studio she asked Mother if I could join her school. Ash-faced in shock, I listened as Mother pleaded, 'Will she become a dancer?'

'She will if she starts ballet classes on Friday and boards next term.'

'But she's studying for her GCE exams.'

'She can start on Friday and board after her studies. Our fees are paid each term in advance.'

Popsey drove us home. I was shocked, unable to comprehend what had happened in the last half hour. 'Not good enough,' according to Miss Hale – yet Mother was giving me this wonderful chance to train with my idols.

After my last class with Miss Hale, I stuttered as I tried to give her her fee, 'I'm joining Pitt-Draffen next week.'

She stared at me in disbelief without uttering a word or wishing me well. Crying, I raced home on my bike to Mother.

'How did you go?' she asked fondly.

'Oh Mother, it was awful.'

'Don't let it bother you, Pamela. You'll get good training soon. Go and do your homework me duck.'

I grimaced. It was impossible. All I could think of was the impending ballet class in a new environment.

Pitt-Draffen Dancing Academy

On Friday night after school I ran to the town bus station clutching a new vanity case of practice clothes. Scrambling to the top of the green double decker green bus, I settled down to see the countryside as the bus travelled fifteen miles to Northampton. Alighting at the end of the main road, I walked the length of a smaller street lined with elegant houses and colourful gardens. On the corner a large, white building confronted me – the Pitt-Draffen Dancing Academy.

Inside, the walls were decorated in a delicate light green with lilac ceilings, a strong contrast to the harsh wooden hall I was used to. Two bars lined the side walls while a huge mirror covered the entire front, with no photographs or advertising to be seen. I never saw the larger studio upstairs until I boarded.

The babbling noise in the dressing room was incessant, yet no-one spoke to me. The Peggy Hale logo was still attached to my black leotard. With my hair twisted into a tight bun I followed them into the studio. The pianist played as the teacher took us through exercises, noting every mistake. Total dedication was required as we were pushed to the limit of our abilities, with legs extended in unison. Placed amongst the pupils I learnt a valuable lesson – the ability to dance on a postage stamp.

The classes on Friday nights continued for a year, with no dancing displays or competitions mentioned, and I hardly ever saw Miss Pitt-Draffen as she employed highly qualified teachers to train us.

At home on Sunday afternoons they showed old dancing films on TV, and in the evening we watched *Sunday Night at the*

London Palladium. The George Carden dancers paraded around the stage in exquisite jewelled costumes and my heart ached, longing to be one of them.

Boarding wasn't what I'd expected. It was so strict – and only a tiny, oblong room upstairs containing a bed, inbuilt wardrobe, a chair and a small window overlooking a side street. Aunty Bett, Denise Pitt-Daffern's mother, was a competent cook. Bed time was at 9 pm. Relishing the freedom of weekends at home, I went to the local dances and stayed up late.

The plusses were ballet, tap and Greek classes all day long, with ballroom and keep-fit at night. Aunty Bett realised ballet was my weak point and insisted I take the lower grade classes to improve technique, and elocution classes to improve the dreadful Kettering accent. *'Ent, kent, shent, wunt, ennagunna'* became 'isn't, can't, shan't, won't, and I'm not going to.'

One day Aunty Bett told me to come to the studio on a Sunday afternoon. Jo Cook, the lead dancer of The Silhouettes and appearing on the TV program *The Billy Cotton Band Show*, was returning from London to teach me routines for competitions. I was thrilled. Young and graceful with a warm, firm voice, she explained how to dance with your soul.

The Northampton and Banbury Festivals were getting closer when Aunty Bett realised my potential as a tap dancer. 'Can you get a grey jumper and slacks for next week?' Knitting furiously, Mother and I finished the jumper in time and I gained first place, a third for ballet, and won the coveted gold medal.

A catastrophe occurred. Pedantic about my feet in ballroom class, I refused to dance with a farmer with clod feet, scared he'd tread on my precious toes and ruin my career. Miss Pitt-Draffen burst into the studio in a rage, dragging me away to the other studio while screaming, 'How dare you do such a thing! No pupil of mine does that. I'll expel you.' She grabbed a stool and, placing it in front of the big mirror, pushed me onto it, shouting, 'Look at your precious feet as long as you want! My dancers work with everyone. I'll expel you.' She slammed the door as she left me alone in the studio.

After ten minutes, red faced with tears streaming down my face, I froze as the door opened. My older brother came in, looking splendid in his RAF uniform. Completely shattered and sure of expulsion, I blurted out between sobs, 'Did you know about this? Does Mother know?'

'No, I know nothing. I was in the area so thought I'd come to see you.'

'Promise me you'll say nothing.'

'I will.' Seeing how distressed I was, he left as Miss Pitt-Draffen came to the door, barking, 'Go to bed.' It was never mentioned again, and a valuable lesson learnt.

Pene, a brilliant student destined to join a ballet company, was not so lucky. She came to class with a big love bite on her neck and was threatened with expulsion. The following week the love bite was so massive it couldn't be camouflaged. She was never seen again. Boys? I didn't dare look at them.

One Saturday Popsey took me to the manor house in Kettering where you could read specialised magazines, and I discovered *The Stage* Magazine. It reported news on the latest shows and auditions for dancers. To dance for an audience was a dream, and if I could get a dancing contract Mother wouldn't have to pay for dancing fees. How long would it be before she could escape the drudgery of factory work?

A week later in March 1961 adverts appeared for dancers to audition for the Tiller Girls summer seasons and The Marie de Vere Dancers for the Butlin holiday camps on the same day at different times. I approached Aunty Bett, asking if I could audition for the Tiller Girls. She'd expected me to continue training for two years, but agreed I could try. Jo lent me a smart grey suit.

On a sunny Saturday morning, Popsey drove me to the bus station. Exploding with excitement, I boarded the bus with a vanity case full of rehearsal clothes and shoes. It was an exhausting journey, passing through villages, the main town of Bedford and onto the new M1 motorway.

Arriving early in London, there was time to reach the first audition at the Max River Rehearsal Studios. I found it after traipsing around dark, pokey alleyways and main streets located off Shaftsbury Avenue. The dancing was difficult and I learnt a short routine, including high kicks, with several girls for the audition.

'You're too short,' they announced. 'Try for pantomime work in September.'

The second audition was held in a smaller room. A pleasant looking, middle-aged woman sat in front of a wooden desk as five girls waited to audition separately. We performed our own routines in modern, pointe ballet, tap and the splits.

The same story. 'No,' she said, 'you're too young. I'll give you work at a later date.' Failed again.

Disillusioned, I returned to the dressing room and listened as another girl who'd completed her audition was asked, 'How old are you, my dear?'

'I'll be seventeen in May.'

'All right my dear, come and sign a contract for Filey.'

I couldn't help myself. Standing in the doorway of the dressing room, I yelled out, 'But mine is in June.'

The woman looked up and smiled. 'Alright my dear, come and sign a contract for Pwllheli.' My parents were ecstatic.

The Marie de Vere Dancers had appeared in the 1951 Royal Command Performance. Thrilled and light headed with success, it was hard for me to believe I was going to become professional and live my dream, aged sixteen.

The Actors Equity contract said I'd receive eight pounds a week with five pounds for rehearsals, and twelve hours of Redcoat duty to pay for board and food. Cancelling the contract would incur a huge fine. Popsey was tickled pink. His pay was a mere five pounds.

The weeks dragged by as classes continued. One day Aunty Bett took me aside to her garden, off limits to pupils and parents. She took my photograph amongst a mass of green ferns and coloured flowers. 'Never wear cheap jewellery,' she insisted. Her word was gospel and to please her was a miracle. When she remarked, 'You'll make a good wife for someone,' it confused me. After Pene's expulsion, the opposite sex was untouchable.

A postcard arrived stating rehearsals would commence in two weeks and a flurry of activity followed. I booked into the Girl's Theatre Hostel in Soho, London, and bought a suitcase. A special gift from my parents was a blue, tin make-up box. It lasted for years, although the suitcase was soon in tatters.

Popsey drove me to the bus station with our dog. I boarded the coach with an overloaded suitcase, excited. Seated at the window, I waved a loving, frantic goodbye as two pairs of eyes glared up at me. Eager and enthusiastic, how was I to know this was the beginning of many journeys and I'd never return to live permanently in Kettering again?

Pwllheli, Wales

The hostel in the middle of Soho was big and sparsely decorated, with a lonely piano standing in the corner of the lounge. Mrs Bell, our warm, chubby, middle-aged warden, welcomed me. The hard bed in the dormitory and the excitement at attending my first day of rehearsals in the morning made sleep impossible.

In the morning I caught the Metro and arrived early. The hall was crowded with girls and the Pwllheli group were ordered to go to the small room. The girls were excellent dancers. Several of them had previously worked for Mrs de Vere. Confusion swept over me as I'd expected to start rehearsals with a few barre exercises. Twenty minutes later it dawned on me it was a high precision military routine. My spine shivered each time the head girl looked my way. What was it this time? Wrong arm or foot? After a bad start I focused and learnt fast.

During the ten minute break I chatted with Maureen, who was staying in the hostel. In the afternoon we learnt another routine but I was worried about the steps I couldn't remember from the military routine. Maureen explained, 'We'll rehearse again at Butlins.' What a relief, although my body reeked of sweat and my limbs were almost at bursting point from exhaustion. Youth has a strange way of recovering quickly and we returned to the hostel for dinner. In two weeks we learnt seventeen routines, but the aching limbs didn't stop us seeing a couple of musicals at night in the West End, the theatre land of London.

In the second week rehearsals moved to a church hall in Belsize Park, North London. It required rising at the crack of dawn. Gladys Morgan was an old musical comedy star from the 40s and the comic Norman Caley, seeing how tired and young I was, gave me vitamin C tablets.

After costume and shoe fittings we boarded the train for the journey to Wales. Assistant choreographer Helen and wardrobe mistress Caroline were to be with us for two weeks to check the shows were running smoothly. During the journey I sat wide eyed, listening to them discuss gambling and show business.

Soon the scenery changed as high mountains towered over the tracks while vast stretches of sand and sea could be seen from the opposite window. We reached the camp in the early evening and dumped our suitcases on the ground as two robust, cheeky guys hugged Maureen. Boarding the camp bus we were taken to the annex for a meal and I was welcomed to the 1961 summer season at Butlins in Pwllheli.

The town was located in the North Western tip of Wales four miles away from the camp. It closed in 1998 and has become a holiday park today. Sir Billy Butlin had seven of them in Britain, but his empire was taken over by the Rank Organisation when cheap overseas holidays were introduced. His slogan 'A Week's Holiday for a Week's Pay' included three meals and entertainment and attracted the masses. Camps were famous for family games and loud tannoy wake-up calls with messages advertising events throughout the day. Each camp had heated indoor and outdoor swimming pools, games areas, ballrooms and theatres. The Pig and Whistle bars were alive at night with boozy singing and the equivalent today would be a holiday on a cruise ship. Dressed in the smart, redcoat uniform of white blouses, pleated skirts and bright red blazers, we felt special and signed many autographs. Previous Redcoats who later became famous were Benny Hill, Des O'Connor and Cliff Richard.

At a local aerodrome outside the camp, four of us had publicity shots taken in front of a plane in our bikinis, and the pilot offered us a free flight. The others declined. I never forgot the thrill and rush of adrenalin as the Cessna 172 took off and landed, along with the aerial view of the camp, miniature houses and paddocks.

Rehearsing all day at the theatre on Friday, we prepared to perform for the campers who arrived in droves the next day, springing the camp into life as the miniature train chuffed merrily to the beach and back. The shows lasted an hour and were presented twice nightly on Tuesdays and Thursdays.

A long bench lined the dressing room with a large mirror placed along the wall. Under it we kept shoes and stockings, and the racks behind held the costumes. My make-up box was full of Leichner greasepaint, powder, lipstick, false eyelashes and cleansing cream. During the dress rehearsal we discovered a quick change was necessary for the Can-can. With frantic pleas of, 'Fasten me up,' heads disappeared among a tangle of costumes. Shoes were thrown everywhere, but Caroline's expertise ensured we arrived on stage for the first beat of the music. We'd changed into wigs, hats, stockings, garters, panties, shoes, chokers, gloves, petticoats and dresses in Olympic time. Simple comical routines such as 'Gotta Wear a Hat' made the audience laugh as we turned our backs to reveal a fancy hat attached to our bottoms. The Can-can and kicking routines were strenuous but clever Caroline kept a close eye on each costume, cleaning and repairing them instantly. The tap routine danced to the music of 'Poet and Peasant Overture', received rave reviews and dressed in glamourous feathered costumes to introduce the stars the audience was introduced to a fantasy world.

It started with a titter in the front row, then a giggle and raucous laughter spread throughout the theatre. Buster, the head girl, glared at us from the end of the line, shouting, 'Keep kicking.' We struggled, thinking the routine would never end. Landing in a heap in the wings, we found the culprit. A lapel had come away from a dancer's costume and was dangling between her thighs, bobbing up and down with every kick.

Red-headed Sue with a photographic smile was attractive, although elegant Linda was caring. Glamour pusses Iris and Wendy were full of boy talk and Margaret the fibber we never believed. Lanky Annie and I often sunbaked together in front of our chalet and she taught me how to sizzle with a home-made lotion of cooking oil and vinegar. Buster the head girl was heavily built, tall and respected. Nothing escaped her attention.

My seventeenth birthday arrived and the girls held a surprise party with scrumptious nibbles. I laughed so much I chipped a front tooth on the table. It was soon fixed in time for the show, then I sprained an ankle, always a hazard for dancers.

As for boys, I listened intently to conversations about these fascinating creatures. Perhaps because of my youth and enthusiasm, the Public Relations Officer took me to see the film *Annie Get Your Gun*.

One day a pang of restlessness surged within me. Tired of eating eggs and greasy chips after the show and sleeping on a bunk bed, I felt an enormous pressure to return home. Homesickness had set in and there was no-one to confide in. What could I do?

Now I was earning money, I decided to invite Mother for a short holiday. A weekend later she arrived with Popsey. She loved the shows and my life returned to normal.

At home Mother played the Ouija board, thinking she possessed psychic powers. She took me to see a clairvoyant who resided outside the camp. The gypsy woman looked at my fingers tips, stating, 'You are artistic.' Rolling her crystal ball several times she looked into my brown eyes, predicting, 'I see many bottles of champagne, but no marriage.' I laughed as I rarely drank, and Mother must have told her I was a dancer.

Before they left, Mother confronted me. 'Are you coming home after the season?'

'Oh no, I'm going to London to find another dancing job.'

'You can go if you save your money.'

What was this? I thought I was free. Deciding to say nothing I meekly agreed, but saved half the amount she suggested.

Pwllheli is close to Liverpool, and teenagers came to let their hair down and dance to the Rory Storm skiffle group, with a young Ringo Starr beating the drums. One afternoon they invited Margaret and I to listen to a jam session in their chalet. For two hours they played with Ringo bashing his drums and we left with the music pounding our eardrums. Margaret rushed to the girls, yelling, 'I'm going to marry Alan from the skiffle group,' but no-one believed her fancy talk.

As the season was closing, the cooks held a barbecue on the beach for the entire staff. Exhausted campers were tucked up in their beds as the cooks came with trays of meat and lit a big bonfire. It was a great party and we ate, drank and danced until the wee hours of the morning. We'd lived and danced together for five months. Packing up the costumes was depressing and I was miserable leaving the girls and friends I'd made, wondering if I'd ever see them again.

Neil a tall, slim, blonde haired redcoat approached me, 'Are you going home after the season?'

'No, I'm going to London to find another job.'

'If you like I can give you a lift and show you the sights of Cardiff for a couple of days?' he offered. 'It's on the way to London.'

I decided to trust him, and was pleased that I did. We drove through high mountains dotted with quaint villages and reached Cardiff at dusk. My room was pleasant with a soft bed and Neil invited me to dinner in a quaint, local Welsh restaurant.

Cardiff Bay was breathtaking, with the 2,000 year old castle situated in the heart of the city. I stared in awe at the opulent interior with murals and stain glass windows.

At the station Neil bid me farewell, declaring, 'You're brave to venture to London alone.' I felt like Dick Whittington as the train sped out of Cardiff towards London, wondering what new adventures fate had in store for me.

The Windmill Theatre, London

As the train chuffed into London, jubilation swept over me. Grabbing the heavy suitcase I stopped. Monkey arms were growing and with the vanity case perched on my shoulder I attempted to skip to the underground station. At the hostel Miss Bell was delighted to see me again and asked, 'Where are you going to dance this time?'

'I don't have a job, I've come to London to find one.'

'Look in *The Stage* Magazine, my dear,' she suggested. 'If you can't find one try the Windmill Theatre.'

Thrusting the magazine into my hands, she directed me upstairs to another hard bed. There was an audition for dancers for a nightclub on Wednesday. Good news.

Exploring major icons and roaming through pebbled streets and markets was exhilarating. Massive crowds queuing for cinema tickets and the dazzling lights of the West End sent me into a trance. I was unsuccessful at the audition. It was the same old story – too short.

Tired and miserable, I walked through a market and asked a stranger if he knew where the Windmill Theatre was. He glared at me and in language I hardly understood replied, 'Go dewn the lane missy un turn roit.'

The Windmill Theatre, London

The Windmill Theatre's history is interesting. A windmill stood on the site and in 1909 a cinema showed silent films. Laura Henderson purchased it in 1930, transforming it from a picture theatre and renaming it The Windmill Theatre. 'Revuedeville' commenced in 1932, running for several years at a loss.

During World War Two, the theatre remained open at the height of the blitz. 'We Never Closed,' or humorously, 'We Never Clothed,' became the theatre's famous motto. Inspired by the Follies Bergere and Moulin Rouge in Paris, the manager Vivian Van Damm introduced motionless nude poses, known as living statues, convincing the Lord Chamberlain it wasn't obscene. The shows were a huge commercial success and toured provincial theatres. London theatres copied Van Damm's format, reducing patronage at the Windmill. Mrs Henderson left the theatre to Mr Van Damm, who ran the shows successfully until his death in 1960. His daughter Sheila Van Damm struggled to keep it going when seedy nightclubs and strip clubs opened and the Windmill closed as a theatre in 1964.

The film *Mrs Henderson Presents* gives an accurate picture of life as it was at the theatre and brought back wonderful memories. When I worked there, Kenneth Bandy was the Press Representative, Ben Stiller the doorman, and Keith Lester the chief choreographer was responsible for the legendary fan dance. Other famous artists who 'trod the boards' were Jimmy Edwards, Harry Secombe, Bruce Forsythe, and George Carden.

His directions were correct and I found it in a side street off Piccadilly Circus. Gigantic posters at the side advertised a non-stop revue, highlighting the comic star Jimmy Edmundson underneath the caption 'We Never Closed'. The front entrance was shut, but on either side were black and white photographs of dancers, scantily clad with a nude girl posing in the centre.

Stunned and confused, I hesitated. This wasn't what I'd expected. What now? Take a chance or go home? Looking a second time, I noticed trained dancers and elaborate scenery. Relief! No strip club. Taking deep breaths I walked around the corner to the stage door.

An elderly man with darting eyes stood inside the doorway. With years of experience, Ben Stiller deterred anyone from entering without his permission. Clutching my vanity case, I asked him for an audition and, noting my youth, he reached for the telephone. 'Go upstairs. Someone will see you.'

I wasn't the first seventeen year old girl to approach the Windmill alone. Heart pounding, I clambered up the narrow, iron spiral staircase over three floors high.

It led to a large rehearsal room without mirrors, with a canteen at the back. A rehearsal was in progress and girls were being whipped behind a gauze screen, directed by a portly, middle-aged man shouting commands. Seeing me, he told them to take a break and they disappeared as flies do.

'The dressing room is there. Go and change,' choreographer Keith Leister ordered. 'Perform a few steps.'

My nerves were frazzled. Dancing the best that my muscles could muster, my confidence grew.

'Change into your tap shoes,' Mr Lester then demanded. 'Put on your pointe shoes. Kick high.' It was the most thorough audition I'd experienced, including ballet, tap, modern, pirouettes, kicks and splits.

Mr Lester smiled, his decision made. 'Go change, and come to my office to sign your contract.'

It lay on the desk, signed by the entrepreneur Sheila Van Damm. As Mr Lester explained the terms, he scrutinised my face for signs of nervousness. In the first revue I wouldn't be asked to pose in the nude, but later if asked I'd agree or leave the show. An attempted smile surfaced while I signed on the dotted line. No nudity in the first show. Performances were five shows a day, three times a week, with each revue lasting seven weeks. Rehearsals were on alternate days and the pay thirteen pounds a week.

My stage name was changed to Petra Kennedy and rehearsals commenced on Monday. The show ran non-stop six days a week using two companies A and B. Dancers learnt two roles in each number, alternating them according to the weekly schedule. I'd only been out of work for a few days. How lucky.

Sprinting to a phone box, I called Mother. 'What?' she gasped. 'How wonderful.' I would've loved to have seen Popsey's face when she told him the news. He must've visited the Windmill during the war years.

Needing accommodation to get away from the hostel, I approached an estate agent. He had a room in Notting Hill Gate not far from the West End, the heart of theatre land – at the end of Kensington Park Road, on the fifth floor of an elegant white building. It was a simple bedsitter, with single bed and a gas cooker and sink to complete the furnishings. The window didn't open and the communal bathroom was on the floor below. A metered gas heater gobbled up sixpenny coins. Happy with a roof over my head, I found a grocery store, bought food and cheap pots and pans, and settled in.

Delighted with freedom I decorated the bedsitter with Spanish posters of bulls and toreadors. The mystique of Spain had always captivated me.

Busy with rehearsals and shows at the Windmill left no time for loneliness to creep in. I bought a record player, modern jazz records and often walked down to Portobello Market on a Sunday or travelled to Kettering to spend a few hours at home.

Happiness was shattered when two young ruffians moved into a bedsitter opposite mine. They rather intimidated me – laughing and sniggering in whispers behind my back. Aged seventeen and far from home, I was petrified when they knocked on my door consistently asking for tea or coffee, and I thrust the goods at them through half an open door. Several days later when I didn't respond, they taunted me, yelling, 'Lady, come and talk to us, we can party together,' while thumping wildly on my door. It left me frightened, and after the continual harassment my private world had disintegrated with no one to turn to. I was innocent and knew little of the opposite sex. I'd heard of rape and young girls becoming victims. Petrified, I grabbed my coat and rushed out into the darkness as tears mingled with the rain.

At the local snack bar, between sniffles I blurted out my fears to the shop keeper, asking if he knew of other accommodation. Behind me a tall, robust man wearing a tweed hat replied, 'I do. It's just a few doors away. I'll take you there,' and I followed him with caution.

We came to a house close by and he knocked on the door. A middle-aged lady with short, grey, half curled hair, humped shoulders and inquisitive eyes opened the door. The man, known later as Alex, explained the situation. She replied in a gentle, tinny voice, 'I've got an attic flat costing three guineas a week, which needs vacuuming.'

Struggling with a suitcase, record player and pots and pans up six flights of stairs was not easy. Living out of home was a breeze, living in a cosy flat on the sixth floor. Dark red velvet curtains covered the window with a matching bedspread. The table, chairs and mirror were adequate. On the right a fixed ladder led to the kitchenette in a cubby hole. There was no gas meter and a communal bathroom one floor below was easy to get to. No room to display the Spanish posters, but a safe living environment. I unpacked and vacuumed the flat and stairs and the landlady was happy.

A month later I invited several of the girls for dinner. The same day my brother phoned – a rare occurrence. He came looking smart in his RAF uniform and insisted on wearing an apron to cook the steaks. They all loved the flat, and my brother reveled in his new role cooking a meal for the Windmill girls.

The girls were pleasant and several of them considered the Windmill their home. It was exhausting with non-stop shows and rehearsals. One day I was late. Glaring at me with blazing eyes, Mr Lester bellowed, 'If you're late again, it's instant dismissal.' Waking up late again, horrified, I powdered my face with talcum powder and told them I felt sick. They were kind and allowed me to rest. Relieved, I rehearsed as normal and bought a large alarm clock on the way home.

We shared costumes, although personal starlet sequined pasties were used for spectacular numbers. Routines were lively burlesque or classical, and tastefully presented. My favourite numbers were the Can-can, Charleston, and Spanish dances. The *Fleet Street*, *Hareem* and *Chicago* production numbers were mini musicals which included dialogue, singing and dancing with original musical scores and were always successful. Two sets of glass panels with coloured lights flashed upwards at the front of the small stage, and combined with stage lighting and spotlights they created a dazzling tableaux. When a production number finished, stage hands rushed out and clothed the nude girl in long, dark wraps, and the audience was never allowed to leave the theatre until the safety curtain was lowered. Often men loitered around the stage door hoping to catch a glimpse of us if we popped out for a coffee, but they never got past Mr Stiller.

The fan dance required four girls passing a nude girl between them using enormous, heavy, ostrich fans. Few steps were required so we learnt the number on stage. 'Don't drop the fan, Petra,' Mr Lester yelled from the stalls as I felt an unbearable pain in my hands and wrists. I revelled in the role of a Honky Tonk girl speaking in a broad American accent, with sassy dancing choreographed by a South American.

In the 'Sheik' scenario I wore starlets, a long, extravagant skirt and a three feet high head dress. In spite of hundreds of hairgrips it still balanced precariously on my head and pulled out numerous hairs. A slight tilt of the head and it would crash. I would elegantly walk to centre stage to meet Jenny and we parted, posing at either side of the stage. Jimmy Edmundson, the comic, tried to make us laugh, pulling weird faces and gags. Keeping a straight face was almost impossible and the challenge was rewarding. The audience adored it.

My parents came to see the show, bringing three car loads of family with them. I had a few minutes to spare between shows and popped outside to see them. Mother laughed and pointed at my photo. 'Look at you, a Windmill Girl and now Miss Fleet Street.' I was wearing a costume covered in imitation newspapers.

Revue No 325 heralded 30 years of 'Revuedeville' at the Windmill. To my surprise, a photo of several of us in Charleston costumes, posing in a line with Mrs Shufflewick, a star of the TV show *Coronation Street*, was published in *The Stage* newspaper.

Sheila van Damm was rarely seen and one day a list for the new show was put on the board, including a solo Spanish dance. My name wasn't there and I longed to do it. Taking a deep breathe I went to her office. She was interested and said, 'You can perform it in the fifth show at night.'

Alas, tit for tat, my name was there for 'nude' for the next revue. In despair I didn't know what to do. The show and lifestyle were perfect and I could stay there for years. The temptation was over powering. No, I just couldn't do it. It was March and summer seasons were starting soon. When I told them my decision I was in shock as they banished me immediately, without time to say goodbye to the girls. Dejected, heartbroken and crying I rushed out of the theatre, not knowing what to do next.

Kensington Park Road

I loved Notting Hill Gate. Redeveloped in the 50s, it bristled with cosmopolitan life. There was a busy intersection, blocks of modern flats, office buildings, cafés, restaurants, supermarkets, record and book shops, a cinema and an old Christian church on the corner. The subway services from the Metro station covered most of London and iconic red buses ran frequently. Kensington Park Road branched to the left and Portobello Road ran parallel to it with antique shops and the famous market. On Saturdays the market leapt into life with colorful bohemian characters, musicians and gypsies meandering through bric-a-brac stores in chaos. Towards the end of the market at Westbourne Grove was a dangerous area to visit, with decrepit buildings and rubbish scattered everywhere.

At my new accommodation, the hive of activity on the ground floor intrigued me, with people carrying unusual costumes back and forth. Curious, one afternoon I opened the door and took a quick look. Joan, the landlady, caught me spying and invited me in. Wide eyed, I saw elegant dark blue velvet curtains cascading down the large bay window. There was a settee by a wall and on the other side several framed, faded photos of theatre productions from the 1930s surrounded a full length mirror. The small curtain draped across one corner to serve as a makeshift dressing room. Stacks of old theatrical magazines were perched on a stool and there was a small table and chairs by the window. Costumes of all descriptions hung around the walls as old ladies sat in the middle, squawking like hens as they sewed in time to soft music from a radio.

A small black and white TV sat on a chest of drawers close to a door on the left, which led into a huge room. Inside, sturdy racks held thousands of costumes. A cupboard as high as the ceiling overflowed with pretty bonnets and hats, and a double chest of drawers had compartments bursting to capacity with cottons, ribbons and laces, and tights of all colours and sizes. At the far end was a large table for cutting out costumes with scraps of material everywhere. A tailor's dummy, an ironing board with a continually hot iron, and two sewing machines completed the wardrobe. Large glass doors opened onto a spacious lawn where Rina, a dachshund pup, was chasing a fly.

Returning to the front room, Joan sat me down and introduced me to Esme, Margaret and Gwen, who in their youth had starred in West End theatre productions. She brought out a circular satin skirt for me to hem, an impossible job for a beginner. Mortified, I glared and picked up a needle and thread. Inadvertently, I'd begun a sewing apprenticeship at the Joan Luxton Theatrical Costumiers. 'Tie three knots at the end of the cotton', 'Wear a thimble on your finger', 'No, don't rip the cotton with your teeth you'll break them', 'Don't put pins in your mouth, they'll rust,' they squawked, and after several clumsy attempts I found it became easier. Machining was shoddier and crooked lines and material bunched up, resulting in knots. Joanie, as I now called her, didn't blink an eyelid, showing me what to do and allowing me to progress at my own pace. It was a challenge and I often popped into the wardrobe as I became more absorbed in this fascinating new world.

Joanie's history is amazing. She emigrated from Sydney to London with her parents as a young woman. An accomplished dancer and actress, her business, The Children's Theatre Company, appeared on the inaugural BBC Television programs in 1937, which gave her many theatrical contacts. Complete sets of costumes for amateur productions were cleaned, checked for rips and stains and sent throughout England. New outfits and uniforms were made to order, and in busy times Alex, acting as a manager arrived to help us pack up the costumes. Frank kept the books up to date in the office upstairs, although over the years the business lost money. Joanie was over fastidious hiring out a costume. If it wasn't perfect in every detail, irrespective of time or money, it wasn't allowed to leave the premises. Customers waited as we sewed minute details to a bonnet or sleeve. When Joanie decided it was good enough it was sent out.

Mortgages forced her to sell the house, with the provision that the business, along with ground and basement floors, were hers until her demise. I always returned to Joanie's between contracts, sleeping on the couch and worked as her girl Friday for a few pounds and meals. It was a wonderful opportunity to learn the intricate facets of sewing costumes and a great friendship flourished between us. In the 60s she was like a second mother to me as I struggled between contracts to find work. We'd sit up late at night sewing and discussing the politics of the day or playing word games.

In the late 60s a tall, flamboyant middle-aged man swept into the wardrobe declaring, 'I'll show you how to make an Edwardian costume in two hours.' Grabbing the tailor's dummy, he draped brocade material around it with precision, cutting, pinning and machining a masterpiece. We applauded him. Richard Cattermole was a talented costumier and had designed the costumes for the show *Camelot*. He was also making 300 Balaclava helmets for the film *Dr Zhivago*.

One day Joanie asked me, 'Have you seen the film *The Red Shoes*?'

'No, I haven't.'

'Every dancer should see it. They filmed some scenes in the church on the corner of our road. It's playing in Chelsea at the moment. Why don't you go and see it?'

I returned mesmerised with the dancing of Moira Shearer and the delightful story by Hans Christian Anderson. The scenery in Monte Carlo was overwhelming and I vowed to work there in the future if I could. I also paid closer attention to the church on the corner. The building next to it housed the famous Marie Rambert Ballet School, and sometimes I'd order a cheap curry in the restaurant opposite to watch the pupils arrive for their classes, wondering where they'd be in a few years' time.

One day Joanie dressed me in an authentic Elizabethan costume, complete with neck ruff, pinafore petticoat and bonnet. I frolicked around the wardrobe pretending to be Ann Boleyn, with Frank attired as Henry VIII. A photo was taken in the garden, which was published in the Kensington Post to advertise the company.

After a while Mother asked me, 'Why do you stay in London between contracts and don't come home?'

'Please understand Mother. I have to stay in London for auditions and sew for Joanie for meals and pocket money.'

Reluctant, Mother accepted my explanation. She was missing her daughter.

Bognor Regis, England

Life was bliss and I was happy living in my attic flat with Joanie as my landlady. But my sudden sacking from the Windmill left me devastated. My world had turned upside down and I fled from the theatre.

Unaware of people or traffic, I found my way back to Notting Hill Gate. Avoiding Joanie at the front door I struggled up the stairs to the flat and flung myself onto the bed crying. I'd danced for six months in a West End theatre and now it was coming to an end. I was confused and upset with nothing to look forward to. It was almost dark before I felt the peaceful calm of nature take over, and closed my eyes.

The light from a window woke me up early. Trying to focus, I clamoured down the wooden stairs to the kitchenette, made a cup of hot tea and toast and sat at the table, looking at myself in the mirror. A youthful seventeen year old with puffy red eyes glared back, a few hairs missing each side of my head caused by the huge hats. The realisation hit me – no rehearsals, no shows, and no money. Darting to the fridge, I grabbed an ice pack and held it over my eyes for a few moments.

What to do? Three options. Return to Pitt-Draffen and train to be a teacher, stay in London and wait for auditions, or return home to Mother. But how without money, and how long would it take? Or I could go back to Butlins if there was a vacancy. This was the best choice.

Whacking make-up on, I hurried to the ground floor to see Joanie. Trying to look away, I implored, 'Joanie, could I make a call please?'

'Yes dear, what's happened? You don't look good.'

'I'm fine,' I lied as she handed me the phone. Heart thumping, I dialed Miss de Vere's number. She answered immediately and trying to keep my voice composed, I said, 'Hello Miss de Vere, I'm Pamela. I worked for you at Pwllheli last year. Do you have a vacancy?'

'Yes, I remember you, but unfortunately I haven't.' My heart sank to the pits of my stomach. 'But there's a new camp at Bognor Regis,' she continued as I held my breath. 'I've got a vacancy there, but you'll have to audition.'

'Yes, when can I audition?' I replied, relieved. Joanie was still hovering, keen to know what was happening.

'Tomorrow afternoon.' Miss de Vere gave me the details and I spent the rest of the day washing my hair, checking my leotard, tights and shoes and practising a few pirouettes and kicks.

The audition was held in the city and a tall, impeccably dressed man greeted me. When I'd changed into rehearsal clothes he asked me where I'd worked. Nodding his head, he then said, 'Perform a few steps for me.' I performed a few pirouettes and kicks, then he raised his hand. 'Ok, you'll do fine.'

Overjoyed, I returned home and told Joanie everything. But what was I going to do for six weeks until the contract started?

A couple of days later Joanie handed me a message telling me, 'A gentleman called asking for Petra and wants you to phone him back.' I was surprised as only people at the Windmill knew me as Petra. It was Raul, the South American choreographer. 'Can you audition for a walk-on part in a new play which is 'trying out' in the East End, with the possibility of transferring to the West End?'

'Sorry Raul, I've just signed with Butlins and don't know if I can get out of it.'

'Come and audition anyway.' I did and was accepted, but disappointed I couldn't get out of the contract. Raul told me to keep in touch and phone him towards the end of the season, as he could have work for me. Another dilemma – should I go home for a few weeks, or stay in London as a girl Friday? Being almost penniless, though, how could I pay the rent? The solution was to find casual work.

I left the following day and walked towards the main road. Great, there was a shop advertising for a sandwich hand. It was midday and packed with office workers queuing up to buy their lunch. The supervisor put me to work instantly. Buttering a huge pile of bread furiously, slopping the butter on recklessly, I chatted to the girls and committed the youthful sin of blabbing to them, 'I'm really a dancer and won't be here long.' They told the supervisor, who instantly escorted me out after paying me a few shillings for two hours' work.

There had to be other work, but to console myself I went to the Gaumont cinema in the main street, an elegant tall building in a state of neglect. I saw the afternoon session of *The Inn of the Sixth Happiness*, an inspirational film. Leaving the cinema, an idea occurred to me – perhaps they had a job. I asked to see the manager who was delighted, and promptly ushered me inside to a small room, telling me to change into a uniform. And there I was dressed in a smart, maroon smock uniform, complete with a small, triangular hat, escorting people to their seats for the second showing of the film. On the third day I developed a massive headache caused by the constant loud noise all day long. It returned the next day during the first showing of the film. The Manager understood and, reluctant to let me go, paid me a few pounds which paid the rent.

Hunting for work again, I noticed a small restaurant a block away with the sign 'Waitress Wanted' in the window. 'No,' the Manager snapped, 'you're too young.' Battling my hurt pride, the next day the sign was still there and I asked again. 'No,' he snapped, exasperated at me for wasting his time. On the third day I inquired again. 'Oh, come in then. You do want the job.'

The restaurant was open for lunch with two set meals on the menu and was packed to capacity. I served one side while a Greek waiter worked in the other area. The four hour shifts were hectic and made my feet ache, but the money and tips were good and the Manager was pleased.

It was Easter at the weekend and I was surprised when the Greek waiter invited me out. I refused but he persisted aggressively, not pooling tips, hissing a tirade of insults into my ear such as 'Nasty girl. You think you're too good for me. Ugly duckling. You're evil,' when we passed each other. His pride had been hurt and I refused to answer or become upset, which annoyed him further.

Watching television at night with Joanie, we saw the film *The Easter Parade*, which was filmed at Battersea Park in London. What a lovely idea. I decided to go there on Easter Sunday. In a new, blue suit, taking extra care with make-up and hair, I went to see Joanie before leaving and asked her, 'Do I need a hat?'

'No, no dear, you look lovely. Come and meet my father.' She took me up to the third floor, where a table was set with delicate chinaware plates filled with cream cakes and an aroma of strong coffee permeated the air. Her father was old and delighted to meet me. I joined them for coffee and a delicious cake but was eager to be on my way.

It was a glorious sunny afternoon, the park a kaleidoscope of colours and people everywhere with children screaming as they enjoyed the Big Dipper and other amusements. Long queues of people waited for rides.

Thirsty, I looked longingly at a tea stall. A handsome young man approached and politely asked, 'Would you like a cup of tea?'

'Yes,' I replied feebly. He disappeared into the crowd and came back swiftly with two steaming hot teas. I admired his tenacity, cheeky grin and twinkling eyes. He was in his mid-twenties, of medium build, wearing a sports jacket and a cute dicky bow tie.

Grinning, he asked, 'Would you like to go on one of the amusements?'

We spent the next couple of hours getting to know each other as we queued to go on the Big Dipper. It was the start of a wonderful adventure with Simon. He owned a revved up Mini Minor and drove it like a racing driver. At weekends we went to pubs and various other places. One evening he put his arm around me, purring soft animal noises in my ear, drawing me closer to him. My legs trembled as new sensations pulsated through my body. Bringing my face closer, he kissed me. Now I understood why Pene at dancing school couldn't resist the advances of her boyfriend and was expelled.

It was almost time to go to Bognor Regis. One evening Simon drove me to London Bridge and we walked across it, staring at the full moon and the lights beaming across the ripples of water made by boats chugging up and down the river. We were oblivious to everything except each other.

We stopped. He took me in his arms and whispered, 'I love you.'

Startled, I pulled away, 'Oh no, I can't, I belong to dance.'

The words had erupted from my lips without any thought of his feelings or my inner emotions. I was too young at seventeen to understand the enormity of such sensations and bliss, but dancing was in my heart and had to take precedence. Would I regret this later? Was dance so essential? Quiet for a few moments he took me home, never mentioning it again but insisting on driving us to Bognor Regis.

On my last day the Manager at the restaurant thanked me, while I ignored the Greek waiter.

As I was about to leave, Joanie asked to talk to me. My sewing was improving and I could machine in a straight line and do simple sewing jobs. What could she want? She sat me down with a serious face, saying, 'Pamela, I know you have difficulty staying in London for auditions. You don't have to waitress. When you return, come here. You can sleep on the couch and I'll give you meals and pocket money if you'll sew for me and do other odd jobs.'

'Oh Joanie, how fantastic. I'd love to, but … '

'What is it?'

'The Windmill choreographer believes he has work for me when I finish at Butlins.'

Joanie smiled, 'That's no problem. Come here any time you like and sew for me.'

The doorbell rang. It was Simon and time to leave.

Bognor Regis is an hour's drive from London, a seaside town on the Southern coast and boasts the most days of sunshine in an English town in summer. We took the little meandering country roads, laughing and happy as we passed through quaint little villages until we reached our destination. We didn't go directly to the camp as Simon took us to the beach, where we ran along the water's edge for a few moments to stretch our legs, breathing in the fresh salty air and reveling in the joy of being by the sea, away from the city.

Simon stopped and picked up a handful of small stones, throwing them as far as possible into the ocean and watching the ripples they created. He was deep in thought. What was he thinking? I'd refused to commit to him on London Bridge. No, I didn't want to settle down. An exciting career lay ahead which I'd trained hard for, yet he'd stirred my emotions to a new height. I wanted to be with him but couldn't commit to him. Dancing was my career and words were left unspoken. 'Time to go,' he whispered before taking me to the camp gates, giving me a quick hug. As he drove away, I waved goodbye with my heart aching for him, and walked towards the staff annex.

The camp opened in 1960 with new amenities. It then almost flooded and the campers were transferred to another camp with free bottles of champagne.

In 1962 the camp was ready for a blockbuster summer season. The format was similar, with idolised redcoat hostesses, ballroom dancing, swimming, competitions, shows and a flurry of non-stop activity. We rehearsed for two weeks at the Gaiety Theatre. I was now confident and had devised my own system of learning steps fast. During spare moments I'd let the music run through my head and used two index fingers to mimic the steps on the seat of a chair. The system worked. The kicking routine opened the first show of the week and the audience adored the glitzy sequined costumes from the Black and White Minstrel show in London. In one unique number a large chess board was placed on the stage, slightly raised so the audience could see it. Dressed as pink pawns, we danced on or around the squares, trying to become queens.

In our spare time we danced the twist in the ballroom. I loved it, flinging myself up and down and round and round.

The theatre's orchestra leader had been watching us, and when the music stopped, he took me aside and asked, 'Would you be interested in doing the twist in my band show? On Thursdays we perform two shows in the Gaiety Theatre. In one number, while my singer performs on one side of the stage in a spotlight, I'd like you to dance on the other side.'

My face beamed, 'Oh! Yes.'

'I can't pay you.'

What madness! As a professional dancer I expected to get paid. He smiled, 'I'll offer you a drink with me at the bar between shows. After the second show, the boys will take you outside the camp for a steak meal at one of the pubs, which you won't have to pay for.'

'That sounds like fun. Do I have to rehearse, and what do I wear?'

'No rehearsal. The curtain rises as you start to dance. At the finish you dance into the wings. Wear what you have on, or a fuller skirt would be better.'

When I told the girls they weren't jealous. Everyone was happy and most of the girls were flirting with gorgeous hunks, mainly the male redcoats – or was it vice versa?

How wonderful to be dancing solo, a dancing starlet at last. The strenuous movements made me sweat profusely and the live music enticed me to dance to the limit of my ability. One minute brilliant dancing, two minutes good and after three minutes I wanted to crumble into a heap on the floor. As I danced to the wings, unexpectedly I saw an armchair and flopped into it. Five minutes later after I'd recuperated, I went to the bar for the promised drink and the orchestra leader was happy with my performance. For the second show I took a short towel to soak up the sweat.

The orchestra boys were fun. A succulent beef steak with crispy chips, salad and chunky bread was bliss after the soggy camp food, and was more than enough payment. A bonus was the home brewed apple cider, but we always arrived back on camp in time for the boys to play their last session of the evening in the ballroom.

My parents came to see me for my eighteenth birthday, a lovely surprise except half the family arrived with them. They all admired the redcoat uniform and there were no demands from Mother. She praised me, 'You've done well,' and, 'Oh my daughter, you are truly a redcoat.' Popsey was always a magnet by her side, although we did manage secret father and daughter jokes over the heads of the rest of the family.

Towards the end of the season I phoned Raul, hoping for news. An urgent voice replied, 'Petra, I've been waiting for you to call. I've got work for you. When will you be in London?'

'On Saturday.'

'Good. I need you to audition on Sunday. Don't worry, it's just a requirement. You have the job. Betty Lunn wants to see you before rehearsals begin on Monday.'

'Thanks Raul I'll be there, but where am I dancing?'

'In hotels in London and the suburbs with the Cavalcade Cabaret. It's for six months and I'm the choreographer.'

'Wonderful Raul, you can count on me.'

After exchanging a few more details, I wandered back to the chalet in a state of exhilaration. Immediate work. The impossible had happened. There were no mishaps and it was an enjoyable summer season.

After the final show and packing up costumes, with the inevitable sad goodbyes I was on the train, heading towards London for another exciting contract.

London Cabaret

Joanie greeted me with open arms, pleased I'd secured a new contract. She showed me how to make the sofa into a bed and hide my suitcase among the rails of costumes in the back, then spoiled me with a home cooked meal.

'Hello my dear,' she said cheerily, giving me a cup of tea in bed at the crack of dawn. 'You've got to get up to go to Chiswick. Use the bathroom on the second floor.' I resolved there and then to sew and help her whenever I could.

Carrying my vanity case of rehearsal clothes, I gave her a hug and caught the Metro to Chiswick. Chiswick lies in the Western suburbs of London and was a country retreat in the olden days. It's on the District line, with many bus routes passing along the main road. Chiswick High Road, the main shopping area, is full of retail shops, banks, pubs and restaurants. Wide streets display a mixture of Georgian, Victorian and Edwardian housing and close by are the River Thames and Kew gardens.

The church hall was easy to find and I was early. Raul wasn't there, but a mature, chubby man sitting at a piano greeted me. 'You must be Petra.' I nodded. 'I'm Jack. You look nervous.' I probably was, but he laughed and took a small flask from his pocket. 'Have a sip of gin to calm the nerves.' I did and enjoyed his boyish banter. 'Not a word to anyone. You'll breeze through the audition, mark my words.'

It was great to see Raul again, and after watching a few steps Betty Lunn gave me the six month contract. Pay per cabaret was good if we had many performances, but disastrous if there were only a few. It wasn't a Standard Equity Contract but I signed it, glad to be in work again. Pick up times by van or coach were at Turnham Green Station and we were returned to our front doors if it was late.

During rehearsals I stayed at Joanie's and she enjoyed listening to me retell the day's events. Gwen, an actress from the 1940's, was plump, sturdy and humourless with school mistress mannerisms, and lived in a house in Chiswick. When Joanie asked her if she could rent me a room so I could be closer to rehearsals, she grudgingly agreed. When I paid the rent she never ventured into small talk or asked about the cabarets.

One week she shocked me, 'Pamela, you've got to leave by the end of the week.'

'What?' I was dumbfounded, 'What's wrong? I pay my rent on time. Why?'

'You arrive home at all hours of the night and your light is on all the time.'

'You know I'm dancing in cabarets travelling the country.' It was pointless to argue.

When I told Joanie she replied, 'Oh, Gwen's a strange one.' Anything was better than an antagonistic old woman for a landlady and I found a decent bedsitter for the rest of the contract. The cabaret was a half hour show involving quick changes with a female singer performing while we changed costumes. After the show we packed our costumes into suitcases, easy to carry to the next venue.

The opening number was dazzling with silver sequined leotards and feathered hats, but the feature of the show was the finale. In white blouses and short red and green skirts we walked in a line to the front, each holding a hand bell. Each bell chimed a different note as we played *The Bells of Saint Marys*. During the applause we walked to the back, unhooking another skirt to reveal a Scottish skirt while playing another tune. After the Irish and Welsh songs the audience were stamping their feet, roaring for more.

In the van we travelled throughout London, performing in many town halls and the Dorchester, Park Lane, Savoy and Grosvenor hotels. The highlight was dancing at The Royal Albert Hall. We travelled as far as Birmingham and to my home town of Kettering. My parents saw the show but other cabarets were scheduled for the next day so I couldn't stay. During long coach journeys we'd twiddle with our fingers, wondering what the audience would be like as our driver told us a few jokes to pass the time. It was excellent for the first few months and during the festive season we performed up to eleven cabarets a week. From February the number of shows dwindled, until there was only one cabaret in the final week at the beginning of May.

In England the brutal winter of 1962-63 was the coldest in 200 years, with sub-zero temperatures persisting for two months. Snow covered the entire country from late January. Fog and vegies frozen in the ground sent prices soaring. Rivers and canals froze over and children delighted in skating over them. Even the sea froze a mile out from the shore in several places. A blizzard exploded its way throughout England and Wales, stranding villagers with snow drifts up to eight feet high. Cars were buried under snow and ploughs used to clear the roads. In March when the thaw came, the snow turned into a muddy slush and many parts of the country were flooded. The smog was appalling. Since then clean air legislation and less coal fires have been effective.

Venturing outside I held a scarf tightly over my mouth to stop black coatings of grime and dirt forming on my lips, as cold blasts of wind made me shiver. Returning to a bleak room with the gas heater gobbling up sixpenny coins, I performed a few high kicks, ran up and down on the carpet to keep my circulation going, and slept with a hot water bottle.

Life continued as usual. The main roads were kept open and we didn't miss a cabaret. Bored and lonely with time on my hands and no spare cash to buy clothes, I bought thick balls of wool to knit my first polo neck jumper without dropping a stitch. It helped to combat the cold and became a hobby I continued for years.

Once the cabarets commenced I phoned Simon. Would he want to see me after six months?

'Hello Simon, how are you?'
'Pamela, I'm glad you're back. Where are you?'
'I'm living in Chiswick, dancing again.'
'That's fantastic. Love to see you. When are you free?'

'Sundays.'

'Great, I'll take you to dinner.' As I put the phone down I could sense the chemistry brewing between us. My face flushed as my body trembled with excitement. What to wear? The old skirt? The Mini? No. He'd have to accept me as I was. The blue jumper was appealing and cheap perfume was all I could afford.

As I opened the front door my spine tingled. His cheeky grin and cute dicky bow tie melted my heart. *Still the same courteous Simon* I thought as he opened the car door with a flourish to let me glide inside. He kissed my forehead, smoothing a stray hair from my face as I struggled to keep warm. We looked at each other. Magnetic. As he drove us to a posh restaurant in Knightsbridge, I almost bit my finger to stop caressing his hand. We talked incessantly, enjoying a couple of wines, succulent steaks with salad and the special dessert prepared at our table – hot pancakes with Canadian maple syrup dribbled over them, saturated in cream.

As he ordered coffees and chocolates, he took my hand as I gazed lovingly into his eyes, unprepared for the shocking news to come.

'Pamela, it's difficult to say this.' A long pause. He tightened his grip on my hand as I drew back. What was he suggesting? 'Pamela, I have to tell you.' He gripped my hand tighter as my blood shot from cold to hot. Was he proposing? Watching me intently, he blurted out, 'I've met someone else, but she's gone home to New Zealand to be with her family for a few months before coming to live permanently with me.'

Shocked, I tried to keep my composure, while the bleary eyes and red face told another story. 'Simon, I don't understand why you're taking me out. Why didn't you tell me when I phoned you?'

'I wanted to tell you in person, not by phone.'

'What about me?'

'You have a career and I enjoy our friendship.'

'What about her?'

'Pamela, she's not here and I love your company. We're friends.'

'It's not fair on your girlfriend, but I'll probably leave London soon.'

Trembling, I waited as he paid the bill, trying to stop tears ruining my make-up. When the car stopped outside my place, he hugged me, whispering, 'I still want to take you out.'

What were the options? He needed an answer there and then.

'Tell me Simon, if she returns,' I uttered as he purred softly into my ear, nibbling it.

I saw him afterwards and enjoyed a few dinners. It didn't feel right and I still cared for him, but the problem would soon be resolved, or so I thought.

Unexpected, my next contract was to dance overseas, although I didn't know it at the time. Longing to return to theatre work, in October I attended an open audition at the London Palladium.

George Carden, the resident choreographer, had advertised for tall dancers for a new revue he was choreographing. Hundreds of girls of all shapes and sizes attended, crowding onto the stage trying to get noticed. He leapt onto the stage screaming, 'I asked for tall dancers. How dare you come here? Go, go.' As he touched their arm, they ran to the wings. This choreographer knew what he wanted and didn't waste time. Straggling at the back, straining to see him or hear instructions, I rushed away before he saw me and left. My height of five feet four inches didn't meet his criteria. There had to be another way. Why not contact a theatrical agent?

Walking around the streets of the West End, I found an old building with a sign outside for a Theatrical Agency, First Floor. Good. Worth a try.

Clamouring up the wide, concrete stairs to the office, the door was opened by a secretary, wearing a dull dress and large reading glasses perched on her nose.

'What do you want?' she inquired with keen eyes.

'I'm a dancer looking for theatre work.'

Noting my youth she ushered me through a door to another office. Above a large desk, a portly man sat smoking a cigar with signed photos of stars on the wall above him.

'And what can I do for you?' he asked with a huge smile.

'I'm a dancer and I want to sing. I've worked at Butlins and The Windmill Theatre. Now I'm dancing in cabaret in London hotels. I'd like to get more theatre work and try singing.'

He sat back in his plush, brown, leather chair and between smokes on his Havana cigar inquired, 'Do you have photos?'

'No, I don't.'

He rose from the seat smiling, the cigar between his fingers, noting my innocent young face. Was I in luck at my first attempt? 'Here's the address of a photographer. He's the best there is. Once you have them come back and see me, and I'll see what I can do.'

Early the next morning I phoned. 'Hello, are you Michael Barrington-Martin? I'm a dancer and need good photos.'

'My fee is twenty five pounds for five professional ones. If you want more, I charge half price for each photo. Book a sitting for thirty proofs. When you've chosen five photos they'll take three weeks to complete.'

Without hesitation I agreed and made an appointment. It was an astronomical fee but I didn't care. 'Make sure you bring your leotard, a pretty dress, some slacks with a blouse, and get your hair styled at the hairdressers,' he replied firmly.

I kept my plans to myself. Everyone would think I was mad. A hair appointment was booked at the prestigious Vidal Sassoon Salon who created a brilliant style piling my long, dark brown hair into a high bee hive with gentle waves and curls.

Mr Barrington-Martin was small with a beard and wasting no time on pleasantries. In his studio in a back alley off Oxford Street, large umbrellas and lights surrounded a white backdrop where the photos were taken. He took many shots, continually changing the lights and umbrellas for shading, and we both made suggestions for poses or dancing gestures. It was an exhausting two hours and when the proofs arrived I was astounded. The finished photos showed a lovely, slim young girl with dancing technique.

When the agent saw them he promised to contact me when a theatre show required dancers. Several weeks passed, but in February he called me.

'Pamela, there's a singing audition for George Carden for a show he's producing in Amsterdam. Are you interested?'

This was perplexing. Did Mr Carden employ singers? I'd never sung professionally, 'Yes I am,' I replied, without thinking of the consequences.

'Be at the Victoria Palace Theatre on Sunday morning at 10 am.'

What a good agent. I rehearsed a few old songs, soon realising I was out of practise. What the hell, I'd go. Nothing ventured, nothing gained.

I phoned home to tell my parents the news. Popsey replied, 'All the best Pamela, feel tall and you will be. Raise your heels half an inch off the ground but no more or you'll topple over.'

Relief! Only two cabarets scheduled for Saturday night. The vanity case was packed with dancing shoes, leotard and make-up and the alarm set for 6 am.

The Audition

Rain battered the window as I grabbed a brolly and ran to the Metro dodging puddles, annoyed with the rain ruining my make-up. The train was punctual and my thoughts were scattered everywhere. Was it stupid to try to sing?

Arriving at Victoria Station I took deep breaths. I could go back but it was a golden opportunity and I couldn't disappoint the agent. Dodging slush, melted snow and keeping the rain away with the brolly, I entered by the stage door. Shivering, the back stage manager ushered me into a warm dressing room where girls were changing.

When they called me, I walked to centre stage. Dark shapes of the managers could be seen half way back in the auditorium. The pianist played and stopped in the middle of the first line. Mr Carden and I both knew it was a terrible rendering of the song. My agent rushed down the aisle with my photo in his hands as Mr Carden waived him aside, staring up at me. 'Are you a dancer?'

'Yes.'

'Can you come back this afternoon at 2 pm?'

'Yes,' I replied, stunned that he wanted to see me again after the lousy singing.

Victoria Street was hectic with red double decker buses, taxis, people and puddles everywhere. What to do for three hours? I bought a newspaper and nestled into a small café. Time dragged as concentration became impossible. Jumbled thoughts explored every avenue of previous auditions. What steps would be asked for? High kicks and pirouettes were good and arm movements needed to be precise. I craved success.

As I returned to the theatre Mr Carden almost bumped into me as he walked to the auditorium, noticing my red suit. Later I learnt his dancing groups wore suits and gloves to the theatre in the 50s.

Chatter erupted from the dressing room. Girls were pulling on tights and leotards, brushing hair and tinkering with make-up. Joining them, I tried to learn as much as possible.

'It's my third audition. I got a call last week.'

'How many girls?'

'Dunno. No idea.'

'It's the last audition. There's fifty here.'

The banter continued until a woman called us to the wings and gave us a number as auditions commenced. The first dancer performed a combination of steps, followed by pirouettes, high kicks and splits. Almost the last to audition, I executed the steps perfectly and thought I detected a slight smile on Mr Carden's non-committal face.

Auditions over, we returned to the stage to listen as he called out several numbers. 'Thank you girls, you may go.' We formed a circle and were told to walk slowly and stop. More numbers were called for dancers to step away, and the few of us left formed a line across the stage. I recalled Popsey's words, 'Think tall, and be tall,' and raised my heels half an inch off the ground. Discussions took place in the auditorium as we waited. My calves hurt, shooting pains everywhere – but I felt nothing as the possibility of success grew.

An agonising wait. Oh! How much longer?

Dreams shattered as Mr Carden beckoned me to come forward. 'No, not you. The girl standing next to you,' he demanded. The poor girl left as I raised my heels again. He walked along the line, scrutinising each of us. With a sudden spurt of energy, he yelled out, 'Come this way to the stalls!' He then waved an arm for us to follow.

Thump! My high heels crashed to the floor as I felt a slight tap on my shoulder from an unsuccessful dancer, who whispered, 'You went to Pitt-Draffens. I knew you'd do well.'

Mr Carden gathered his chosen dancers around him and, looking at our excited faces, raised an arm. The god of choreographers was speaking. 'Are any of you under eighteen?' Nothing registered as the stabbing pains in my calves reduced to a dull ache. Gazing at me, he was trying to read my thoughts, knowing I was young. No-one replied. A huge grin spread across his face, as the sun does when it peeps out of the clouds in the morning. Triumphant with his decision, he announced, 'You're going to Amsterdam for a year. Rehearsals begin in June for two weeks. Pay is fifteen pounds a week and costume fittings are in London. Come and sign your contracts.'

Euphoria swept over me with firecrackers exploding in my head as the realisation of my achievement sank in. Who could I tell?' My first thought was Popsey. What would he think? Contract signed, I looked at my watch. Five o' clock. No cabarets until Wednesday.

Oblivious to the cold, hunger and fatigue, I flew out of the stage door to Chiswick and packed an overnight bag. Grabbing a heavy coat and scarf, with chattering teeth I ran to the Metro which took me to St Pancras train station.

'You've just missed the slow train to Kettering, but the fast train is due in half an hour,' the ticket man stated. Paying for a return ticket, I was almost penniless until pay day. As I waited in the coffee shop, the warmth and hot tea soothed away the gnawing, hunger pains rumbling in my stomach.

The fast train screamed its way non-stop through mini-towns to Kettering. Bubbling with excitement, I stepped into a colder temperature with the scarf strangling me against a blistering wind, my hands clutching the insides of the coat for warmth. I was relieved to see there were no taxies outside the station. No money! Exhausted, the temptation to take one would have been too great. Walking past the twelfth century Parish church smothered in a foggy haze, its spire a landmark in the countryside, I struggled along the High Street void of traffic or people.

Arriving home, I glanced at my watch. It was nine o'clock. The glimmer of a TV shone through the window, illuminating the darkness. They weren't expecting me. Opening the front door, an unexpected blast of warm air greeted me. I rushed down the passage to the kitchen to make a cheese sandwich before bursting into the lounge to greet Mother and Popsey. Sitting on a stool between them, drained of energy and the stress of the day's events, I couldn't speak.

'What's the matter?' Mother inquired as Popsey turned off the TV.

Between gulps of bread soggy from joyful tears streaming down my face, I uttered, 'Amsterdam, Amsterdam. I'm going to Amsterdam to dance for George Carden.'

Popsey leapt to his feet and hugged me as Mother crooned, 'When it's spring again I'll bring again tulips from Amsterdam.'

Two days of home cooked meals and sleeping in scented sheets were bliss.
Returning to London I kept silent, but couldn't resist telling Susan, who I trusted.

At the end of February, the cabarets were infrequent and it was a struggle to pay the rent. Glowing with excitement, one evening Susan suggested, 'Petra, I'm going to work at The Ideal Home Exhibition at Earls Court for a month. You can, too.'

'Wow! What about the cabarets?'

'It's easy. We work all day and finish at six. There's plenty of time to get to Turnham Green for seven o'clock.'

'Gosh that'd be a godsend. I'm in dire straits at the moment, almost at my wit's end and can't pay the rent. Do you think they'll accept me?'

'Of course they will. Here's the number.'

Together we started work on the Monday morning at the Jiffy Starch Stand and were paid weekly, with the added bonus of a commission on sales at the end of the month. At the back of the stand were a large washing machine and spin dryer with several ironing boards in front. The supervisor stated, 'Take a child's garment from the spin dryer, spray and iron it, and pop it back into the washing machine. Grab another from the spin dryer to demonstrate our product.'

The clothes were never washed and taken wet to the spin dryer, fooling the public. At the end of the day they were hard boards, and Jiffy starch sold like hot cakes. I delighted in making up stories on the effectiveness of Jiffy Starch, but one day a man listening to my spiel looked me squarely in the eyes.

"How do I know if it really works as you say it does?' he demanded.

'It works on all clothing,' I boasted.

He produced a clean handkerchief from his pocket and placed it on the ironing board. 'See if you can make my handkerchief stiff.' I squirted double the normal amount onto the hanky and after ironing it stretched it between my hands.

The trick worked. He felt it and mumbled, 'Alright, I'll take two.'

A small crowd had gathered to watch the results and promptly delved into their purses to purchase the starch. Sales escalated.

There were over 300 stands in the Exhibition, ranging from wine tastings to various demonstrations on cooking and household equipment, to larger exhibits of bathrooms and houses.

Sauntering down an aisle in a tea break, I stopped in shock. Ahead of me, perched on a ladder fiddling with a light shade, was Simon, with a blonde woman staring up at him. He hadn't seen me. Who was she?

Deciding to ignore the woman, I called to him. He turned around surprised. 'What are you doing here Pamela?'

'I'm working on the Jiffy Starch stand. There aren't many cabarets and I've got to pay the rent.'

'Oh, I'm busy with company work. I'll call you later.' He called as usual and the dinners were delicious. It didn't matter. I was going overseas to Amsterdam in June, which would ease my tormented heart.

After the exhibition closed in March the two or three cabarets per week were insufficient to pay the rent. Time to job hunt again. I headed for Chiswick High Road and found a small restaurant advertising for a waitress. No-one was in sight except for a cheerful, middle-aged man. Telling him about the cabarets and my being unable to work on a Saturday evening didn't seem to bother him. 'Can you can start tomorrow lunch time?'

He was a one man show, cooking the meals and serving the customers when I wasn't there, leaving everything spotlessly clean. There were no frantic meal times, only a constant trickle of people coming and going. The mediocre pay incremented, with the odd tip payed the rent, and I loved being in charge of the restaurant and greeting the customers. The boss always inquired where a cabaret was performing and we were both delighted with the arrangement.

One night a group of young men and women came into the restaurant and sat at the main table. The leader of the pack asked, 'What do you have on the menu?'

'What would you like Sir? Quack, quack soup?'

'And what's for main course?'

'Puppy dog tails served with vegetables and gravy.'

'And for sweets?'

'Rose petals and cream.'

Raucous laughter filled the restaurant. When they left I was disappointed. Twelve empty plates were on the table without a tip. When I picked up the first plate I was shocked to see a shiny half a crown coin underneath it. Grabbing the other plates revealed similar coins. Elated I felt as though I'd won a mini lottery. In May there was one miserable cabaret and Betty Lunn cornered me in the dressing room.

'Petra, I can offer you a short, summer season at the coast.'

This was the chance I'd been waiting for to let her know my news. 'No thank you Betty. I won an audition to dance for George Carden in a theatre show and I'm going to Amsterdam in June.'

Dumbstruck, she never wished me good luck and I wasn't sad to leave. It'd been difficult to survive on the wage but I would miss the girls. On my last night at the restaurant the boss chuckled, 'Pamela, I'm going to teach you to be a good waitress.' What did he mean?

'You fill the salt and pepper pots first, sauce bottles are next, fold the serviettes neatly and don't pirouette between tables.'

'Yes Sir,' I giggled, 'Thank you Sir. I'll keep the pirouettes for Amsterdam.'

Amsterdam, Holland

Costume fittings took place at the legendary Alex Shank Costumiers in Garrick Street London, created by Anthony Holland who was the leading designer of the day. He produced costumes for musicals, revues, plays, ballet and opera. In awe I watched as assistants measured and pinned half-finished costumes of silks, velvets, satins and taffeta around me. Crispy new costumes with meticulous sewing and the smell of new material were intoxicating. No expense was spared as they outlined my foot on paper for shoes. Returning to Joanie's homely wardrobe for a few days, the time dragged before my departure to Amsterdam.

It was the first day of summer in 1963 as I made my way in a trance to the departure lounge at Heathrow Airport. Several of the cast were already buzzing around. We were the lucky ones as it was rare for youngsters to travel overseas. They called our KLM flight and we settled into our seats. How different from the joyride I'd experienced in the light aircraft in Wales. The massive engines roared into life and we were soon airborne as the city of London lay beneath us, with miniature ships bobbing up and down on a dim, grey ocean as dark clouds threatened to destroy the view. The miniature salt and pepper packets served and plastic cutlery served with the meals were fascinating.

Landing at Schiphol Airport in the early afternoon, people spoke a different language and no-one wore clogs. Mr Carden greeted us with a huge grin and bundled us into a coach.

Travelling along the main highway, the countryside resembled a green pancake without the hint of a hill, tulips, windmills or water. A boat was gliding among the fields. It was a mystifying, strange sight compared to the English countryside. Where was the water?

As we approached Amsterdam her fairytale magic cast a spell on us. Tall, centuries-old buildings appeared and we passed side streets, with shimmering water from the canals with overhanging trees coming into bloom. Houseboats and quaint stone bridges, markets, flowers and people dawdling on the pavements with thousands of bicycles – it was all so bright and inviting compared to the hectic pace of London traffic. The coach stopped twice.

Glancing around I noted only ten of us were left. A sharp turn onto a road running parallel to a large river led to six storey high buildings rising out of the water. The coach stopped at our home for the next twelve months. As we left Mr Carden announced, 'Settle into your digs. Tomorrow afternoon you're going on a tour of the city and I'll show you where rehearsals will be on Monday morning.'

Our landlady, a tall mature Dutch woman, spoke English with a strange accent and allotted us our rooms in military fashion. My room on the first floor was adequate with simple furnishings and a tiny electric heater. How I longed for the comforts of home, but the view from my window of the lights on the river and majestic buildings was a dream. The bathroom on the fifth floor was sufficient and the breakfast room comfortable.

Over the large table at breakfast we'd chat for hours, discussing the show, artists and music, while digging into peanut butter, honey and jam. A cooked dinner was provided before the show and supper was 'help yourself' in the large kitchen, although we loved the smell and taste of the landlady's thick percolated coffee.

Refreshed and bubbling with excitement, twenty of us boarded a mini coach which could manoeuvre through the side streets. Amsterdam is in the North of Holland and full of museums. The main square was originally a dam built in the twelfth century and scores of bicycles dodged the long, electric trams.

After visiting the main tourist attractions Mr Carden laughed, 'Would you like to visit the Red Light District?' The boys in the group screamed as we howled, and the fun began.

We approached a narrow, cobbled lane and on the right hand side were bay windows. At each window a voluptuous woman with pouting lips full of gaudy red lipstick was selling her wares. Dressed in black fishnet tights with ornate garters, miniskirts, six inch high heels, feathers and sassy bows, the women looked like live dolls for sale, gesturing in subtle movements for potential male clients to come in. Thinking over my career, I realise Mr Carden was the only choreographer to take care of his artists and give us a tour of the city.

On Monday morning we decided to walk to rehearsals. With the sun shining we leapt forward, with Ron and Tudor from our group leading the way. We laughed, giggled and danced over the Magere Brug (meaning thin) bridge which is a tourist highlight and stretched across the Amstel River. Ron stopped, so we stopped. At the end of the big square was a huge sign displaying two elaborate letters 'VD'. Ronnie shrieked, 'It's the venereal disease department store.' Still giggling we found the rehearsal room at the back of the store. Mr Carden was already there and pleased to see we were early.

Choreography was precise. If Mr Carden yelled, 'F.O.T', fingers were placed on thighs. Straggly arms and hands were forbidden. Elegant steps were used to create works of art and rehearsals lasted two weeks. Professional photos were taken in our costumes on stage for the program and we received lyric tuition to sing in Dutch for the finale.

Snip and Snap was a revue produced by Rene Seerswiyk, starring Willy Walden and Piet Muyslaar, the Dutch equivalents of the English comics The Two Ronnies. Bill Stanford, a famous English orchestra leader, conducted Dutch musicians. We adored being called The English Starlets, and the boys were proud to be known as The West End Debonairs. The theme of the show centred on two comics travelling the world on holiday stopping at various countries. The first scene was in London visiting *The Talk of the Town* theatre show, where they paraded with lovely ladies as their confused spouses ran after them. In Paris we were different characters depicting Parisian life and in Vienna we danced the romantic waltz. Before the interval, the 'Festival in Rio' number involved the whole cast dressed in lavish, colourful feathered costumes.

Dressed as horses in another number, the male dancers guided and pretended to whip us as we cavorted around the stage. The costume was a figure hugging, white jersey body suit with the replica of a horse head as a hat, light and comfortable to wear.

The body suit was torture. Cleaned every two weeks, they were returned four sizes smaller. We swore under our breath while heaving and trying to pull them on. Even the two dressers couldn't help. It was a tug of war as the kicking routine took every ounce of energy to kick at waist level. What should have been a good number to perform became a living nightmare.

In cute Tyrolean costumes, we were grouped behind the operatic singer Christine Spierenburg, dressed in different shades of green and mauve mini-skirts with satin shoes dyed to match the costume. Blistering pain crept through our feet as we sat on the stage. The shoes had shrunk with the dye. We could never have danced in them.

Don Jones, a celebrated American singer, sang as we danced around him, pretending to play various musical instruments. At one section of the routine we bent over in a circle around him as he simulated playing a trumpet. One evening I was suffering from flatulence, trying to contain it. The trumpet reached a high note and in the split second before the entire orchestra played the uncontrollable blast had to go. Everyone on stage convulsed in laughter. One girl left the stage returning with a toilet roll and threw it at me. I became known as the Champion.

For the finale, dressed as cute Dutch girls we paraded around the Passarella (a platform extending from the stage in a half circle), singing in Dutch to the audience. They loved it and always gave us a standing ovation.

The first three months of the show flowed smoothly, giving us time to discover the city in detail, visit museums and shop for clothes. Life was good.

The Carre Theatre was vast. The auditorium was a large half circle and cold compared to the intimacy of the Windmill Theatre. It was built by the German circus director Oscar Carre to stage circus performances in the winter and opened in 1887. Later vaudeville shows were produced but in the late 60s it was almost demolished. The municipality bought the building and completely renovated it retaining its historic façade. In 2004 it was renamed The Royal Carre Theatre.

The American Alvin Ailey Jazz Company came to town and we were given a class with the famous dancer. He taught us how to dance from the heart. One Sunday we even got to see Sammy Davis Junior, one of the greatest talents of the twentieth century, who came to the theatre to perform a live Eurovision telecast. We were invited to see him and sat in the 'gods' seats up the back of the dress circle. He sang, tap danced and played various musical instruments. It was incredible to see him performing live. We didn't meet him but heard he'd hidden in the box office to watch the invited public arrive.

One Friday night as I was leaving by the stage door, I was shocked when a voice I knew called out, 'Pamela, it's me.'

I felt as though a bomb had hit me. Grinning, with another young man by his side, there stood Simon. Composing myself, I inquired, 'What are you doing here?' There'd been no communication with him at all.

'This is James my brother, and we're on our way to a trade fair in Brussels for the weekend.'

'How did you find me?'

'Easy. There's only one good theatre in Amsterdam. I knew you'd be here.'

'Did you see the show?'

'Yes, you were fantastic. Come out with us. Can you get a girl for James to make up a foursome?'

Behind me, Elaine yelled, 'I'll come.' What choice was there? We went to a nightclub and danced until the small hours.

When we were alone I inquired about his New Zealand fiancée. 'Oh! We got married.' I froze as I took in the news but he held me in his arms pleading, 'When you come back to London call me and I'll take you out.'

'Yes,' I lied. My mind was in a whirl-wind, tormented. My youth shattered. How could I live like this or see him again?

Tears flowed as I scurried up to my room. He'd been my first love and was married. Between sniffles, I realised there was only one thing to do. Grabbing my address book I ripped out his phone number and tore it into a thousand pieces, stamped on it in a rage and buried my face in the pillow. Distraught, I realised there was no-one I could turn to as the memories surfaced and sleep became impossible.

After opening night we didn't see Mr Carden for several weeks. One night Mr Keats, the Stage Manager, gathered us all together. This was unusual and we were curious.

'Management will use all of you this year to dance in four TV shows. Mr Carden wants you for rehearsals at 10 o'clock sharp on Monday morning. You'll rehearse for two weeks and transmission will be on a Sunday. If you complain of tiredness or perform badly on stage you won't do the shows.' We were speechless. As he closed the door we exploded with excitement.

Hilversum television studios was an hour's coach drive from Amsterdam. At 10 am on a Sunday, there were lighting, orchestra and camera rehearsals. It was different to dancing on a stage as the steps were minimised and we performed like puppets.

At four in the afternoon a small audience arrived, sitting directly in front of us. Usually programs were recorded live but a new video taping system was being trialed and we were told not to stop the show for any reason. Adrenalin flowed as we changed hair styles and costumes on time. Today, few recordings are left of the 50s and 60s as most of the shows were broadcast live. The first time stage fright hit me was during a studio rehearsal for the cowboy number. I sweated, my mind froze and my body was riddled with nerves. It involved a simple 'step ball change' sequence. A frustrated Mr Carden showed me the steps three times. Inwardly I felt doomed, expecting to be ordered off the set. Shaking, I mastered the steps. The shows were televised before Christmas.

It was tiring performing at night and rehearsing in the daytime with a matinee on Saturdays, but my previous experience of working long hours at the Windmill proved to be invaluable. The television numbers were short and lively and included a circus, disco, Christmas theme, a cowboy number and others, which we performed between acts. I was one of four girls chosen to parade white Afghan dogs around a circle set in black and white triangles. Mine decided it liked the middle camera and in front of millions of viewers sat and did its business. I waited smiling, and escorted her away with poise and dignity.

One night early in November, a terrible rumour spread throughout the theatre. President John Kennedy had been assassinated in Texas. Stunned at the news, we continued dancing. Was it true? If it was, how would it affect us? It was still the Cold War and everyone was fearful another bloody war would start. We were safe, but how would America or Russia react and who could take his place? Kennedy had been an amazing President thwarting a war in Cuba and to be killed at the height of his power was unthinkable.

At Christmas we flew home for two weeks at management's expense. Joanie was delighted to see me and being close to Christmas the wardrobe was buzzing with activity and people hiring fancy dress costumes. I stayed a week to help, but the festivities at home with Mother and Popsey were a joy.

Returning to Amsterdam the show went on tour, performing in all the major towns every week. The coach arrived at our digs at 5 pm and returned at midnight. Tired, we'd sleep for most of the day, although Sundays were free, giving us time to relax and recuperate.

On a Saturday matinee towards the end of our contract in Rotterdam, our horse costumes had been dry cleaned overnight and as always required super human strength to kick in them. The kicking line was messy and I struggled to kick to waist level. During the interval Mr Carden stormed into the dressing room, screaming, 'That's the worst show I've seen in my life. You should all be ashamed. How dare you! I'm not taking you back next year.' We cowered and I was in tears. Silence. 'There are three girls I will have back.' When my name was the second one to be called, relief flooded through me.

There was a six week holiday in England before the new contract commenced, which was to include ten TV shows. I divided the time sewing for Joanie in London, spending weekends at home and attended costume fittings at Alec Shanks Costumiers.

The week before I was due to return, unexpected pains and nausea attacked me. 'Mother, what am I to do?'

'Go to the doctor. You can't dance in your condition.'

'What about Amsterdam?' I pleaded. 'I have to fly there on Saturday.'

'We'll go together and see what the doctor says,' she replied, worried. The tests were vital and could only be returned on Monday. I was heartbroken, and no-one could console me. My career was spinning out of control. On Monday, the doctor explained it was a small problem and medication would heal the problem.

I flew to Amsterdam on the first flight out and went directly to rehearsals. I was hesitant to enter, and as soon as I did Mr Carden noticed me, turned the music off and walked up to me.

'I've been sick and was only given the all clear yesterday,' I mumbled.

Staring at my miserable face, he replied, 'I'm sorry Pamela I had to get another dancer.'

I threw my belongings into an old trunk and headed for the port to catch the ferry home. Memories of happy times surfaced as I passed quaint canals, majestic buildings, trams and bicycles. I'd never see this fairy tale city again.

The journey took three hours on a choppy sea. Miserable, it was a relief to stand on English soil. I'd hired a porter to help me with the trunk.

With nothing to declare, I was passing through customs when an officer stopped me, pointing at my wrist. 'Where did you buy that gold watch?'

Dazed, I muttered, 'Amsterdam.' Looking at the trunk, I noticed one side was dented and a lock had been smashed. I yelled, 'What's this? Who did this? Are my clothes safe?'

To avoid a nasty scene he ordered me to go and I arrived home intact.

Mother insisted I stay a few days, smothering me with kindness, but I was keen to return to London. Joanie was sympathetic, insisting I'd soon get another contract. I bought *The Stage* Magazine. The Billy Cotton Band Show wanted dancers for an eight week theatre contract in Jersey, one of the Channel Islands. I breathed a sigh of relief. I'd soon be dancing again.

Jersey, The Channel Isles

Jersey in the English Channel is close to the coast of Normandy and part of the United Kingdom. Captured by the Germans in WWII, many of their fortifications remain today. Warmer weather from the mainland and gentle sea breezes attract thousands of tourists, and the highlight of summer is the annual Festival of Flowers held in July.

The Forum cinema, in the capital St Heliers where the show was held, was a huge, bleak building without ornamentations. The massive auditorium had no side boxes, although the dress circle featured a large organ. During the war, the Germans used it to show propaganda films, but in 1981 it was demolished to make way for office buildings.

Starring in the show was Billy Cotton, the top post-war band leader of England, who was a national institution on British TV and radio during the 50s and 60s with his war cry, 'Wakey, Wakey.' Also starring were singers Alan Breeze and Kathie Kay, the happy-go-lucky pianist Mrs Mills, Edwin Braden playing the organ, the magician John Wade who'd just returned from a season at the Windmill, and the Lesley Roberts Silhouette Dancers.

The audition was easy and I was surprised to see Anna, who I'd worked with in Amsterdam – so we agreed to share digs. With four simple numbers to learn, no weekly rehearsals, one show a night and no matinees, it was a paid holiday after all the trauma, and exactly what I needed.

In the finale we threw cotton wool snowballs at the audience and one night the temptation proved too great. Billy Cotton was centre stage, singing. I aimed at his head and caught him on the nose. Shocked, he turned around to see who'd thrown it, but I was composed. He could only guess who the culprit was. The show wasn't popular, with empty seats in every show except for Saturdays.

Anna and I settled into our digs, a double room converted from an old cellar with the window at pavement level. We didn't complain as the room was cosy and cheap, but one day we noticed slugs crawling up the window pane. She soon found a boyfriend and I enjoyed soaking up the sun. Every morning I went to the beach, swimming and sunbathing until sunset. There was a tiny island close to the shore which fascinated me. The old ruins from a past era perched on the hill were too small to be a castle. Could they be the relics of an old abbey? Against a background of blue skies and a glittering sea, it was a delight to the eye. I sizzled and fried in the hot sun as my porcelain white skin transformed from a lobster pink to a dark, chocolate brown.

I'd often sunbake with Kim and Jenny who were older, and we became good friends. They met two guys on the beach, but my experience with Simon lingered. Aged 19, I was young and vulnerable and wary of strangers.

One day they invited me to the pub after the show. We were laughing and having fun when the publican suggested we play a drinking game. 'Have you heard of Cardinal Puff?'

'No.' I replied.

The publican put a shot glass in front of me. 'Take the glass with your thumb and index finger,' he explained. 'Then you say, "Here's to the health of Cardinal Puff Puff for the first time." Drink it in one gulp and bang the glass on the table once. Repeat it with two fingers, and say, "Here's to the health of Cardinal Puff Puff for the second time", drink it in two gulps and bang the table twice. The third time with three fingers say, "Here's to the health of Cardinal Puff Puff for the third and last time", drink it in three gulps, then bang the table once, a second time upside down, and the third time normally.'

It looked easy, but for every mistake you had to drink up and start again. The more I drank the more pathetic and confused I became until I was dizzy. They rushed me home and I reached the toilet in the nick of time. No more pubbing.

My parents came to see me and the show, along with the Flower Festival. When Mother saw her idol Mrs Mills she rushed to greet her. They clacked together like Peking ducks. Embarrassed, I hid behind Popsey.

The Battle of the Flowers was inaugurated in 1902 when the islanders wanted to celebrate the coronation of King Edward VII and Queen Alexandra. The floats were horse drawn and petals and flowers thrown into the crowd. This was stopped in 1964 due to unruly crowds and the clean-up operation afterwards. Today it attracts tourists from all over the world, and the battle has been replaced with a competition for the finest float.

In 1964, 50,000 people attended the festival and Billy Cotton heralded the crowds, shouting his famous slogan 'Wakey, Wakey' with his elite stars in a car ahead of our float. Our Russian costumes were short with flowered headdresses and we sat on the sides of a big float filled with white, pink and yellow flowers. Without any warning Kim screamed, 'I'm going.' She slid off the float to mingle with the side jugglers and street performers. 'Your turn next,' she yelled at Jenny, while Anna sat prim and proper, oblivious to our antics. Jenny returned jubilant. 'Your turn now, Pamela.' I pranced among the performers, waving at the crowds and relishing the atmosphere.

Returning to the theatre tired and exhausted, we flopped onto the stage until it was time for the show. I was chosen to appear in a skit with John Wade. As he played with a rope pretending it was a snake, the orchestra played oriental music. Dressed as an oriental belly dancer I glided across the stage behind him, holding a basket above my head. It wasn't funny. On the final performance, knowing they couldn't sack me, I improvised. I stretched a black leotard over my knees, put a white shower cap on my head, wore white shoes and socks and bounded onto the stage. The audience screamed and howled. John was shocked but said, 'We should've done that every night.'

Returning to London, no auditions were advertised. The wardrobe was idle yet Joanie had commenced a new line of hiring out historic and period costumes for weddings. She sent me to buy materials and taught me how to measure people, but I was bored and lethargic, dreaming of shows and wondering when I'd get another contract. Absent minded, I flipped through *The Stage* Magazine, not reading it properly. Glancing through it later, I stared in disbelief. There was a small advert for dancers to audition for the Beat Girls for a TV show. Could I make it in time?

Arriving late, I walked into a large, rehearsal room crowded with dancers huddled around the walls, guarding their belongings as they watched a routine. Six girls were dancing together as an American man shouted out movements. I changed fast with my back to everyone. The steps were unusual, modern American jazz. When they'd finished, the American called me to the centre of the room. He'd noticed my late arrival and asked me to perform a weird movement squatting like a frog, pushing my back up and down and swinging my arms up and down. Everyone laughed but I'd impressed him.

'Can you stay behind?'

'Yes,' I replied in disbelief, knowing he'd already chosen his dancers.

Surprise! One of the chosen dancers was Jo Cook, who'd taught me at Pitt-Draffen's. She'd recognised me and my eyes lit up as she approached me. 'Pamela, how'd you like to take my place at the Pigalle Nightclub in Piccadilly Circus?'

Spellbound, my confused mind envisioned late nights, expensive taxi fares and dancing in a nightclub. I loved the theatre, though. 'No,' I replied to her amazement.

The choreographer was Gary Cockrell who'd danced in the 1957 Broadway musical *West Side Story*, which later transferred to Her Majesty's Theatre in London. 'You need to take classes with me in jazz,' he stated.

'How can I afford that?'

'You can wash our dishes on Monday afternoons and I'll give you free classes.'

I agreed.

He lived in Covent Garden in a town house with several other show business colleagues. Every room was pristine white with large, exotic green plants adding colour to the glaring whiteness. The kitchen featured the latest equipment, although I was mortified to see a mountain of greasy pots, dishes and cutlery stacked high on every inch of the sink and bench. It was spotless when I left.

Returning to Joanie's, a limp rag doll crawled up the steps. But the classes were brilliant and as I learnt the latest American jazz steps my style improved in leaps and bounds.

One day Gary took my photo, explaining he'd arranged an audition for me for the musical *Hair*, which was coming to the West End. His strict instructions were, 'Wear beatnik clothes, loads of jangly jewelry and wear your hair in plats or loose.' What stupidity! I wore my pretty, black dress with hair piled up high and was dismissed in seconds. The musical became an international success from the hit songs. The theme of the show centred on beatniks and the whole cast appeared naked in the finale.

I'd told Joanie about the classes but not the cleaning. Returning after a hard, washing up session she confronted me. 'Look at you. You look dreadful. What on earth have you been doing?' I blurted out the truth. Anger swept over her face. I'd never seen her like this. 'How dare you,' she exploded. 'Isn't sewing here good enough for you?'

Frightened of the outcome I whimpered, 'I only wanted dancing classes.'

She glared at me for a few seconds as she made up her mind what to do with me. Red faced, I waited for what seemed like an eternity. Abruptly she stated, 'I'll phone my agent. If she's got a job you'd better take it.'

Meekly I agreed. Shaking, I waited as she made the phone call. All ambitions to dance in a London musical were crushed forever. I had to stay in London for auditions as Kettering was too far away. How could I live between contracts?

She returned triumphant declaring, 'You've got an audition on Wednesday. It's for pantomime in Scotland and you'd better take it.'

'Oh,' I replied in relief.

Life returned to normal, with no greasy dishes to wash, no classes and sewing for Joanie. The private audition was brief. Pantomime would be a new experience.

I didn't know I'd signed a contract with one of the best theatrical establishments in Britain. The acclaimed Howard and Wyndham Enterprise Group. Scotland, a land of mystique and legends, was waiting for me.

Scotland

The train chugged and rattled at an annoying pace, steam mingling with heavy, grey skies. Heading north it meandered through quaint villages and towns filled with terrace houses, stopping at all stations. Passing through Robin Hood country, the colossal furnaces in Newcastle opened the gateway to Scotland with smoking furnaces and extensive ship yards.

Tired and relieved, I reached Edinburgh twelve hours later. The platform was deserted, apart from people exiting the train. Dragging a battered suitcase from the warm train into the cold air I shivered, realising I'd need a new one soon. Suitcases didn't have wheels in those days and were carried by hand unless a porter was hired.

At the taxi rank I asked the driver to take me to the Kings Theatre. 'Okh hai hen,' he said, grinning. I stared in disbelief at his reference to women as farm animals. Laughing, I replied, 'Okh hai cock,' and he chuckled. Scotland has its own currency but accepts English money, so paying him was easy.

My first impressions of Edinburgh were of admiration. The characters of the town and the mediaeval streets were unique. The large castle on the hill protected the old capital city and in past centuries it would have been filled with knights and fair maidens, feasts and merriment and the odd ghost.

Reaching the theatre, I noticed how small it looked. The outside façade was deceiving, resembling an office building with double windows, but the central entrance was designed with

Grecian pillars. Large billboards advertised the forthcoming pantomime *A Love for Jamie*, the second in a trilogy produced by Freddy Carpenter and the brainchild of Stewart Cruikshank. The fairytales told the adventures of Jamie in the highlands of Scotland with Scottish songs and dances, lavish sets, comical characters and spectacular tartan costumes.

Relieved to have arrived, I dumped my luggage in the foyer and gasped at the grandeur. The foyer doors displayed mahogany carved frames inset with stained glass. Marble pilasters attached to the walls and the shiny parquet floor seemed too clean to walk on. Venturing into the large auditorium, tiered boxes were arranged on three levels at both sides of the stalls and circles. The theatre was owned by Howard and Wyndham, a production company founded in Glasgow in 1895. Today it's controlled by the Festival Theatres Trust, who plan to refurbish it to modern day standards.

The cast of the show were arriving in dribbles and drabbles. I reported to the stage manager who told me to find my digs, and to attend rehearsals on Monday. Stage managers are gods, responsible for the smooth running of a show. Cause a disruption and they'll sack you on the spot. Their command is absolute.

Walking down a side street full of terraced houses, a sign 'Bedsitter to Let' caught my attention. Close to the theatre it was a stroke of luck, and a cheerful housewife greeted me. The room was cosy, clean and comfortable. As I was leaving to collect my luggage, she told me she had another double room to let. Two tired dancers came back with me and were delighted they didn't have to search for digs. We stayed there for the entire season without incident.

The dance routines were learnt on stage but the final two days were filled with dress and lighting rehearsals. Freddy Carpenter, the producer, created special effects tranforming plain sets to colourful tableau with soft hues of green, brown and gold. For the fairy glen he used dry ice to create smoke and haze, bringing the fairytale to life.

The show was a knockout success, with every matinee and evening performance filled to capacity. During the Christmas and New Year festivities we performed three shows a day. Forget the aching limbs – the electric atmosphere and joy of dancing in a spectacular show was magic. During the festivities, management hired a coach for the cast to visit the Royal Children's Hospital. Dressed in our tartan costumes, the children were thrilled to see us.

Due to the cold, frosty days of winter I rarely ventured out. No sun or swimming or lazing on a sandy beach. My skin colour had changed to a pale white and I missed a golden opportunity to explore the town and culture. The main shopping area was in Princess Street and the magnificent castle on the other side looked fascinating. Bored, I returned to my new hobby of knitting and racing against the clock between numbers I finished three jumpers in record time.

One evening in the barnyard scene we were performing as chickens while the boys partnering us were roosters. A large hut was erected on stage left and we came out of it to the delight of the audience, prancing towards stage right. Smash and crash. The entire audience gasped as the entire hut collapsed, missing us by inches. The orchestra continued to play as we danced but by the next performance the hut was restored as new.

Towards the end of the season, in the opening scene in the fairy glen a male dancer decided to show off. He'd persuade one of the girls to give him her long length pink ballet dress with flimsy wings attached for him to dance in for a laugh. Knowing how strict the stage manager was, I rushed to the wings and confronted him. Dragging the dress from him, I struggled into it before the curtain opened.

The girls whispered, 'Walk to the back and wait, then extend your right leg back in an arabesque, come to the front, cross your hands. Kneel. Get up. Cross in front. Pose and don't move.' It worked, but involved changing at lightning speed for my number. Although comical, the boy would have been in serious trouble. Later, I tried to pick up the missing stitches on the needles – a hopeless task.

What a long panto season. In London few if any summer season contracts were available. Nothing was advertised in *The Stage,* but an unimaginable twist of events took place.

People were always coming and going in Joanie's wardrobe, and one day a tall handsome man came to talk to Joanie. Seeing me, he asked casually, 'Hello, and where are you from?'

'I've just finished a panto in Scotland. I'm a dancer,' I replied with pride.

'Ah, show business. I'm the boyfriend of the choreographer George Carden,' he declared with amusement.

'What?' I exploded as my cheeks turned bright red. 'I worked for him in Amsterdam last year and couldn't return because I was sick.'

'I saw him last night and he told me two girls have pulled out of a show he'll be doing in Glasgow. He's looking for someone.'

'Tell him about me,' I implored him.

'He's waiting outside in his car for me. Do you want to come and see him?'

With no make-up on and dressed casually, I was horrified. 'Oh no. Tell him I'm looking for work.'

The following morning he returned and looked for me. 'Here's George's telephone number. He wants you to phone him at 2:30 this afternoon.'

I couldn't contain my excitement and phoned on the dot. He wasn't there. Phoning every five minutes, Joanie became distraught. 'Stop it Pamela. You're disrupting the wardrobe.' Half an hour later, Mr Carden answered and told me to go to his apartment the following afternoon.

Nervous, I arrived at a modern building in Knightsbridge, and entering the foyer the automatic glass doors opened – a new age phenomena. The apartment was grey and bare. A large circular table was at the side with a big, cardboard box placed in the centre, surrounded by several papers. Mr Carden greeted me, wasting no time.

'Where've you been working?' When I told him, he was impressed. I'd worn a long, woollen dress, not expecting to dance. 'Lift up your dress and turn around slowly,' he requested in a firm voice. I clutched the skirt up to my waist line holding my breath, praying he'd take me as I turned like a fairy in a musical box.

'Come and sign your contract,' he stated as my face radiated happiness. Opening the door for me to leave he smiled and said, 'Don't forget costume fittings at Alex Shanks.'

I'd signed a contract to appear in the brilliant *Five Past Eight* show in Glasgow, Scotland at the famous Alhambra Theatre. It'd be the most spectacular show I'd ever danced in, surpassing any West End show for glamour and spectacle. Dick Hurran, the producer and impresario, travelled the world searching for show-stopping items and unique artists to create magnificent, extravaganza shows each year.

In the six month run there were three separate shows. We rehearsed at St Andrews Church Hall, although specific numbers were learnt on stage. The dressing room was spacious with a large mirror for each dancer. It also contained a shower, unheard of in those days. All the girls were in the same digs but with the constant gossip and preferring to be alone, I found a bed sitter close to the theatre.

Glasgow is very different to Edinburgh. It's a sprawling metropolis and the largest city in Scotland. With a population of half a million it boasted a large port and a ship building industry on the river Clyde, shopping centres, museums, theatres and pubs. Scotch whiskey is claimed to be the best in the world and walking home from the theatre at night I'd occasionally see a drunken body lying in the gutter. The climate was cool, wet, humid and overcast. I missed the Jersey beaches but dancing again for Mr Carden in such a historic show made my heart and mind pulsate with joy.

The *Five Past Eight* show had been running for several years and always started at this unusual time. Apart from guest artists, the major drawcard were the Scottish comics Rikki Fulton and Jack Milroy, and the theatre was packed to capacity every night. Acts who appeared in the shows were the Scottish singer Sheila Paton, the singer Peter Regan who'd appeared in many London musicals and the soubrette Elaine Taylor who later starred in the musical *Chess*. Johnny Hart had just returned from Las Vegas and thrilled the audience, making doves and budgies disappear and reappear. David Nixon, the magician, astounded the audience sawing a lady in half and used one of the girls for a disappearing act. Patsy Ann Noble, the young Australian singing sensation, was warm and friendly, laughing and joking with us. Everyone adored her.

At exactly five past eight the loud noise from the audience subsided as the orchestra commenced playing. The red curtains parted and entering in a kicking line we were welcomed with thunderous applause, wearing pink, satin leotards with hair bundled into bee hives adorned with feathers. There were amazing production numbers and it's hard to pinpoint which one was the best as they were all different. 'Shades of Blue' included the polka, tango and the blues. I danced in a blue ballerina length dress as Patsy Ann glided down a white staircase, her rich voice captivating the audience. To exit I ran to centre stage to a male dancer, who lifted me high above him with my legs in an arabesque position. Bliss. I was a bird in flight.

The finale was breathtaking. The stage floor parted to each side as five grand pianos rose up to stage level while pianists played 'Rhapsody in Blue' and waterfalls cascaded in the background.

Fete Espanole portrayed a typical Spanish fiesta with the full ensemble. In one scene the backdrop was a mirror, which reflected the picture of a Spanish tavern which covered the entire stage floor. A flamenco couple danced at the side, and dressed as a waiter I improvised steps, jumping onto the reflected pictures of tables and chairs. It gave the impression I was an Olympic athlete performing gigantic leaps.

The Paris number featured the Living Screen, presented by arrangement with the Tropicana Hotel in Las Vegas. A large screen filled the stage, composed of many one feet wide elongated elastics. A film showed a manor house in the centre with a white grandiose staircase on either side. Parisian characters appeared and ran down the steps and onto a garden. As our character reached the bottom of the screen we burst through the elastic in the same costume as the figure on the screen disappeared. We ran around the pasarella in front of the orchestra to the other side. With exact timing we broke through the screen as our figure reappeared on the screen to run back up the stairs and disappear into the mansion.

Opening the second half of the last show, the orchestra platform rose up from the pit in its entirety on an iron grid and slid to the back of the stage. Cabaret style numbers completed the rest of the performance. Other small numbers included being dressed in hooped crinoline gowns and balancing on wooden, orange boxes around an enormous clock as Peter Regan sang 'Hickory Dickory Doc'. While Sheila Paton sang 'Climb Every

Mountain', we stood at the side dressed as nuns. In another number to open the second half, four of us were dressed as black panthers perched on the shoulders of the male dancers, and I was severely reprimanded for having a hole in my black tights. Any unusual detail in the show was never missed and reported instantly, as they had seamstresses to repair the costumes.

Patsy Ann held a party for her 21st birthday at her apartment and a week later kindly offered to celebrate mine there, too. My parents came but, waiting for them after the show, to my horror I'd missed everyone. Getting lost in unfamiliar territory, they sang 'Happy Birthday' in a dead end street. Seeing a long line of cars and hearing the music, we found the party in full swing – and Mother presented me with three Revelation suitcases which all ended up in tatters after the constant journeys. I became friendly with some university professors and students who showed me how to drink whiskey the Scottish way. Placing a bowl of thick, hot soup in one hand and a minute glass of potent 80 per cent whiskey in the other was an enjoyable, heady contrast. One evening they implored me to go to a party on the outskirts of Glasgow. I agreed if they promised to drive me back in time for a 10 am rehearsal. After much merriment we flopped onto the couches and chairs at 3 am.

Waking up late and hung over, one of them drove me at lightning speed to the theatre. I raced onto the stage, five minutes late. We were rehearsing a number climbing on tall ladders and an angry Mr Carden bellowed, 'Get on the first rung and hang upside down.' I held on for dear life, blood gushing into my head. Aching arms were no distraction, I'd hold on until death. After what seemed like an eternity he demanded, 'You can come down now, get to your places everyone.' Payback for being late. Why be in Glasgow and not see Loch Ness? Grey skies below the high peaks of the mountains smothered the silent landscape. The boat pierced though the still waters of the lake, breaking an eerie silence. No birds could be seen or heard, only the gentle commentary of the captain telling us about the famous monster who lurked below. Straining our necks, we never saw it.

In the final week of the show, we were stunned to learn one of the girls was sacked by the stage manager before she entered the dressing room. No explanation was given and we never saw her again.

George Carden offered us a contract for a Christmas season in Newcastle. No – the dream of escaping the chills of winter to pursue the warmth of a new country was calling …

Madrid, Spain

My family had been delighted to see me, but within days after my arrival in London, a contract to dance in Spain for a year was advertised. Packing a new suitcase, I'd waved goodbye to Mother's taunts, 'Don't bring back a matador.'

Sleepless, I'd travelled since the crack of dawn from Kettering, experienced another choppy voyage on the ferry and a chaotic train journey to Paris, then changed trains from Gare du Nord to Gare du Sud.

Slamming the *Teach Yourself Spanish* book onto the shuddering, wooden table, I wondered if I'd ever master this peculiar language or understand the gallant Spaniards I'd dreamed of meeting. Gazing at the dull French landscape and listening to the constant yanking and clanking of the heavy wheels as they tore the train forward, I recalled the film *Carmen* and Spanish dances I'd previously performed. Vibrant fiestas with flamboyant gypsies partnering flamenco dancers as they swish their long, polka dot costumes with passion and clack their castanets; feet beating in unison to a background of melodious guitars; powerful bulls pitted against richly clad matadors whirling their capes to the roar of the crowds …

Spain thrives on the dark history of wars and horrific, anarchist, religious rebellions. Kings reigned in splendid palaces and castles, but in 1966 the Republic was headed by a tyrannical, balding Franco, the reincarnation of the devil who had treated Spaniards as aliens, hunting them down for mass killings. Yes, I was determined to experience it all. As darkness approached, I crept past the other sleeping travellers and settled into my seat.

The jolts and hissing of the train woke us up as it came to an abrupt halt at Irun, the border town between France and Spain. Struggling onto a bare platform, we proceeded along an unending path to customs and strained to put our luggage onto the Spanish train. Our weary bones slumped onto hard, uncomfortable seats. The complete journey would take 36 hours and we were only half way to Madrid. In darkness we'd missed the beauty of the magnificent, eloquent mountains of the North Basque country where rebels fought during the Civil War. The land was smothered in parched, dry earth, the sky a clear blue with a hot, blazing sun in the distance. Yellow stoned villages seemed abandoned with no sign of life and the odd tree refreshing the landscape, while towns revealed church spires peeping out of a mass of structured, medieval buildings.

The ballet consisted of twelve girls and six boys and at day break we continued to get to know each other. Dark, frizzy haired Nematalla (known as 'Nem') fascinated me with her bubbly enthusiasm. Exploring our backgrounds and being the same age, we agreed to share digs together. Passing through Don Quixote territory, Nem screamed out, 'Look at that!' In the distance rising above the uninspiring yellow plains, a massive poster of a black bull appeared and these continued to appear intermittently until we reached Madrid.

As we arrived at the main railway station Atocha, head girl Mary, who'd renewed her contract with choreographer Miss Baron, took us to our digs. Exhausted and grubby from the epic journey, the thought of sleep was paradise and we took no notice of our new surroundings until we reached our accommodation, known in Spain as a 'pension'. The tall building with wooden shuttered windows stood among a host of similar ones on a street close to the centre of Madrid. Our hearts missed a beat when we saw the winding staircase and the single iron cage lift, which jerked each time a suitcase was thrown at it. Reaching our room, Nem and I took one look at the high ceiling and bare furnishings, said goodnight to each other and crashed onto the creaky, iron beds, oblivious to the outside noise of heavy traffic. Madrid is a majestic city, rising above the barren plains in the middle of Spain. It's also the driest capital in Europe. Conquered by the Moors in the Medieval Ages they brought with them a wealth of mosaic culture now preserved in the southern parts of Spain. The river flowed alongside the city with the luscious green foliage of the Campo del Moro surrounding the Royal Palace.

The Grand Via, the main highway, was crammed with department stores, expensive shops and the major banks. We loved it and gazed in awe at the historical Post Office with its cascading fountains. At the heart of Madrid, the Plaza Mayor was a fascinating arcaded square, with authentic eateries displaying hunks of cured ham and other delicacies, and exits leading to cobbled lanes full of tapa bars.

Miss Baron looked to be about seventy, with gold bracelets dangling from her fleshy, bronzed skin. Although strict, her routines left much to be desired. In the opening number, we strutted like peacocks through doors at the back of the stage dressed in blue bikinis with fluffy, feathered hats, and stepped elegantly down a large, white staircase. Exiting at the wings, we repeated this three times to create the illusion of a large company. Honestly, did the audience really believe there were hundreds of dancers? In another number, she placed us on gaudy, wooden horses on a revolving carousel. Other numbers involved posing in the background as the comics joked and laughed, and she used the same ladder routine from the *Five Past Eight* Show in Glasgow. All we did was throw out an arm or a leg as monkeys do, with no fluidity of movement. The show named *The Policeman and the Taxi Driver* starred the popular comedy duo Zori and Santos, who'd toured Spain for many years with successful reviews.

Lasting two hours, the shows commenced at 7:30 pm and 11 pm every night except Sundays. The money was good but we earnt it. We were pretty English girls and the Spaniards would love us as we were.

Frustration set in. Where were the intricate steps or creativity? Madrid had captivated me and I couldn't break my contract. I resolved to spend my time learning Spanish, explore Madrid and its culture and travel with the company to learn more about this fascinating foreign land. Spaniards live a different lifestyle to the English. Shops close in the afternoons for 'siesta time', and for urgent repairs they reply, 'Manyana, tomorrow.' Dinner was eaten late, but we soon accustomed ourselves to the late hours and we loved to shop and enjoy the sunshine.

The show commenced in Valencia for two weeks to flush out any inconsistencies before opening in Madrid. The problem was the blue bikini costumes. Under Franco's rule, freedom of speech was prohibited. Revealing a belly button on stage was censored and two lengths of blue material were hurriedly crossed over from the bra to the top of the bikini bottom to hide the wicked culprit.

Before opening night in Madrid, we stifled giggles sitting in the eighteenth century boxes at the side of the large auditorium, in a theatre destined to be condemned for the sake of humanity. It'd been an old cinema. By the final performance of the show we knew we were replacing the pathetic, tatty, plumed costumes reminiscent of the 1930 Hollywood films with glamour. Our show opened to rave reviews from the critics and we settled down to enjoy the Spanish way of life.

It was during this time an unexpected friendship developed with Alan and Paco, two of the male dancers in the show. They'd worked together in a theatre show in Denmark and were as frustrated with the choreography as I was. Paco was the walking portrait of a tall, dark matador, whereas Alan was an English rose, small, white skinned and balletic with flaming red hair – an odd couple, who I respected more as our friendship grew. Paco, impressed with my futile attempts to learn the language, suggested Alan and I take language classes.

Alan loved classical dance and, loathing the thought of losing our technique, we hired a studio to practise. I wanted to learn flamenco dancing and bought the proper shoes and castanets for genuine tuition. The basic steps were good, but my lower arms ached and hardened trying to play them, and I couldn't master the intricate art of dancing and playing them together. Nem didn't mind the loud clacking noise in the flat as she was secretly seeing one of the stars. It suited us both.

Sometimes Nem and I would stroll along under the shady trees of the Avenida_del Prado by the lake, settling down at a side café for a welcome 'caffe latte' to write our postcards. 'Adios Pamela,' she'd say as I walked to the Prado Museum to gaze in awe at the works of geniuses. I wondered what they were thinking when they painted their masterpieces. Their clothes were so different to ours, the royals flamboyant with many jewels and lavish costumes. War paintings portrayed human suffering on a large scale. As for the peasants, their lives must have been hell. Faces were weather beaten and their clothes were torn rags falling from emaciated bodies. It made me shudder and I was shocked at the disparity between nobility and the poor.

Between shows, Paco led us to trattorias for cheap, delicious food hidden away in side lanes where the locals ate and we'd order the plate of the day, washed down with a glass of watery red wine suitable for children. I relished the cold 'Gaspacho' soup, a recipe taken from the countryside peasants, with plump, bright green cucumbers, sun scorched tomatoes and old breadcrumbs mixed together with oil and water. Thirst quenching! Crispy salads were filled with lettuce, ripe bulging olives, red tomatoes and Spanish onions with pure olive oil dribbled over them. Added to succulent, grilled steak or tender, juicy chicken, the meals were a delight to view, smell and enjoy. Fish, a major part of Spanish cuisine, was not on my Mother's menu, and I adored tasting and trying the exotic dishes.

One day Paco ordered prawns. The plate of the dormant see-through pink creatures horrified me. The spindly long legs seemed curled in pain. I looked again – dead, black, pin-pointing eyes stared up at me. Were they demons from underneath the ocean? I touched one and shuddered as Paco laughed, then peeled back the crispy shell and gave it to me. Delicious.

'The best part is the head,' Paco explained.

Alan had devoured most of them and told me to shut my eyes. 'Suck, suck,' ordered Alan as I tried to alleviate my fears. 'Suck it gently.' With closed eyes, praying I wouldn't be poisoned, I sucked. Surprise. The taste and rich flavour of the sea awakened unknown taste buds and a desire to try more fish delicacies.

As the months passed, my Spanish improved. Speaking pidgin Spanish and understanding what the locals said, Paco allowed me to shout, 'Oiga', to get the waiter's attention, and corrected my pronunciation when he allowed me order meals.

Sometimes the girls would sunbathe naked on the rooftop of a local swimming pool. White marks on our shoulders would look dreadful with the costumes. It seemed a safe place from prying eyes, or so we thought until a helicopter hovered overhead.

My parents came for a holiday. What should've been a happy time became a nightmare. Mother was treating me like a teenager. 'Don't do this, don't do that. Can't you wear something else? Surely you'll get sick eating all that seafood?'

I couldn't bear it. Aged twenty two, I'd looked after myself for years. A cruel plan formed in my mind. Arguments wouldn't lead to a peaceful solution.

They came back to the flat after the show and Nem was out. I made us coffee and before I chickened out on the idea told her, 'Mother, I've something to tell you. You're not going to like it.' Her body tensed as Popsey sat quietly in the background and I announced, 'I'm going to become a nun.'

'What?' she stammered. 'You must be joking. You can't do that. What about dancing and boyfriends?'

'No Mother, I've made up my mind.' It was as though a bomb had struck her. The tirade continued for ten minutes until she conceded defeat and I released her of the pain. 'Mother, I'm not going to become a nun.'

Relief flooded her face as she exclaimed, 'Thank God for that.'

I gave her a hug and it wasn't mentioned again, but I'd felt guilty at hurting her. On their last night I took them to the Plaza Mayor, where I'd seen a small night club advertised flamenco dancing. The low lit tavern was as I'd visualised it. Castanets clacked in unison to foot stamps as dancers passionately threw skirts at their partners. Guitars played in the background and the men sang, leading to a tumultuous finale with the deafening noise of hand claps, singing and fast heel beats.

We were finishing our drinks when a tall Spaniard dressed in an expensive black suit approached us, and sat down in the spare seat beside me. What happened next was totally unexpected.

He leaned across, extending his hand to Popsey, then said in English, 'Hola, my name Antonio. I, matador. You good man. You holiday?'

My father was shocked. Something had passed between them. After a few pleasantries, we escaped and returned to my flat for a coffee. Popsey explained, 'He belongs to some sort of guild or masonic society. When he shook my hand he put three fingers into my palm.'

Mother roared with laughter as she shrieked, 'I thought Pamela would bring home a matador, but you've still got what it takes.'

In Spain, Holy Week leading up to Easter is a time for celebration. The Spanish are overly religious, with churches and cathedrals holding long, spectacular processions. It was a national holiday and Nem and I were intrigued, and decided to go to Puerta del Sol on Good Friday in the early evening. Mingling with the massive crowds, we heard trumpets as we arrived. Rolling drums pounded our eardrums as monastic figures paraded before us. It was a somber occasion. They carried metre-length white sticks through the streets, dressed in mauve tunics and conical pointed hoods covering their faces, with slits for the eyes. It was eerie in the twilight and felt like a death march. We didn't stay long, and returned to the safety of our flat after noticing the bars were full of religious worshippers.

On Easter Sunday we went to the Gran Via to see a magnificent procession. Heralded by trumpets, massive floats passed us, carried by young monks who must've been heavyweight champions to carry such a weight on their shoulders. The holy images of Christ and the Virgin Mary were life-size, adorned with ornaments and candles. We enjoyed it – a far cry from the sombre procession on Good Friday.

Summer posters advertised a forthcoming bull fight on Sunday with a famous matador. My heart quickened. I'd longed to see the glamorous parades and bravery of a matador. His photo was plastered on all the women's magazines on the front covers. I approached Alan and Paco hoping, they'd come with me. Paco was concerned.

'Pamela, don't go,' he implored me, 'It's cruel. The bull gets killed. You won't like it.' Nevertheless, I was intent on going, and set out on Sunday morning alone.

It was hot and I'd put a small fan in my bag. Taking the Metro to Las Ventas, I joined the hustle and bustle of the stampeding crowd, following them towards the Moorish-inspired stadium. Purchasing the cheapest ticket I was delighted my pidgin Spanish was understood. Halfway up the vast stadium I settled on a hard, stone seat in the sun, where I had a complete view of the huge, yellow arena and action. The Royal Box, where the

President of the Bullfight sat, was directly in front of me, along with a red barrier with several entrances surrounded the ring. The stadium filled up quickly with not a spare seat to be seen, as people buzzed with anticipation of the forthcoming fight. A bugle sounded the commencement of a parade, and a deathly hush swept over the stadium. The show was about to begin.

A band entered, followed by matadors and picadors marching in time to the music. Holding pink and red capes, they waved to the cheering crowd and saluted the presiding dignitary in the Royal Box. Their costumes, designed from ancient, Andalusian clothing, delighted the audience. They were magnificent in jeweled boleros and thigh-hugging black trousers. Three matadors would fight two bulls each, with the famous matador appearing last.

As they departed, quiet reigned until a ferocious bull with massive horns charged into the ring, followed by a matador holding a large, pink cape. The bull snorted as the matador manipulated it over its horns, making several passes. The crowd roared their approval. The atmosphere was electric and I shouted with them, enjoying the excitement.

However, what followed next was a living nightmare. The matador retreated as picadors rode out on horseback. The horses wore padding over their eyes and heavy padding covered their torsos. I couldn't believe it! They rode directly towards the bull to pierce it between the shoulders with two barbed sticks with small ribbons attached to the ends. In retaliation the bull turned its attention to the horses, banging horns into the side of one who caught his attention, pounding harder and stronger, trying to gore it and knock it down. Petrified and unable to see, the horse reared up its hooves high into the air, led by the horseman he trusted. Once the sticks entered the bull they galloped away at hurricane speed, leaving it angered, agitated and weakened. A picador on horseback entered the arena holding a lance in his hand. Alongside the bull, he threw it with all his strength into the shoulder blades. It aggravated, pulling and twisting the shoulder blades and giving the bull pain each time it moved. Torture.

Feeling nauseous and sick in the gut with the sun beating down on my head, I furiously waved my fan to blow away beads of perspiration. Squashed between two loud mouthed Spaniards with my blouse drenched in sweat, I was determined to stay to see the end of the fight, curiosity my worst enemy.

The bull heaved, its nostrils steaming in the harsh heat as the crowd jeered and whistled. It was panicking with the trauma of pain and deafening noises. Jumping up and down aggravated the wound, making the lance cut deeper. No escape. Wracked with pain, delirious and weak, an inner strength kicked in. Animal instinct dictated it to fight to the death and gore the enemy. The matador entered the ring again with a red cape to tumultuous applause. Flaunting it and waving a steel sword to the crowd, the matador hid the sword beneath the cape, taunting the animal to the end of its energy. Swishing his cape with precision, he brought the captive animal closer to mortality. The crowd stamped their feet, giving thunderous applause as the matador swirled the cape closer to the exhausted bull. He knelt before the desperate animal as it sat to the ground. No more pain, green grass, sky or earth. Take the pain away.

As if on cue, it lowered its head in defeat. In a single movement, the sword thrust between its shoulder blades to the heart. It keeled over dead. The crowd waved white handkerchiefs – a symbol of their exhilaration with the fight. An ear of the bull was cut off and the matador paraded around the ring, holding up his trophy to the crowd as four workers in overalls dragged the body away before the next fight.

I'd never witnessed such barbaric torture and had to escape. Struggling to get out of the arena, I pushed past people ordering ice-creams.

I reached the bottom, disorientated and lost. Where was the Metro? Walking for miles around the arena, as I turned a corner the foul stench reached me first. Horror! The recently killed bull was hanging upside down on two large hooks. Stripped of its hide, heavy steam was rising from pink flesh and a vivid green in the gut was visible from its last meal. I couldn't sleep at night. The meat is sold at exorbitant prices and the hide is made into winter coats. A bull is colour blind, and the red cape dates back to medieval times, used to camouflage blood. Today, bull fights continue throughout Spain.

Spanish Tour

As the Iberian plane flew into a storm, shuddering and crashing through black clouds, the torrential rain became a nightmare. It zoomed up and down, spilling crockery everywhere as lightning flashed past the windows. What a relief to land at Heathrow Airport.

I popped in to see Joanie, who loved listening to my Madrid adventures. At home I caught up on family news and relaxed. The journey back to Madrid was as smooth as an eagle soaring through the sky and reignited my love of flying.

We toured Spain, crisscrossing the country in a large coach and staying a week in each town or city as they celebrated their annual fiesta. Journeys varied from a couple of hours to half a day or night. The coach would stop at the theatre and we'd explore nearby streets for cheap digs. Some had bare necessities while others were comfortable with delightful patios. The theatres were large, cold and ancient, packed to capacity for every performance.

Nem and I continued to share digs together. Dear Nem and her clandestine affair – she never mentioned where she was going, often disappearing all night. She'd get hurt but it didn't bother her. My lips were sealed tight. Able to converse in Spanish, I enjoyed chatting with the locals and exploring new towns on my own or with Alan and Paco.

One night heading north through Basque mountainous territory towards San Sebastian, the coach stopped half way up the mountain. Two soldiers holding machine guns and wearing dark green uniforms entered the coach. Walking up and down the aisle, they glared into each face. Rigid, fearful of the outcome, no one moved. As they left the coach, the driver explained, 'It was just a routine search. They were looking for rebels.'

San Sebastian is a wonderful coastal town packed with tourists. During one show, the lights went out while we were dancing, leaving the stage in darkness. The orchestra stopped playing and, disorganised, we waited in the wings. The comics appeared and entertained the audience, while stagehands hurriedly placed lighted candles along the footlights. The audience didn't move as they'd paid for their tickets and expected to see the show. The orchestra played and we repeated our number. The candles reminded me of a true story I'd read. In the nineteenth century in France, a young dancer was destined for fame. Her long ballet dress caught fire from the gas lights in the footlights and killed her!

The show continued as normal in a spooky atmosphere, although we kept well away from the candles. Half an hour later the lights returned. Someone had managed to get a generator to work and the stage hands grabbed the candles.

At Salamanca another bizarre incident occurred in our first show. As the curtain rose and the carousel began to move, it caught one of the side curtains, dragging it to the back. Chaos! The comics ran around not knowing what to do as we rode around on the wooden horses, smothered in curtain. The audience thought it was hilarious and part of the show.

Vigo is a town with a massive port, surrounded by inland mountains leading to the Atlantic Ocean. It's located in the North West in the municipality of Galicia and close to the Portuguese border. While there, I met some university students who were surprised to meet an English girl who could understand a little of their language. I told them how much I admired the beauty of their country and they invited me to join them for a trip up a mountain at the weekend, promising to return me to the theatre in time for the show.

There was not a cloud in the sky as they arrived in an old car, bringing with them a bottle of white wine and local cheese. Leaving the outskirts of Vigo, we continued driving up a steep, rugged road leading to the top of a mountain, miles from civilisation. Perched at the top of the peak we laughed, sipping wine and eating cheese as they pointed out various highlights and places of interest. It was breathtaking with a panoramic view of the town, the harbour, other mountains and distant islands in the glittering blue sea.

After an hour or two it was time to leave and we clamoured back into the car. The unimaginable happened. The car wouldn't start. It coughed, spluttered and died. They thought quickly. 'No te precoupes', 'don't worry', and told me they would free wheel the car down the mountain to a small café at the bottom where they could call a mate to collect me.

With the three boys and girl I helped them push the car to the narrow road. It worked. One student sat on the bonnet, shouting instructions to his mate who was steering the car. It was hair raising as the car sped faster down the winding road until we arrived at the café unscathed. It took an hour for the other car to arrive and I was frantic that I'd miss the show. After hugs and thanks, their friend drove me at neck-breaking speed to the theatre and I arrived with only ten minutes to put on my make-up and scramble into the opening costume.

The show was performing in La Caruna another costal town in Galicia when I met a young Spanish business man. In limited Spanish I told him of the amazing places I'd visited, how I adored the culture and historic buildings. He told me he was going on a business trip to Santiago del Compostela, the capital of Galicia, the following day, and could take me if I was interested. It was a couple of hours' drive away and had a spectacular cathedral built over the supposed shrine of St Paul, which I shouldn't miss. He said I'd have to sight-see on my own, though, and we'd be back in plenty of time for the show. Thrilled at this golden opportunity, I agreed.

He arrived in a modern car. The scenery was plain with many green fields as we travelled inland. It rained as we arrived at the city, adding a shimmering glow to the historic buildings. He left me at the door of the cathedral, giving me a few hours to explore. I gazed up in awe at the spires, and enjoyed the magnificent statues and ornamentation as I ventured inside. Traipsing around the old part of the town through arched, cobbled streets was awe inspiring, surrounded by ancient, historic buildings. My new friend was there at the appointed time.

We were driving along a country lane, heading back towards La Caruna and discussing the cathedral, when a bizarre and unexpected incident happened. Out of nowhere a fat, brown cow leaped into the road, hitting the bonnet of the car and meandered away, limping into the countryside. The car wouldn't start. No traffic, and we were miles from the nearest town. 'No te precupes', 'Don't worry', he said, 'A car come soon. You theatre OK. No worry.'

I was restless. It was an impossible situation and we could do nothing but sit and wait. I told him how much I'd enjoyed the sightseeing but I was unable to concentrate, fearful we'd be stuck here for hours. He understood.

At last a dilapidated, ancient car driven by a middle-aged country larrikin appeared, and my new friend flagged him down. They spoke together in Spanish and after reassurances the larrikin could be trusted I accepted the lift. We bumbled along with no other cars in sight as I was bombarded with fast unknown Spanish words.

Approaching Vigo, he drove slower as I looked at my watch. With no traffic jams I could make it in time for the show. To my surprise he opened the door for me in front of the theatre, bowed and kissed my hand. I dashed into the dressing room with minutes to spare before the opening number, regretting I was unable to speak good Spanish to thank him.

After a long coach journey and approaching Barcelona on the Eastern Coast and the second largest city in Spain after Madrid, Paco told me, 'They speak a different language here.'

'Oh dear,' I exclaimed, 'I won't be able to practise Spanish.'

'Yes you can,' he grinned. 'They speak Catalan, which is based on Latin. You'll be understood.' It was Paco's home territory. Alan and I spent the entire week being led to trattorias off the beaten track which catered for the locals. We ate delicious fish soups, strange meals of squid, octopus, mussels and clams, and the popular rice dish paella. Mother would have been horrified.

Heading south to Andalusian country, the home of gypsies and flamenco where the Moors left their greatest influence, there are mountains in the North, farmland in the South and glorious beaches at the coast. It was mid-summer and hot. We danced in Jaen, Murcia, Cordoba, Seville and Granada. Bull fights were advertised in each town and in the carnival atmosphere high-spirited children danced in flamenco costumes with parents. I visited cathedrals with Alan and Paco and stared in disbelief at the tombs of the old medieval kings – they were midgets, only four feet tall. One day we visited the famous Alhambra. Old royal palaces, castles and fortresses adorned with intricate mosaic patterns and arcades, serene patios, fountains and terraced gardens greeted us. We sat on a wall to admire the view the silence, broken only by the soothing trickle of water entering the clear ponds, an experience I never forgot.

Towards the end of the tour Alan confronted me. 'Look at you, you're getting fat. You've got to stop eating chips and bread rolls if you want to dance in a good show. Grilled steak and salad for dinner and no bread rolls.'

One day I was so hungry the temptation was too great. I hid a delicious cheese roll in my bag to eat during the show. I couldn't believe it when he saw me sneaking a bite and chased me around the dressing room to the delight of everyone. When he caught me, he grabbed the roll and took out the mouth-watering, doughy portion explaining, 'It's the white part that's fattening, but you can eat the crust.' He handed it back to me minus the delicious gooey centre piece.

Saying goodbye to Spain, I wondered if I'd ever return to my favourite city Madrid, but I could never work for Miss Baron again. The urge to dance in a show with good choreography was strong.

After another long, tedious, train journey, I arrived back in London. The latter part of October was cold, dreary and uninviting after the scorching heat of Spain. It was also too late to audition for the pantomime season. Joanie was getting costumes ready for several amateur musical productions and I often worked throughout the night to help her.

At last an advert appeared in *The Stage* wanting dancers for the Casino in Monte Carlo. I obtained an audition for the following week and rushed home to prepare to be in tip-top condition.

Monte Carlo

Arriving home briefly, I told my family a strict diet was on the agenda. However, an uncle I'd never met came to visit us from Derby and brought me chocolates as a gift. Reluctantly I handed the box of mouth-watering chocolates to Popsey as Mother laughed and joined in the fun. Scavengers with eager eyes surveyed their feast, waiting until the door closed.

'Don't worry Pamela, you can eat a lettuce leaf and carrot,' Mother laughed with a mischievous twinkle in her eyes. 'I'll soon get you slim.' She served me a miniature potato with meat and beans, sitting in a thimble full of gravy.

Popsey reacted differently. Brilliant at solving problems, he disappeared into his shed and returned with a length of thick plastic, one foot in width by two yards in length. I stared in disbelief. What could this weird thing do to help my waist line?

'Wrap it around your waist, wear it all day long and take it off at night.'

'What's that going to do?'

'It's an old trick a jockey uses before a race to lose weight quickly. The plastic will make you sweat.' Clever Popsey! I followed his instructions.

Mother was amused to see me dart around the house, doing pirouettes and high kicks every spare moment, with the yards of plastic wound around my waist under my jumper. Sweat poured out, with the belching noise of wet skin against plastic increasing during the evening. Torture, but worth it. Leaving for London I was slim.

I arrived confident at the private audition and the woman showed me a few steps which I mastered to perfection. 'Would you like me to repeat the sequence to the left?' I inquired.

'No need,' she replied smiling, 'Come and sign your contract. It's for twelve weeks and you take the train to Monte Carlo on Friday.'

Ballet Bentyber was an international troupe I hadn't heard of, as they were based in Monte Carlo and had never worked in England. I'd read fascinating stories and seen the old films about Monte Carlo and the famous people who lived there. Grace Kelly, the American film star, became Princess Grace when she married Prince Rainier of Monaco and lived in a palace. Onassis, the Greek tycoon with an empire of ships, was cruising there. The world famous ballet dancer Rudolf Nureyev recently defected from Russia was dancing at the Opera House in the Casino, and the high-status annual car rally brought in the crowds. The French Riviera was a playground for the rich and famous and in 1966 I was impatient for new adventure. I was 23, and nothing could go wrong.

Rushing back to Kettering, I threw out the dilapidated suitcase and chose the bigger one of the two I'd received for my birthday.

'Bring back a millionaire Pamela, we'll welcome him with open arms,' Mother yelled as I was leaving.

'Mother, I can't do that in a few weeks. I'll write and be back soon.'

In early December the channel crossing was rough and then the journey crossing through Paris to Gare du Sud usually took one hour. The taxi from Gare du Nord crept forward, unable to meander through the heavy traffic-jams. Distraught, two hours later I arrived at Gare du Sud at a deserted train platform. The train had gone.

A young girl with long, twiggy legs looked lost, too. Approaching her, I asked hopefully, 'Are you joining Ballet Bentyber?'

'Yes,' she replied, relieved to know there were two of us. She phoned the Casino and we were told to take the next train.

Palm trees lined the foreshores with impressive mansions in the towns. Approaching Monte Carlo, there was a wonderful panoramic view of the harbor, full of expensive yachts and the town nestled under a mountain beside a calm, blue sea. This excited us both as we exchanged dance histories.

The Grimaldi family, who owned the tiny principality of Monaco, were almost bankrupt in 1863 and a decision was made to build a casino. Monte Carlo was born in 1866 as tourists and celebrities flocked to the casino in the magical country. Money poured in. Later, the Café de Paris and other palatial hotels were built. It's the second smallest country by area in the world and the most populated. With no taxes, it's also a wealth haven for millionaires.

I gazed in admiration at the majestic Casino and terraced pathways. A velvet green lawn stretching as far as the illustrious Café du Paris displayed groups of flowers around a small fountain. Other grand hotels complemented the scene – one named the 'Place du Casino.' Signs of splendour, luxury and wealth were plentiful.

We couldn't dawdle as Mr Bentyber was waiting. Dressed in a suit and of medium build with short, black hair, from his smile you could see he was a jovial person and was relieved to see us. He took us to our living quarters in a house close to the Casino, telling us to be ready for rehearsals at 10 am sharp. The room was adequate and nothing to write home about. Weary from the turbulent journey I slept, dreaming of millionaires.

Mr Bentyber escaped from Hungary in the early 50s and was well established. His ballets travelled the world and he used Monte Carlo as his home base. We were twelve highly trained girls from England, America, Denmark and France, there for the Winter Season at the night club in the Casino. Residents were forbidden to enter the gambling area and the same rule applied to us, but the fancy poker machines displayed in the Café du Paris lured tourists and locals to try their luck.

In the large rehearsal room on the top floor, our ballet mistress spoke in English to teach us the routines. Her attention to detail was immaculate and the numbers were often fifteen minutes long, but changed weekly. We rehearsed for three days, with costume fittings on a Thursday. A dress rehearsal with the orchestra occurred on Friday and the new show commenced on Saturday. No expense was spared.

The night club was decorated in soft hues of pink and grey, with a medium-sized stage. We opened the show with international cycling, acrobatic, and juggling acts performing afterwards. Nervous with the fast pace of learning routines, it took me a while to settle into the routine.

It was mandatory to arrive at the dressing room an hour before the show. Make-up is a work of art. Mine consisted of mixing together Leichner grease sticks No's 9 and 13 to form the face foundation and fluffing a light brown powder over my face to eliminate shine. A thin, black eyeliner applied to the lower eyelid widened the eyes and applying a soft blue or green powder softened the effect. For the final touches, I'd paint a small white dot at the corner of eyes, outline the eyebrows with a brown pencil, add false eyelashes and mascara, daub the cheekbones with pink and paint my lips a blood red. I'd used this method for years, knowing it looked good.

When I arrived at the dressing room, the ballet mistress took me to the wash basin. She had a bar of soap and a small container of pancake compressed make-up in her hands, and explained, 'We all have to have identical make up. Watch carefully what I do.' I watched intently as she wet the soap to moisten it and applied some to her fingers. Smoothing the soap over my eyebrows, it dried after a few minutes and they disappeared. Taking me to my seat in the dressing room, I watched in amazement as she wet the pancake with a sponge and smoothed it over my face with skilled strokes. Looking at the mirror, I saw a tan-coloured death mask. When this dried, she took my black eyeliner and drew a line from the beginning of the eyebrow in a sweeping curve up and out. Next, she repeated the process under the eyes and said, 'Now you can continue with your normal make-up.'

When I'd finished, I gazed at the mirror, astonished at the transformation as the face of a swan with large appealing eyes looked back at me. My dream was about to be realized – to dance in one of the most prestigious places on earth.

My favourite costume was worn for special galas. Sequined blue bikinis with masses of light blue feathers cascaded down to calf length, held on our backs by a wire rectangle frame. The headdress consisted of a jeweled tiara with blue ostrich feathers shooting up from a single central sheath. As I executed the superb choreography, the jewels, sequins and floating feathers overwhelmed the audience.

We were to perform at a gala at the Café du Paris Hotel ballroom for British Centenary Week at the Café du Paris Hotel in the ballroom, a lavish affair with socialites, film stars and royalty attending. After rehearsals, my adventurous spirit resurfaced. I wanted to know who the film stars were and decided to sneak into the ballroom to find out. If caught, the consequences could be disastrous.

The ballroom was on the ground floor. Heart beating wildly, I inched the main door open and looked inside. It was all clear, no hotel staff or bodies to be seen – and I entered quickly, hoping to look like an employee. Small tables were set for four people and flawlessly decorated. The long main table in the middle caught my attention. I sprinted. Above, enormous, crystal chandeliers sparkled. Gold shining cutlery and fine china dinner plates trimmed with gold were waiting for unknown delicacies to be placed on them. Twelve places were set for the elite guests. Princess Grace and her husband were placed at the centre of the table and opposite them were Elizabeth Taylor, Richard Burton and Sir Alec Guinness. I'd seen enough and headed out the opposite door. Mission accomplished.

At night the ballroom was packed and while dancing in the half-light I could see Princess Grace sitting regally with the Prince by her side. In front of her Elizabeth Taylor wore a black dress decorated with yellow and orange horizontal stripes, an unusual attire for her figure. She looked anxious. Richard Burton was slumped over the table with one arm outstretched.

After the show Mr Bentyber told us to dress in normal clothes. He wanted a photo taken of us with Richard Burton on the steps of the Casino. We gasped. He returned disappointed, declaring Richard Burton was drunk. What a pity. We'd have enjoyed two minutes of fame if the photo had made the international newspapers.

The other girls were pleasant, although no special friendship developed. We played cards to pass the time and a couple of times dined together. Steak fondue was delicious. A large pot of bubbling olive oil was placed under a burner in the middle of the table and with a fork we dipped into it, cooking the meat to our own satisfaction. Eaten with crunchy bread sticks, it was sensational. Other delicacies were not so succulent – grainy snails and frog legs tasted of tough, sinewy chicken.

How was it possible to run into rally drivers? I did. There were a group of English men who'd been coming to Monte Carlo for years. We were chatting and laughing when one of them chuckled, 'Have you seen Monte Carlo from the top of the mountain?'

'What do you mean?'

'At night the view is spectacular.'

'I haven't, but I'd love to.'

'How would you like to see Rudolph Nureyev? He hangs out in a small café shop after his show.' Stunned, I couldn't reply. Nureyev was my idol in the world of ballet. 'We'll take you after your show tonight.'

The show dragged on and I was there to meet them early, tense with excitement. The cafe was crowded except for a spare seat on the other side where Nureyev would sit.

'When he comes in don't stare or look around, act normal,' they lectured.

'Oh, I won't,' I replied with butterflies in my stomach.

'C'mon,' said the jovial one as he stood up. 'Before you see Rudolph, let's take you on a joy ride to see the lights.'

'How long will you be?' the tall one asked.

'Five minutes.'

'That's pushing it a bit. I'll time you.'

Buckled into my seat, the car blasted its way into the darkness at hurricane speed. I started to enjoy it, holding on for dear life. As a racing driver he knew his skill and I'd be safe. Soon the town was behind us and we tore up the steep, winding, narrow road to the top of the mountain, passing through a long tunnel. As we came out the other side a spectacular view greeted us. The town beneath us sparkled, looking like a huge Christmas tree against the darkness of the mountain.

'Enjoying it?' the driver asked, not taking his eyes from the road.

'Yes, thanks.'

On the way down he drove at bullet speed. Entering the café again, the tall one exclaimed to us, 'Six minutes, not bad!'

No sooner had our coffee arrived, the door opened. Rudolph

Nureyev, the world renowned dancer came in taking elongated strides in his tall boots, swishing his black cloak over his shoulder and laughing greetings to his friends. There was another quick glimpse of his famous square jawbone and the tousled blonde hair as we left.

The whole evening had been an amazing experience. I'd seen my idol Nureyev in person and the hair-raising ride with a professional rally driver had thrilled me.

The season was closing in a week and I was expecting to return home. One afternoon Mr Bentyber asked to see me. I'd danced to the best of my ability, was never late and wondered what could be wrong. He was hesitant as I entered his office.

'Pamela, I've had a phone call from Miss Doriss from the Moulin Rouge. She asked me if I can spare a dancer for a six month contract in Majorca. Would you be interested?'

Smiling I replied, 'Yes.' The chance to return to Spanish territory was wonderful news.

'You have to go to Paris tomorrow morning. I'll drive you to the airport in Cannes.'

'Yes, Mr Bentyber,' I replied, bewildered at such short notice.

A line of swaying palm trees along the Cannes esplanade made me feel sad to leave. Would I ever see the south of France again? I was living a dancer's dream – continually working with the best choreographers, travelling and exploring new places. I was happy.

Paris Rehearsals

On the short plane trip, my thoughts crisscrossed over the possibilities which lay ahead. I'd proven my dancing ability, but what if I was too small and they sent me back to England? Surely they'd wonder about my swift departure from a world renowned dancing troupe, and had thousands of dancers they could choose from at a moment's notice? Or was it my destiny to rehearse at the Moulin Rouge where the Can-can was born? I'd already proved my ability to perform the dance at the Butlins' holiday camps, the Windmill Theatre in London and performed high kicks for the George Carden Dancers. How difficult could it be?

I sighed as I settled into my window seat on the plane, gazing at the golden sun blazing through blue skies, bathing the dotted palm trees along the South of France and the famous Riviera. Miniature yachts resembled white lilies swaying on the blue ocean. Yes, I was sad to leave paradise but I was eager to see Paris the city of love, with its Eiffel Tower and bohemian Montmartre. I thought about the origins of the Can-can and how it developed in the early eighteenth century from the 'Chakute', a crude, sexy dance, consisting of high kicks and splits performed in the slums by laundry girls. A dancer was holding one leg high above her head while gyrating her hips without wearing knickers, as the male audience judged her talents.

During the Universal Exhibition, a café concert hall was opened at the bottom of Montmartre hill. Red windmill sails attracted the masses to night time pleasures and the Moulin Rouge became a household name. Entertainers were introduced and four dancers performed erotic steps, throwing themselves at the audience. Interspersed with singers and other acts, it became a raucous night full of booze and entertainment, attracting everyone from aristocrats to the lower classes.

In my youth I recalled the thrill of seeing the Hollywood film *Can-can*, starring Frank Sinatra and Shirley Maclaine, with the vibrant Can-can music of Jacques Offenbach complementing the choreography. Apart from flamenco and ballet, Can-can is one of the most energetic dances in the world. Studying dance as a teenager, I was overwhelmed by the quickness and precision of the high kicks and the swirling, frilly, white petticoats. It was the opposite of classical ballet – the cheekiness of the dancers, with skirts held high, showing knickers and garters.

I'd read the biography of the celebrated painter Toulouse-Lautrec, and became fascinated with the black caricatures of men in top hats as they watched the wenches dance. He'd been influenced by the Japanese movement which had come to Europe, showing cut out black forms. In his posters he immortalised his favourite dancer, the petite Jane Avril. She threw a leg high above a man, tilting his top hat. The undisputed queen, though, was La Goulou. Through her, the dance became risqué with high kicks and loud screams as she grabbed a drink from male onlookers, drinking it and flirting with them as she continued her performance, shrieking and yelling to the audience.

As the plane approached Orly Airport, grey skies with heavy dark clouds were itching to burst and couldn't damper the excitement brewing inside me. There were no customs to go through, so I swiftly collected my suitcase and stepped outside the building. A blast of cold air hit me and I hurried to the taxi rank, hugging my coat. It was almost midday and people were bustling around small cafés, the buildings grey and unimpressive and the noisy traffic almost impassable. I could only sit and wonder what Montmartre would be like.

The French had suffered a bloody revolution in the late eighteenth century and memories of guillotine beheadings to the famous cry 'Liberty to Equality' still linger today.

In his etchings and drawings, Lautrec captured the spirit of Montmartre, mountain of the martyrs – the sinners, beggars, thieves, vagabonds and prostitute houses in narrow lanes smothered in dirt and filth. Yet it became a haven for artists to recite poems, sing and exhibit paintings. No doubt it would have changed, but the narrow lanes would still exist. What type of people lived there?

As the taxi entered the city centre, my excitement increased. What sort of building was the Moulin Rouge today? It had burnt down and was rebuilt in 1903, and Bing Crosby and the voluptuous dancer Josephine Baker had performed there in the 1930s. Miss Doriss Haug, a German classical opera dancer, became the ballet mistress in 1952 and introduced feathers, glamorous costumes and a new revue on par with the shows in Las Vegas. Her girls were tall and elegant. Would I be too small? I'd just come from the glamour of the Monte Carlo Casino with the colourful, landscaped sidewalks, and was looking forward to seeing a magnificent building with bold posters advertising the revue.

As the taxi stopped at the entrance I looked around in utter disappointment. The building was hedged in with high ones either side. No large posters advertised the show. Above the entrance, there were light bulbs surrounding the oversized letters spelling 'Moulin Rouge.' When lit up at night, it would create a fantasy world to lure people inside. It wasn't what I'd expected. I paid the taxi man, picked up my cumbersome suitcase, then dragged my feet up the grey steps and opened the main door.

Shock! It was like an electric current had struck me. In the foyer there were gigantic Toulouse-Lautrec posters, with Jane Avril preparing for a high kick and the flamboyant Goulue opposite her. Smaller posters showed the current revue, with girls in scantily clad costumes smothered in jewels and feathers. How stupid I was. I should have known nightclubs were different, but my background was theatre.

Relieved, with renewed vigour I decided not to waste time gloating over the posters, and instead go further inside. There'd be plenty of time to pursue this pleasure and examine the craft of the great painter in detail, or so I thought. Reassured and eager to see more, I sprinted to the doors of the nightclub, carrying my suitcase with me. Can-can music and loud screams were coming from inside.

It was huge, with no side boxes, and the stage almost the width of the club with a runway down the middle, surrounded by tables where the audience could almost touch the dancers. Everywhere the décor was a plush deep red with chandeliers sparkling overhead. All the tables were immaculately prepared for dinner and a dress rehearsal was in progress. Girls as tall as giraffes were kicking their legs high above their heads. They were dressed in long, flouncy, frilly skirts and blouses and their hair was twisted in a knot high on their heads with feathers protruding upwards. It was a glorious spectacle to watch.

At the side, a tall middle-aged woman in glasses and a lengthy grey skirt and top was barking orders. 'Kick zee legs high, higher. *Gut.*'

I crept forward slowly and sat on one of the plush red chairs, thankful to lower the suitcase. Inwardly I groaned. Would I ever be able to kick as high as these girls? And why couldn't I have been born at least a couple of inches taller?

Keeping up the fast pace, the girls danced into a circle around the protruding part of the stage. They looked taller and the barking continued. 'More shrieks. More. Loud,' the woman demanded as one by one they exited the stage.

The woman then noticed me. I stood up and approached her, fearful of her judgement of my height or ability. 'Pamela? I expect you,'

'Yes,' I murmured.

She was smiling and didn't seemed to notice my height. 'One of zee girls come out shortly and take you to zee digs. Rehearsal tomorrow at ten zee clock. I zee you zen.' She promptly left.

Light headed, I knew I'd passed the height test but would have to work like a Trojan to master those high kicks. It was going to be tough. After a few moments, one of the girls marched in, wearing a bright green jumper, green slacks, a multi-coloured scarf and a brown suede coat, with calf length boots and a handbag to match. Her handbag was slung over her shoulder and in her other hand she held a long, brown umbrella, with a teddy bear mascot dangling around the handle. We chatted amicably as she escorted me out of the club and around the corner. She wasn't as tall as I'd expected, although she was a precious two inches taller.

'I'm Simone,' she said. 'Not far to go. Lucky you, going to Majorca to soak up the sun and swim. Escape this dreadful weather.'

'Yes, but I've just come from Monte Carlo and the sunshine.'

'How great. You must be a good dancer.'

'I watched your rehearsal. You all looked fantastic.'

'Miss Doriss could only let three of us go to Majorca. We were rehearsing with new girls for the Paris show. Poor girls didn't know what struck them during rehearsals but they'll soon fit in and learn the ropes.'

'Why didn't you ask her if you could come with us?'

'I love my life here in Paris. I've been with the show for five years. After the show we go to discotheques and boogie until daylight. The markets are great to explore, but I've got a boyfriend I couldn't possibly leave.'

Feeling at ease, I decided to ask her the question burning on my lips. 'I've danced the Can-can before and can only kick to shoulder level. How on earth do you manage to kick so high?'

'Don't worry. You'll do well. Before every rehearsal we have Can-can training to loosen muscles.'

We'd walked down a small lane, with houses crammed together on each side of the glistening, cobbled road. After the fine rain, large droplets threatened to engulf us in a heavy shower. I couldn't help thinking these were the haunts of Toulouse Lautrec. He'd visited parlours in lanes similar to this, or was this one of them?

Abruptly we stopped outside a wooden door. Above was a sign in French which I presumed advertised a guest house. Simone knocked on the door and announced, 'We're here,' and in fluent French spoke swiftly to the robust figure. As I was ushered inside, she waved goodbye and wished me good luck.

The room lacked decoration of any sort, only the bare essentials of a bed, a wardrobe, and a miniature window. Home for the next ten days. Monte Carlo was behind me. I didn't want to go back to England and spend hours sewing for Joanie. It was a better proposition to conquer the Can-can. With a smattering of French and English between us, the robust landlady and I communicated and I met the other girls there. Caroline looked like an English giraffe and her friend Margaret was a gigantic six foot tall, long legged, blonde one.

There were eight of us at rehearsals the next day and I noticed Jesse was my height, so I wasn't alone. An English ballet mistress was there but maybe she'd been trained by the Gestapo. Without music we were given rigorous exercises, putting our legs up to the side of the stage, pressing as hard as we could.

'Push, stretch zee leg. More. No gut,' the mistress roared, and later ordered us onto the stage to perform. 'Do zee steps', she screamed, 'Kick zee leg higher. No is gut. Again.'

This was followed by the splits, pressing down as hard as we could to reach the floor. Torture. Dancing classes had never been this punishing, but the thought of quitting never entered my head. We were given a short break and collapsed onto the plush red seats, groaning. Miss Doriss appeared and rehearsals commenced learning normal routines. At the end of the week I was crippled and could hardly walk let alone dance. The pain at the back of my thighs was excruciating.

Sunday was a free day. I decided to try to see Paris while I had the chance. The sun peeped out of a cloud as I began to walk to the River Seine. I'd hoped to make it to the Notre-Dame Cathedral and the Eiffel Tower, but with each step I took it was as though a hammer was banging on my legs and thighs, the pain unbearable.

Defeated, I hailed a cab as soon as I could and headed back to the hostel to take a long, hot bath to soothe the muscles. By the end of rehearsals, the pain had almost disappeared as my muscles realised they had to work harder in order to kick as high as my head.

Our opening costumes were to be bright green leotards covered in jewels with a foot high, bouffant wig on our heads. At last I'd look like a giraffe. For the Can-can we'd wear a delicate pink dress with white lace around a low neckline and a pink feathered hat, with the usual black stockings and white petticoats.

On the last night, Miss Doriss allowed us to watch the show at the back of the club. The show was dazzling with a large cast of dancers and exotic acts.

After arduous rehearsals I was looking forward to leaving, yearning for warmer weather. Early the next morning, we caught the train for the long journey to Barcelona and the overnight ferry to Majorca.

Barcelona, Spain

Dawn approached as the boat sailed into the harbour at Palma, with a magnificent view of sandy beaches and a sparkling blue sea. The sun was peeping its head over the horizon to welcome us to our home for the next six months. Disembarking, we passed several quaint cafés and restaurants with bold paintings of fish, lobsters and huge coffee signs. The drive to our accommodation was short and we were greeted with a spacious Spanish bungalow with stone floors and a courtyard draped in green ferns and flora – pure luxury after living in the tiny rooms in Paris. There were four large bedrooms with a huge sofa in the living room.

Importantly, there was no hovering landlady. We could come and go as we pleased. The wonder of the place after the rain in Paris was exhilarating, along with the thought of the gorgeous hunky men we could meet.

The head girl Jesse and I opted for the front bedroom. Throughout the season we laughed and joked, never argued and went our separate ways day or night, living the joys of youth. But we were the famous Doriss Girls and the show our top priority. The following afternoon we arrived at Tito's open-air nightclub for rehearsals, and were met with the splendour of the harbour-side location. Palm trees lined the promenade and the city of Palma could be seen over the waters in the distance. The semi-circle stage was large where the audience could dance, with a gigantic palm tree towering high to the right, reaching the upstairs terrace. Tables and chairs surrounded the stage as far back as the entrance.

Tito's was originally built in 1923 and is still an exclusive nocturnal night club in the hub of the Mediterranean. When we arrived, Miss Doriss was there and rehearsals were perfect. She seemed content, telling us to return the next day at 5 pm in long skirts and normal make-up to meet officials and the local press. Dilemma! Maureen and I didn't have long skirts. Proud of my Spanish, I told her, 'I speak the local lingo. Come with me tomorrow morning and we'll find them.' The shops were full of summer clothes and we soon spotted cheap, wrap-around long skirts. We posed for the officials in the new skirts and Miss Doriss was delighted.

Tremendous screams had the audience glued to their seats as the Can-can kicks amazed them. The Moulin Rouge girls were no match for us. The show was an outstanding success, the nightclub filled to capacity every night and Miss Doriss congratulated us. There was one show a night and rehearsals to change a number every two months. Otherwise we were free to enjoy ourselves. Discotheques were discovered and we reveled in an island of youth, surf and sun. One day in the dressing room Jesse asked us, 'What are you doing tomorrow? I've discovered a small cove where we can skinny dip. No one will see us.'

'What?' we chorused.

The following night after the show we grabbed two taxies, taking towels. It was a small bay away from the harbour and tourist beaches. We ran naked into the warm ocean, splashing each other in the moonlight and swimming among the fishes as the shadow of a mountain protected us from prying eyes.

Another evening Maureen announced, 'I've been invited to visit the American battleship in the harbour. It's here for two days and you're all welcome to see it tomorrow afternoon.'

Excited, we were helped aboard by young American naval officers in smart uniforms. They showed us the engine room, guns, the galley and 'mess' a minuscule dining room and bar where they socialised. It was a unique experience and I will leave the rest to your imagination.

Other international acts who appeared during the season were Los Indigenous from Paraguay, The Lucky Latinos, Trio Thenee, Ballet Epanole Los Piconeras, and The Ballet of Mario

Maya and Carmen Moya. Sunday was our day off when special gala performances were performed by Mireille Mathieu, Gilbert Becaud, Charles Aznavour and Petula Clark.

Later in the season Miss Doriss returned to change a number. She looked directly at me during rehearsals and asked, 'Why no smile in zee show last night?' I was surprised she'd noticed my straight face. It seemed as though nothing could escape her attention.

Giving her a goofy, toothless smile I explained, 'A front filling fell out. The dentist can't fix it until tomorrow'.

'Buy a white candle, melt zee wax and put on zee tooth,' she replied, a solution for anything.

The new number was a joy to dance. We waltzed and floated in long, white, chiffon pleated dresses, dazzling the audience as the costumes changed colours in the neon lighting. For the last number change, Jesse created a modern pop style dance, buying the outfits locally. The mini-skirts and tops in pink, white and green stripes with a matching cap, white socks and tennis shoes were a radical change from luxurious costumes. It didn't matter. The audience liked it and management was happy. What an idyllic, paid holiday – spending most of our free time swimming, shopping, and dancing at all night discotheques. We didn't want it to end. In the final week Jesse delighted us with the news – 'Miss Doriss has found us another contract for a month in Barcelona and a month in Madrid.' We were relieved to continue working again, enjoying our love of dancing for a living, and I was thrilled to be returning to my favourite city.

Barcelona is a huge metropolis and our pension was on a side lane from the famous Las Ramblas in the old part of the city. It was close to eateries in the boulevard, stretching from the main Catalan square to the Columbus monument in the harbour. Always a hub of activity day and night, it overflowed with shops, stalls and street entertainers. The nightclub was mediocre and rarely filled with patrons, a far cry from the splendour of Titos. There were no photos outside the nightclub to advertise the show. Inside the entrance was different, with elaborate red furnishings – almost a smaller version of the Moulin Rouge. Spanish pictures of flamenco dancers and old buildings of Barcelona decorated the walls. A large bar at the side displayed spirits, and the stage was small.

After the show we'd walk back along the seashore and pop into a local restaurant for supper. It was such a big city so we never bothered with discos. Sometimes I'd walk along the side streets reminiscing, thinking of the fun times with Alan and Paco. It wasn't the same. One day after roaming the streets for an hour, I found myself in the Plaza Cataluna, where two magnificent fountains soared into the air. Gasping for coffee and looking around, I spotted a bar almost hidden from view by tall buildings, although the coffee sign was recognisable. It had to be cheap.

I sat on a stool at the bar and ordered a café latte. The bar tender was a tall, hearty middle-aged man with smooth black and grey hair surrounding a tanned, wrinkled face. Gurgling and hissing noises came from a big coffee machine. He served me a scalding hot, milky coffee and with a beaming smile declared, 'El major café en Barcelona!' (The best coffee in Barcelona). I agreed with him and we began to talk. Realising I wasn't Spanish, he was impressed that I could speak his language. A wonderful friendship began but we never exchanged names. With his limited knowledge of English and my mediocre Spanish, we understood each other or mimed or drew pictures to clarify a point.

I visited the bar every day and enjoyed learning about his country – Argentina, on the other side of the planet. Coffee was all I ordered, and with old fashioned courtesy he'd light my cigarette with a radiant smile.

One day he surprised me. He had a small record player and played a 45 rpm record. The music was different, melodious with guitars, not as dynamic as in Spain. Each visit he played a different record and I became fascinated with South American music, learning about Chile, Brazil and Argentina. But his heart was in the South with the great open plains and cowboys, *Los Gouchos,* and the succulent barbecued steaks they ate. He explained one day he'd return to his homeland.

On my last day I approached the bar with a heavy heart to tell him I was leaving for Madrid. I'd miss our chats. As I paid for the coffee he said, 'Tengo algo para ti', (I have something for you).' Expecting a little fan or touristic gift he put a gold lighter on the bar in front of me.

Stunned, I didn't know how to reply, but he insisted, 'Toma', (take), you need lighter.'

Thanking him I left, amazed at his generosity. The lighter was lost or pinched on my travels, but lovely memories remained.

Returning to Madrid

Giant posters of black bulls could be seen on the dusty, yellow plains as the train neared Madrid. I was thrilled to walk down the Gran Via again and relive memories of the theatre two years ago. The city would be the same, but working in a nightclub with late hours would be different.

Our hostel in Calle de las Infantas, 'Street of the Children', was half way down an insignificant lane, with tall, old, stone buildings towering over the narrow cobbled road. At the side of one of the buildings there was a dark blue plaque dedicated to Cervantes, the celebrated author of the Spanish book *Don Quixote*. The plaque stated he'd lived there in 1607. How inspiring.

At the entrance to the building, massive wooden doors were locked at sunset as the huge figure of the Sorreno, key master, jangled his string of heavy keys and listened for claps to catch his attention. Irrespective of time or weather, he was always there from dusk till dawn, and no crime existed in the streets under Franco's' regime. On his death the monarchy was restored, and people no longer lived in fear of religion – only terrorism and thieves who thrive today on unsuspecting travellers.

The rooms in the hostel contained the bare necessities, the small windows overlooking a miniscule street below.

The owner was Don Antonio. He was elderly, couldn't speak English, and had suffered in the Spanish Civil War. It was essential to be quiet at night to allow his other Spanish tenants to rest and paying the rent were his main concerns. A key for our rooms was provided but not for the front door, as he always opened it irrespective of the hour. The difference between this and other pensions was the small dining area, containing a stove, fridge and sink where you could cook a meal, which was impossible to find elsewhere. We didn't bother to cook. The coffee shop below was frequented every morning, and the location handy for the city.

We walked down the Gran Via to the night club opposite the main department store. I skipped across the pavement, breathing in the Madrid air and smelling the wafting aroma of fish from local restaurants and thinking of past times looking at majestic buildings. There were few tourists, and the whirl of traffic on the highway was incessant. It was a city bubbling with life, gaiety, culture and warmth, with people I could converse with. This made me happy. Why not live here forever?

Content, we waited to rehearse as Jesse spoke to management about what would happen. She returned nervous and red faced, gathering us around her. Concerned, we asked what was wrong.

'There's no show,' she stuttered. 'They want a complete half hour of entertainment with the ballet. We only have dance numbers.' We were aghast. No ballet meant an immediate return to England. Numbed with this information, Jesse continued to stutter, 'Miss Doriss will pay your fares back to England.'

We were trying to comprehend the disaster when, without warning, Caroline stepped forward. 'Stay here. We can do this. I'll go to management.'

Poor Jesse. She'd done nothing wrong, but what did Caroline have in mind? She was away for ten minutes, but it seemed a century. No-one spoke. How could she save the ballet? What was her idea?

Caroline returned. 'I've arranged for us to dance with four girls in each number, while the rest of you perform a quick change. Their singer will perform a number, so we can all be on stage at the same time for the Can-can finale.'

Fantastic news. We were almost crying, and crowded around to give her big hugs.

It was never mentioned, but Caroline was our hero and immediately took charge of the ballet. Jesse understood and reverted back to the role of being one of us.

'Let's rehearse,' Caroline demanded. She instructed us

though a long, three hour rehearsal as though she'd been doing it for years. We didn't care and the audience never knew of the catastrophe which almost occurred. Management was pleased. The month passed. Caroline told us we were going to work in another club. We were surprised. It was only a couple of blocks from the pension and we stared at her in disbelief. How could there be a nightclub in the miniscule street we lived in?

She possessed an inborn sense of knowing what to do at the right time. We followed her down the street, which lead into a small square we hadn't noticed. On one side was a building advertising an indoor circus and on the other a large coffee bar. Next to it was another building – the Casablanca Nightclub.

Entering the front door, we were delighted at what we saw. The whole club was a large oblong shape, with a small balcony upstairs along the left hand side. At the back, there was a stage with sixteen stands for a full orchestra. Behind them, the décor of large palm trees gave one the impression of being in an exotic place. There was also a large square extension of the stage where we would dance, with tables and chairs surrounding it.

Times for the shows were unusual. The first show at 7:30 pm was for early diners, and was often half full. At 1:30 am the club was crowded with patrons who came to enjoy the orchestra, the show and drinks. Apart from the strange hours we loved it, and people came in droves to see the Can-can. During the first week I was approached by a young, immaculately dressed member of the orchestra who was small. Black hair and sideboards enhanced his appearance, but his sparkling, blue eyes captured my heart. Instant chemistry.

When he invited me for a meal between shows I was thrilled. He took me to a local trattoria in a tiny lane, where from the window on the first floor we could see people walking to and from the nightclub. It was always empty early in the evening and we enjoyed the seclusion, getting to know each other. There were mouth-watering dishes of shrimps fried in garlic and oil, accompanied with fresh, crusty bread to soak up the juice, followed by a large, grilled steak with a crispy lettuce and tomato salad.

Five hours was a long wait between shows, so we parted company and I returned to the pension. He'd take me out for a meal twice a week, but on our day off he'd book a small hotel on a Saturday night, where our romance flourished.

Towards the end of the month I began to wonder what was happening. I was besotted with Andres and unhappy at the thought of leaving him.

In the final week Caroline approached me. 'Pamela, you're going out with Andres aren't you?'

'Yes,' I replied sadly. 'He's wonderful. Where are we going next?'

'The ballet is finishing and the girls are returning to England.' My heart missed a beat. I'd realised this could happen, but before I could reply she asked, 'Would you like to stay here?'

'What? How?'

'There's a South American ballet with the choreographers Louis and Violetta coming here next month. Are you interested?'

'Yes, yes.' Colour returned to my cheeks. How fantastic to stay with Andres and dance in Madrid, the city of my dreams.

'The pay is lower,' she continued, noting how happy I looked. 'Rehearsals are spoken in Spanish and held in the afternoons from two until five for three weeks, and the show changes every two months.'

'It's continuous?'

'Yes, and Margaret and I are joining them, so there'll be the three of us. The other girls are going home. I'll let Violetta know.'

This was amazing news, and Andres appeared to be as happy as I was. Blinded with love, I didn't have the heart to ask him about his family. He came from the mountainous region of Asturias in Northern Spain and never mentioned them or where he lived. I was content, although hopeful our relationship might flourish. At rehearsals I was surprised at how full-sized the company was. There were twelve girls and four boy dancers from Argentina, Chile, Spain, Holland, South Africa, Singapore and Japan, and we were the only English girls. Whenever a dancer left the show, they were quickly replaced.

Violetta was a six foot tall Argentinian with long legs, jet black hair and a voluptuous figure. Sizzling with sex and a million dollar smile, she'd dance into centre stage a star. Firm and kind, her choreography was excellent. Her husband Louis was the complete opposite, small and robust with brown hair and a moustache, although together they made a formidable team. Their four year old daughter Alexandria came to rehearsals and was fascinated by the dancers. Perhaps she would become one, too.

Each show consisted of five numbers ranging from tangos to modern musical numbers and always finished with a spectacular feather jeweled finale. The costumes were made by the top couturier of Madrid and were wonderful to dance in. I adored the show and atmosphere. My parents were never concerned as I wrote to them often and were delighted I was living my dream. I settled into the routine of meeting Andres when he was free and made friends with several of the girls. I started sharing a flat with Peta, who danced in another theatre group. It was so refreshing to have lovely living quarters where we could cook and come and go in privacy as we pleased. Andres declined to visit the flat, though, and I wondered about our relationship. Was he hiding something?

The girls and I danced at discos after the show and soon I was invited to the homes of other artists, musicians, choreographers and dancers. This is known as a *tertulia*, a gathering of people interested in Spanish culture. The tradition continues today. I was the only English girl present, but reaping the benefits of speaking Spanish fluently. We sat in a circle as one of the musicians played a guitar, making up phrases to a subject which often changed. Occasionally I'd contribute a few words and surprise them. When a slow cooked paella was ready we devoured it with gusto and went our separate ways.

Sometimes a few of us continued the fun, rushing to a street stall for chocolate and churros. A dough was coiled into a ring, thrust into hot oil and coated in sugar, similar to donuts. It was a delicious breakfast dipped into hot chocolate. Flopping into bed at dawn never mattered. We were young and there was plenty of time to recuperate before an afternoon rehearsal. After six months Peta left Madrid and I reluctantly returned to the pension. I found out there was a film studio wanting dancers. I couldn't believe my luck when I sent in old photos and was selected.

Six of us dressed as natives in long, grass skirts, with our bodies plastered in dark tan make-up. Massive mirrors and umbrellas were set up to reflect the rays of the sun onto the set in a field outside of Madrid as we played cards, waiting around for hours for the shoot. Several African style huts had been erected and we danced for the cameras vigorously and individually, with no formal choreography.

The second film, starring Pier Angeli, was a co-production between Spain and Italy. Five of us were required for a short cabaret scene. Arriving at the studios at 4 am, make-up was applied. Dressed in black top hats and tails, we were called to the nightclub set in the afternoon.

Many film extras were seated at tables around the stage as the director screamed, 'It's getting late. I only want one take. Give me lots of noise and silence when the dancers arrive.' The cameras rolled and the enthusiastic crowd was quiet when the music began, then applauded as we made our exit. We patiently waited for the director's decision as he checked the footage.

'Excellent. Good,' he yelled. 'One take. Go home.' People scurried everywhere, returning the costumes to wardrobe, then left.

Tired with droopy eyelids I looked at my watch. It was six o'clock and the bed looked so inviting. After the excitement and one hour's sleep, I must have nodded off.

Suddenly there was a loud knocking at the door – the landlord, demanding I go to the phone. Half dazed I staggered over. It was Caroline.

'Pamela I know you've been filming all day,' she said, 'but it's seven o'clock. Get here fast.' Caroline had saved me. I bolted out of the pension and made the opening number with seconds to spare. It was a hot, steamy Saturday night as Andres waited for me after the show. We drove down the Gran Via, but instead of turning right to our usual rendezvous, he turned left, past the Royal Palace and through the gardens to the Casa del Campo. The noise of city people could be heard faintly in the distance as he glided the car to a halt.

Holding hands, we entered the magic of nature. Alone, the moon was bright, the sky a maze of twinkling stars and the smell of his masculinity intoxicating. Love was in the air. We lay on the soft grass and caressed each other as passion overtook us. Life was wonderful. Without warning, in the darkness we heard thudding noises. At once Andres sat up, then laughed. Rabbits were running around us, bobbing up and down.

One Sunday he invited me to Toledo, the old capital of Spain, a few hours' drive from Madrid. It's a unique town reminiscent of the fifteenth century and filled with tourists. We walked over the old bridge, past the castle and up and down the hilly, narrow, cobbled streets. The masterpieces of the painters Goya and El Greco were displayed in the old, yellow stone buildings. The highlight was the Catholic cathedral rich in golden ornaments and exquisitely carved statues.

It was a memorable day which brought me closer to Andres. It was a happy time – but changed with an unexpected shock ending. Andres announced he was going to Majorca on a six month contract.

'Don't worry,' I replied, 'I'll still be here when you return.' Without any explanation, he avoided me and I couldn't fathom the reason. What had happened?

An Argentinian girl had recently joined the ballet. One evening in despair, I returned to our trattoria. Horror. From the window I saw him hand in hand with her, walking out of the club. Broken-hearted and tormented, I cried. He'd made his choice. Hurt, listless and alone, nothing could stop my heartache. I needed to forget him and find a normal guy. At twenty five I was young, but could I trust a man again? One day Violetta called me aside. This was abnormal. Looking at her stern face, I knew trouble was brewing. Nothing was wrong with my dancing and I had no idea what was happening.

'Pamela, are you pregnant?'

Shocked at this insinuation I replied abruptly, 'No, I'm not.'

'I can't have a dancer work for me looking pregnant. Have you looked at yourself in the mirror? You'll have to go if you don't lose weight.'

It hadn't occurred to me the rich Russian salads overflowing with mayonnaise, Spanish tortillas filled with juicy potatoes, onions, peas and other vegies saturated in oil and eaten with crispy bread could affect my figure. Returning to the dressing room, in the mirror I saw an image of a plump, young girl with a balloon belly ready to pop outside of a jeweled bikini.

Petrified at the thought of losing my job, I decided on a rigid crash diet. Milky coffees and eggs were nourishing and would give me the stamina to dance without food. The first boiled egg without salt was devoured in slow motion, each morsel relished.

The sugarless café latte, though, was revolting. Hunger pains started with a gnawing sensation in the gut. The second day the pains became too intense. Faint, I boiled another egg and drank a second sugarless latte. On the third day, the pain mellowed as the cravings for food dissipated.

I continued this regime for three weeks. Costumes began to fit, but the problem was mental. Passing restaurants and cafés, the smells and aromas taunted me.

One night Violetta said urgently. 'Pamela I must speak to you.' I'd done nothing wrong this time. 'Pamela,' she sighed, 'you lose weight too quick. You must eat. You look like a skeleton.'

'No. I must lose weight.'

'Tonight I'm taking you home with me to eat vegetables.'

Together with four year old Alexandria and Louis, I sat at her table as she poured hot, steaming vegetables onto our plates. Watching young Alexandria pick up her fork to eat the vegetables I hesitated.

'Eat,' Violetta demanded.

The food slithered down my throat, soothing the withered stomach as I returned to normal.

Relieved to have saved my job, I settled into a natural routine, eliminating fatty foods. I drank a cappuccino before the first show every night.

The heartache was mellowing and the coffee bar by the club had a TV. In the midst of this, I was amazed to see an American man stepping onto the moon for the first time.

Farewell Madrid

One summer night in the coffee bar before the show, a young, bronzed man in casual clothes captured my heart with deep brown eyes and a warm, endearing smile. Returning each night, our friendship blossomed and a wounded heart was healed. As our relationship developed, he fascinated me with stories of his family living in a village outside of Madrid. Memories of Andres wafted away, and thoughts surfaced of a real Spaniard who'd love and care for me. I could stay here forever and be loved.

He never invited me out in the daytime or missed an evening. What was the problem? Later he confessed he worked as a golf caddy, making good tips in the daytime. We'd part company, and the yearning to know more about each other grew each time he returned.

One evening in the dressing room I received an unusual phone call. Racing to the phone I wondered who it could be.

'Hello, who is it?

A husky male voice replied, 'Pamela, I'm back in Madrid.'

Andres. Oh, the thrill to hear his voice again. In an instant I recalled our wonderful times together, his blue eyes and the rendezvous in the forest. I could have him back if I wanted.

The temptation was enormous. But he was a playboy and probably had girlfriends from Majorca in tow crying out for him. I couldn't bear the heartache. José Antonio would never cheat on me.

After a short silence I replied firmly, 'No, Andres. I've met someone else.' The phone went dead and I never saw or heard from him again.

One night José Antonio presented me with a gold ring. 'Wear it for me,' he declared. 'I want you to be mine forever.' Looking in his eyes, I saw sincerity and a longing to be with me. It was no marriage proposal, but was this the Spanish way of committing to an English girl?

After two months, when he suggested moving into the pension, the thought of staying in the city of my dreams was bliss – and nature won.

'Well,' said the landlord, 'if you want him to stay here you must pay for two rooms.' Looking at the gold ring, I agreed.

It was impossible to take him to the tertulia, as he didn't fit into the circle of professional dancers, musicians and choreographers. All contact with them ended. No discos, late nights or early breakfasts – but it wasn't all bad news. Cuddling and laying in his arms at night compensated for the loss of fun. I bought us a small television set for entertainment. We couldn't afford to eat in restaurants any more, and as money was tight we would meander through the markets, holding hands and buying fresh vegetables to cook in the small kitchen.

Chatting with other artists and boarders was fun. Even the landlord joined in, throwing oranges at us. José Antonio became one of us.

This lifestyle continued for several months, although what would happen if the ballet folded? My shoes were thread bare and soon I'd need to buy more clothes.

One day I said to José, 'What will happen if I can't dance?'

Unperturbed at this question, he shocked me. 'I can arrange an interview for you to work in an office.'

Dressed in my posh pink mini-skirt and high heels, with hair swept into a high ponytail, I arrived at the top of one of the modern office buildings in the city. A manager in a smart, black tailored suit ushered me into his office and asked me to sit down.

'Pamela, what office work have you done?'

Posing with legs crossed, I replied with a sigh. 'I've never worked in an office.'

'Can you type?'

'No.'
'What other work can you do?'
'I dance.'
'We can't help you.'

When I told José he was calm, and cuddling me soothed away the fears. It was unusual when Violetta asked to speak privately with me. 'Pamela, the ballet is finishing this month and I'm going to work at the Casino in Lisbon for a month and continuing to tour South America. I've a second ballet starting here. Do you want to stay in Madrid or travel with us?'

A brilliant opportunity. I'd yearned to go to South America for so long it tormented me, but how could I leave a genuine man like José Antonio? The choice was simple – stay with my new love. Margaret and Caroline left for Portugal as I felt a few pangs of regret. The new ballet commenced and life continued as normal. Unexpectedly, José Antonio bought me a second gold ring, insisting I wear one on each hand. A marriage proposal? Was he becoming jealous or scared of losing me? It felt uncomfortable.

One evening, he presented me with a bottle of champagne and flowers.

'What's all this?' Hugging him, I stared at the two gold rings. He loved me. But why the flowers and champagne? What was he planning?

As I put the flowers in a vase and sipped the champagne, he grinned at me. 'Tomorrow morning we're taking the local bus to a small village outside of Madrid where my family live. They're longing to meet you.' We snuggled together after the champagne and I felt lucky to have met such a genuine man.

However, trying to sleep was impossible and the thought of meeting his family was daunting. As I drifted into la la land, my inner emotions surfaced in a dream. Holding José Antonio's hand, we stepped off the bus at the bottom of a hill in the countryside. We began to walk up a small pathway smothered with weeds and grass with large fields on either side. In the distance was a small, stone house. With every step we took, the blades of grass began to smother the pathway. How could it happen? In fear, I cried out and wrenched my hand away from his tight grip. I tried to run haphazardly down the hill as the grass and weeds grew higher, threatening to strangle me. There was nowhere to go. I woke up.

Glancing at José, he was sleeping peacefully with a blissful baby expression on his face. He hadn't heard me as I tried to analyse the dream. I wasn't scared of meeting his parents. Was it thoughts of what the future held for us? Did I want to live this way and never dance again? He would want babies – and without a decent income, how could we educate them? Did he love me enough to accept me for myself? I couldn't think straight. Maybe the nightmare was trivial, even stupid. He'd never know.

Rising early, I pushed the dream from my mind as we held hands and caught the bus. I gasped as the bus stopped at the bottom of a hill. In the distance were the tall buildings of Madrid. We began to walk up a narrow lane with fields on either side towards a large stone house, a replica of my dream without the grass growing.

Glancing at his excited face he pulled me harder as he gathered speed to greet his family. 'Ola,' screamed José Antonio, and his family ran out of the centuries-old house to meet us. Three athletic brothers in their late teens or early twenties talked incessantly as José clasped my hand tighter, striding faster towards the front door. Maria, his schoolgirl sister, ran around us, bubbling with enthusiasm but struggling to get a word in as her soft, brown eyes noted my blue lace mini skirt and make-up.

Juan Carlos, José's father, was slender and towered above us, his crop of brown hair showing feathers of light grey. His rugged, lined, dark face displayed the result of years of hard labour under the harsh rays of the sun.

José's Mamma was different to my expectations. Small and robust her clothes were dull, with the long, grey skirt almost reaching the ground and covering flat, worn shoes. The black shawl around her shoulders covered a drearier, light grey blouse. Her hands were rough from washing, cooking and raising a large family. A sparkle from her golden wedding ring lifted the gloom, but her radiant smile emitted the warmth she felt to see her elder son so happy.

'Mamma,' José cried hugging her close. 'Here's Pamela.'

I extended my hand to greet her, but she leaned forward to

give me a hug. Speaking slowly in Pidgin Spanish, her eyes were shining. 'Pa-me- la, José Good. All good. He happy. I happy.' This was an excellent beginning, and José seemed relieved that his mother had welcomed me into their family.

Autumn was hot in Madrid and Juan Carlos, the master of his clan, ushered us inside to the drifting smell of a spicy meal as we entered the dining room.

The door to the outside kitchen was open. Decoration was sparse with a large table and chairs dominating the room. A few paintings of flowers and trees brightened the coldness from the dim, grey stone walls. Even though they were poor, I felt the warmth, love and laughter from years of happy family life. The boys appeared to be impatient, wanting to leave. They had performed their duty to meet me and had other pursuits in mind.

'Don't be late,' Juan Carlos yelled as they rushed away.

Mamma and José took me to the yard, where a stew of chorizo sausage and vegetables simmered in a big earthenware pot on an open fire. Delicious! Mamma proudly told me she also made her own soap. Washing was hanging on the line, but the view of Madrid in the distance over the hills was magical.

We returned several times on my day off to a wonderful welcome. As long as José was happy, Mamma was happy.

A close relationship developed with his sister Maria. She'd question me about the big city, her appetite for news insatiable and a longing to become a woman evident as she admired a dress or necklace I was wearing.

'I take you my special den,' she whispered one afternoon. We snuck past Mamma and clamoured down some steps to an old cellar. Miniature lights glowed on a wall in the darkness. 'Silk worms. No light. Make silk.'

'Yes,' I murmured as she took a small torch and pointed to a jam jar filled with layers of soil from a bench.

'Geography class. Here two weeks. No move. Layers form.' I admired her innocence and thirst for knowledge and for inviting me into her secret world. After several visits Mamma stated scornfully, 'Pamela. You mini skirt no good.' She pointed to the length of her skirt. 'Please long skirt. No, no mini skirt.'

Horrified I didn't reply and told José when we returned to the pension. It didn't seem to bother him. 'Mamma is old and you can wear what you like. I adore your miniskirts.'

The seeds of escape were beginning to germinate in my inner thoughts. Mamma didn't approve of my clothes. What else would she dislike?

We came from different backgrounds. The subject of religion had never been approached, but with no language barrier we were happy. What about my family? How could we have a lasting relationship or a future together in our present financial circumstances? Looking at shabby, worn out shoes in dire need of repair, the clothes needing replacing with no available sewing machine to make new ones ... the loss of friends at the tertulias, and the missed opportunity to dance in South America. It all hurt. This, combined with the hefty weekly cost of two rooms each week from my wage, was more than I could bear.

Cheerful letters arrived from England full of family events, important births, deaths and marriages. It'd been three years since I left home and I longed to hear Popsey's jokes and Mother's raucous laugh and hug them. They'd rented the family home and moved into a house close to the town centre of Kettering. Christmas was fast approaching.

One night after the show, the burden of the situation must have shown on my face. I didn't talk anymore, not knowing what to do without hurting José. I was still unsure what to do. Noting my glum face, he took both my hands in his, leading me to the bed. Smothering the two gold rings with kisses, he sat down stroking my hair with gentle fingers, trying to read my thoughts.

After a few seconds of silence, he whispered, 'Pamela my darling, you are my life. We can have a baby, and you will be the mother of my child.'

'Oh!' I exclaimed, shocked at the news and trying to hide my true feelings.

'What's wrong? A baby will unite us forever. I love you.'

'Darling, why so quick? Please give me time to think.'

Nestling in the warmth of his arms my worries seemed to grow. I didn't want to be an unwed mother, with a father who would shower us with love and poverty. Escape was the sad answer.

We kissed and hugged, but one afternoon I asked him to take a walk with me in the park, trying to act normal. We sat under a tree by the lake as I explained the 'live happily ever after fairytale.

'José, I love you and would love to have your babies. But we don't have a good place to live in or money to educate them. If I leave and return to England, I'll get another contract, travel the world and return with enough money to buy us an apartment.'

His brows slumped as he thought it through. 'You will come back?'

'Yes, I will.'

There was sadness in his eyes, knowing he couldn't stop me. I wrote to Mother, telling her of my imminent return with no fixed date.

The show lacked the vitality of Violetta and several Spanish dancers who'd been engaged required technique. It was easy to find another girl to take my place, but rehearsing her to the standard required took three times longer, delaying my departure.

At the pension I said goodbye, telling them I'd return but didn't know when. With guitar, suitcase and wig box ready, I hugged José one last time as I glanced around the room. He'd take the television to his parents, who'd be thrilled to own it.

'Don't come with me to the station, José,' I implored him. 'It's too stressful.'

With tears in his eyes, he agreed. The taxi came and I left.

Aged nine years

Amateur Theatrical Society in the Musical Maritza aged 14.

Pitt-Draffen Academy, 1960. A Protuguese Character Dance, won 1st Prize, age 15.

Denise Pitt-Draffen, F.I.S.T.D. Choreographer

Our Chalets with mother, 1961.

Marie de Vere dancers, 1961. Pwllheli, Wales. My debut to Show Business.

Publicity photo for Tourist flights with Gaeity girls Pwllheli, 1961

Windmill Theatre, Picadilly Circus. London

Windmill Theatre, Picadilly Circus. Windmill girls.

Cavalcade Cabaret, London, England.

George Carden.

Professional photos taken for agent and George Carden.

Dancing school, Amsterdam.

Television in Amsterdam, 1963

Dressing room, Amsterdam, 1963

Dressing room, Amsterdam, 1963

Dressing room, Amsterdam, 1963

Touring Holland, 1963

Glasgow 5 Past 8 Show

Glasgow show with Patsy ann Noble

Majorca, Spain

Returning to Madrid

Home sweet home

Leon Grieg

Can-can solo Lunel 1972.
Age 27

Monty in Lunel

Florence Italy. Opening costumes, Robert Kapikian as Manager 2nd ballet from Leon

*Safari Air, Nairobi.
Learnt to fly*

*With Joe Bugner V
Muhammad Ali fight.
Kuala Lumper, 1975*

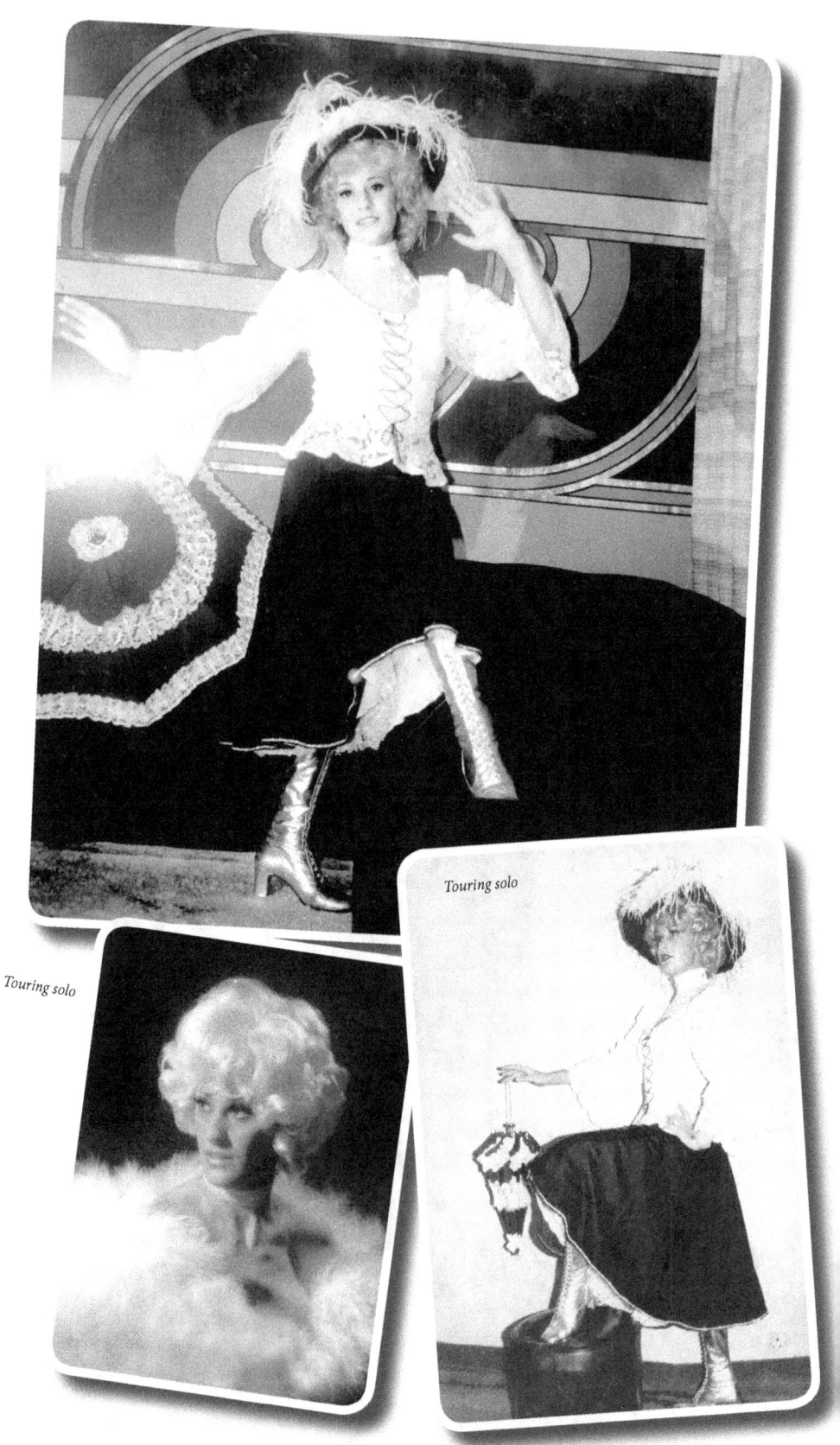

Touring solo

Touring solo

Spanish number

Home, Sweet Home

In the dim overcrowded train, I was huddled next to an old Spanish couple who gossiped incessantly. I kept quiet. The atmosphere was stifling with smells of spicy bocadillo buns full of red meat, reminding me of that horrific bull fight – intermingled with body odour and thick smoke from Spanish cigarettes.

It was goodbye to Madrid, the city I adored. The weight of an impoverished existence lifting from my shoulders was huge.

After three years away I knew my parents would welcome me back, but for how long? I needed a place to put together the threads of an existence. Yes, home sweet home. How I ached to see family and laugh and love again. Would Joanie have changed or be pleased to see me? We never wrote and I always returned to her between contracts. I was heartbroken, however, by my own doing. Would José survive? He was young and when he realised I wouldn't return, he'd find a new love.

The heavy clanking of wheels stirred my nerves. Eager for relief from the constant chatter I left the carriage, stepping over hot, smelly bodies in the passage way to make my way to the toilet. A tear rolled down my cheek and landed on my hand, gliding towards one of the rings on my fingers. I'd forgotten all about them; a dilemma. A symbol of our love and commitment and I'd left him. Tears flowed as I pulled the rings off and thrust them into the bottom of my bag. Patching up smeary make-up I returned to the crowded carriage. What to do next?

On the rough crossing by ferry to England, a cold, cruel wind slapped me on the face, seeping into my bones. Bereft of a hat, scarf and gloves, I was doomed to face the elements.

Tired and struggling with luggage, I sighed as I stepped onto English soil. Red double decker buses struggled for the right of way with black taxies. Men and women in tailor made suits with suitcases and umbrellas to match were a stark contrast to the casual lay-back attitude and attire of the Spanish people. The greatest thrill was understanding every English word. My inner voice told me to run over to people and demand, 'I know I've been away a long time but I understand every word you say.' I didn't know the price of vegetables or the politics of the day, and I'd lived in a foreign country for six months without speaking one word in my native language.

The Midland coach, departing from the corner of St Pancras Station, was the cheapest and longest way to get home. London high rise council houses flashed by with spasmodic gestures of greenery until we reached the M1, heading north. Half way to Kettering, the coach branched off the highway. It was good to see green fields dotted with lazy cows and sheep under a dark, grey sky. The coach meandered along country roads lined with quaint villages with thatched roofs, bare trees, prickly bushes and weeds shooting up where they could. Droplets of rain pounded against the window, but the weather and excitement couldn't deter the growing anticipation to see familiar faces. I craned my neck forward along the window pane, pining to see the landmark for Kettering, the tall spire of the parish church, as my heart beat wildly.

Late in the afternoon the coach stopped at the town centre. I'd been unable to notify my parents when I was arriving and prayed they'd be home. I hurried home, dragging the bulky luggage in spite of the rain and fatigue.

In a fashionable part of Kettering, smart bay-windowed houses lined the street called Broadway. How on earth had Mother managed to find the house on such an unusually named street? No doubt about it she was unique, and I ached to hear her hearty laugh.

The rain had gathered force, splashing the pavement. It didn't matter how I looked, and with dripping, wet hair I pressed the doorbell.

'Oh Pamela, you've made it. Get in, out of the rain,' Popsey exclaimed as he pulled the luggage into the hallway, giving me a huge hug. He led me into the lounge where Mother was thrilled to see me. A fantastic reunion, but exhaustion had taken its toll. We chatted for a while, and after a snack Mother took me by the arm.

'C'mon me duck, you're tired, let's get you to bed. We have all day tomorrow to talk. You can see the house then.' She led me upstairs to the bedroom as Popsey followed with the luggage. In a state of semi-shock, through drooping eyelids I noticed an exquisite luxury confronted me – an exquisite white and mauve satin eiderdown over a double bed, with delicate cream lace curtains covering a large window, further enhanced by two long, velvet red curtains either side. I glanced in awe at a modern white dressing table and drawers.

'We'll always have a bedroom for you,' Mother announced proudly. 'This is yours.'

'Yes Mother, but my shoes are worn out and need urgent repairs.'

The suitcase was flung open and shoes grabbed as Mother took a few clothes and closed the door. It was too difficult to comprehend the change of country, environment, and culture in such a short time. Sinking into fresh, clean sheets I was safe and home. And I slept, slept, and slept. I woke fuzzy eyed the next day to find Popsey holding a cup of tea in his hand, telling me it was one o'clock in the afternoon. 'I've fixed your shoes.'

'What?'

I ran down the stairs after him. Nothing happens quickly in Spain, but England is different. Mother had washed my clothes and pegged them on the line in the garden, and three pairs of shoes were mended and polished, waiting for my inspection. Squeaking, bubbling and popping noises were coming from a room at the front of the house.

'It's alright,' Mother laughed, noting my worried face. 'It's my brewery. I'll show you.' She opened the door to reveal a luxurious cream sofa with matching arm chairs and long, gold velvet curtains at the bay window. Standing in the centre of the room, there were eight huge glass magnums merrily bubbling away as though they had a life of their own. 'I love making wine,' Mother declared.

'But they're all different colours,' I replied in amazement at her new hobby.

'Yes, I make wine from anything, grapefruit, carrot, tea or oak leafs.'

'Mother, I thought you could only make wine from grapes?'

'Good heavens no,' she said. 'Home-made wine is different and more potent. It takes a couple of months to make and the noise is produced by yeast activating the sugar.'

More surprises? There were. 'Later I'll show you the cellar where we've got a hundred bottles stored, and our own little pub.'

'What?' I exclaimed.

Mother always looked and acted sober, but enjoyed a few. 'Your father altered the end bedroom and turned it into a bar and put in a record player for music. We call it *The Hub*. It's strictly closed except for family visits.' Method in Mother's madness. How did she do it?

'Come over here, I want to show you something.' She led me to a table in the corner I hadn't noticed. Several packages wrapped in coloured paper had been lovingly placed there and tied with silver ribbon. 'C'mon me duck, open them.'

'What are these for?' I replied, oozing with excitement, knowing they were for me.

'Gifts to you from us. Each birthday or Christmas we bought you one. We saved on postage.' Perfume greeted me as I opened a soap or body cream and she watched intently, enjoying my reactions. The house was warm. Coal fires had been replaced by instant warmth from gas fires. Mother's creative decorative skills had allowed her to transform an ordinary house into a cosy home. But the back garden was a let-down and I could sense Popsey's frustration. There was no lawn, apple trees or room to grow vegies, only a tiny area where a few roses and other flowers grew.

When my siblings and I left home, Mother retired from the slavery of working in the shoe factory, dividing her time between cooking, making wine, gardening, reading women's magazines and watching TV soapies. On the other hand Popsey seemed content to work full time at the leather factory, contributing to help pay for household expenses and enjoying a pint of Guinness, while playing billiards at the weekends. I was relieved they were reaping the benefits of hard work and living a comfortable life. Dancers always work in the festive seasons and I hadn't experienced the joy of celebrating Christmas at home for several years. Waking up on Christmas Day, I went to the bedroom window. Snowflakes were lazily drifting from above to the street below, coating the dull atmosphere in an ermine cloth of white brightness. Music of carols floated up the stairs and singing to myself I joined them. Streamers were stretched across the ceilings, while mistletoe perched around lamp shades invited the odd guest for a hug. A Christmas tree was draped in silver tinsel, and tiny, electric light bulbs flickered intermittently from the front window.

It didn't matter there were only the three of us. Popsey and I danced a polka down the passageway as Mother buried her head in the kitchen. We dived into roast chicken, pork and the traditional pudding with custard, followed by mince pies, nuts and chocolates, drowned with a tot of Mothers' home-made wine. Hardly able to move, we retired to The Hub for more jokes, laughter and specials until it was time for the Queen's speech.

What a wonderful day! I didn't know what the future held. Would I be dancing this time next year or doing something else? My heart glowed with love for my parents and I treasure the memory of a very special day. In the New Year, memories of previous experiences lurked and played on my restless mind. But the safe haven of home couldn't keep me there. I'd outgrown the lifestyle of living a mundane, ordinary life in a country town, and missed the stimulating benefits of a stage career. The thought of no longer travelling and dancing in big cities, or having unexpected encounters with crazy characters, was depressing. London was calling.

'Pamela,' said Mother, 'I know you've been through a hard time, but me duck, make sure you've recovered and well enough before you rush away again.'

'Yes Mother', I sighed. She was over protective again.

'You were away for such a long time. We got a phone call from Joanie asking where you were.' Mother noted my short intake of breath. Her next few words left me gaping at her insight and intelligence – she could read me like a book. 'I'm sure you'll pick up the threads of friendship, me duck. Let me know when you're leaving. Your home is always here.'

'Yes Mother,' I replied, relieved she understood. She plucked a letter from a pile of others and declared with motherly wisdom, 'There's plenty more fish in the sea. This came today.' She put it on the table and left.

Staring at Spanish postal stamps I was dumbfounded. It was from José. How to cope with this?

The more I read, the guiltier I felt. Pages were filled with words of pure love, heartache and a desperate longing for my return. I'd been gutless not to tell him I was leaving for good. It'd been difficult to let him go as it was, and guilt lingered. He was still living in the pension and wouldn't be able to afford it. No doubt he'd soon return to his parents. To send him a 'Dear John' letter would hurt him deeply. It was better not to reply and I was right. He never wrote again.

Mother never inquired about José or what I intended to do.

What about the rings? Hurrying up the stairs I found my handbag. They were still at the bottom with all the other paraphernalia. They shone in the bright light as I looked at them. Made from eighteen carat Spanish gold, they were exquisite with a delicate leaf decoration curling around the outside edges.

Flawed with indecision I placed them in a drawer until I could decide what to do with them. What? Sell them? No. Pawn them? No. Give them away? No. Too many memories were attached. There had to be another answer.

One day, alone in the house I wandered to the back of the garden. The Christmas Day snow was a dirty, muddy slush in the streets. Everything was bare. I couldn't stay outside for long as the cold wind was whipping my bones. Mother's pruned rose bush caught my eye. The lean trunk devoid of branches and leaves was the perfect place. In summer it would blossom under the care of Mother's green fingers and reign supreme with glorious roses, a symbol of love. A garden tool was easy to find in the shed. Hacking away at hard soil, my fingers froze. What was another solution? Boiled water would soften the ground.

Two kettles of hot water later, I dug a deep hole beside the bush and with remorse buried the rings. A rush of relief overwhelmed me – they were safe. Gold never rusts. Sometime in the near or distant future they'd be found. Maybe they'd dig up the garden looking for more, or perhaps the rings would lay dormant until eternity. As the days passed, Mother's prediction came true. Bored, but recuperated and feeling good, I told her, 'Mother, I'm going to see to Joanie.'

'OK, me duck.'

I needn't have worried. Joanie greeted me with open arms. She looked older, the curly, grey hair slack, her walk slower, yet she was the Joanie I loved, with a sharp business mind. We talked for hours. She'd trained a German girl to sew, to take up a career sewing costumes for the film industry. I told her all the juicy bits of my travels – the ride up the mountain with a racing driver in Monte Carlo, seeing wonderful scenery, dancing for Princess Grace and Elizabeth Taylor and wearing sequined blue feathered costumes. How lucky I'd felt to see Rudolf Nureyev, the acclaimed Russian ballet star, in person in a night café. I declined to tell her about José. It felt as though I'd never left.

One evening Joanie was frantic. 'I've got to get 150 costumes for tomorrow.' They had to be posted to Devon for an amateur, theatrical production. The avalanche of work involved sorting out military costumes and long Georgian gowns.

We worked tirelessly throughout the night, sewing, checking and packing costumes, hats, stockings and gloves. Exhausted, I slumped into a bed she'd hidden in the back wardrobe amongst a line of elegant costumes serving as a curtain. She woke me up two hours later with a hot cuppa tea. 'Wake up dearie, people are coming.'

A few days later she confronted me with the most astonishing offer. 'If you stay in London, I'm prepared to teach you to take over the business.'

'Oh Joanie, it's an amazing offer. I'll go home at the weekend and let you know on my return.'

My parents refused to help. The decision had to be mine. After soul searching, the choice was clear. Aged 26, I was a veteran dancer with ten years professional experience. How much longer could I dance? Few dancers continued as most of them married. There'd be no more overseas travel and I loathed the bitter English winters. Although sewing was becoming enjoyable, I'd be committed to the wardrobe for life. No, dancing was my passion and I would try to dance for as long as I could.

Decision made, my parents nodded their heads and it was time to tell Joanie. I knew she'd be disappointed, but she surprised me by accepting my answer and never mentioned it again.

No dancing jobs were advertised. The pantomime season was in full swing and an unexpected postal strike lasting eight weeks made the situation worse.

Noting my distress, Joanie came to the rescue. 'Pamela, I'm going to phone my agent. She may have something.'

'Do you think so Joanie? There's no jobs with this strike.'

'She has many contacts. She got you the job in Scotland. I'll phone her now.' She returned swiftly, interrupting my thoughts. How lucky I felt to have such a good friend. She was like a second mother and I trusted her implicitly.

'There's a contract for six months in Lunel in the South of France for Leon Grieg for four dancers.' Unusual. I'd never heard of Lunel or Leon Grieg, and always danced in big theatre productions or cabarets with a large cast.

'I'm not sure,' I replied, confused. It didn't sound good at all.

'Oh, stop looking for big contracts.' Joanie glared at me as though I was a zombie, agitated with my reply. 'I've heard of Leon Grieg. Sometimes big things grow out of little things. She says you don't have to audition, but wants an answer this second.'

This was madness with no time to think properly. Six months was a short time and it was overseas, but I wanted to audition to see how the other girls danced. This would give me a chance to escape and leave my options open.

Silent, pondering on my options she requested, 'What do you want to do?'

'OK Joanie, I'll do it but I insist on auditioning.'

At the audition in a community hall, three young, classical dancers were good, although the one with curly, fiery red hair was exceptional. I learnt later her name was Cherry. Her superb combination of soft arm and strong leg movements was a delight to watch. Content, I was pleased I'd auditioned. Being older it would be hard to mingle with younger girls, but their dancing skills were excellent. It didn't matter.

'Hello Mother,' I yelled down the phone, bubbling with excitement. 'I'm coming home to pack. Got a contract for the

South of France and I travel there next week. Have to cross the Channel again. There's no sewing. It's only for six months.'

Lunel, France

'Hurry up, you'll never go anywhere at this rate,' an irate voice boomed in my ear as I fumbled to open the carriage door. Struggling with a suitcase, I was also carrying a guitar. I wondered why I'd bothered to bring it. Strumming on the strings soothed tensions but it was a damned nuisance right now.

As usual it'd been a nightmare crossing on the ferry with the boat swaying from side to side and up and down. Several people were seasick. The incessant chatter of the young girls on their first overseas journey nearly drove me nuts. Had I been like that when I was eighteen? Cherry, the fiery redhead, was talkative, bubbly and interested in everything. Val, with her long, dark brown hair, classical oval face and ivory white skin, was petite and reserved, though I suspected she had a strong will of her own. Ah, Vicki with the flowing mane of golden hair – she would tempt a few men, yet she was coy and self-conscious and walked with a heavy gait.

'Hurry,' the English voice boomed. As I stepped onto the platform to join the girls, a ray of sunshine burst through the clouds. It was nippy but not as cold as England. I'd actually returned to warm weather.

Gazing at the man who'd spoken, he was a modern day Adonis, tall and strong with short, fair, wavy hair encompassing a handsome, fading tanned face. He wore a cream polo necked jumper and brown trousers.

'Follow me girls,' he commanded with a slight smile on his face as his long strides led us out of the tiny station to the taxies. Leon Grieg, the choreographer, wanted everything done yesterday. He'd met us with an urgency to know the way we walked and talked as we were his new dancers.

'Can anyone drive a car?' he asked with a broad smile. 'The previous girls bought an old jalopy. It'll get you around.'

Val leapt into the air as the other girls laughed.

'They left a cat behind you can look after.' Cherry and Val grinned. Preferring dogs, I was quiet.

'Who can sew?' he inquired and I shot my hand into the air without thinking of the consequences.

Lunel is a minute country town built on marshland. Located in the Languedoc wine-growing region, its situated half way between the main towns of Nimes and Montpellier close to the sea, and 200 kilometres from the Spanish border. In 1971 with a meagre population of 13,000, it had one hotel, a café, a few shops and a few old stone buildings. Nothing exciting to write home about.

We approached a white, modern bungalow, almost hidden from the main road by rows of grapevines. It was within walking distance to the nightclub. Parked at the side was the old, run down car. If it worked, who cared what it looked like!

Leon left after announcing he'd bring hats for me to sew in the morning. A few food essentials were in the fridge and we chose our rooms. Outside, a faint meowing intervened in the gossip and Val and Cherry rushed to pick up the big, fat, grey cat, smothering it with kisses. It'd found new owners, and I secretly named it Doormat.

Gulping down breakfast, the girls scampered away to explore Lunel in the old jalopy while I waited for Leon. He came with eight huge headdresses. The half-moon shaped head pieces were covered in gold material. Extending from the top of the hat long, red-dyed pheasant feathers were securely attached with strong, neat stitches. Stunning. He also gave me a small bag of red gem stones an inch in diameter, thin needles and cotton.

'Make your own design,' he suggested.

Difficult and time consuming, I dotted them everywhere on the head dress. Working throughout the day, they were soon finished and I was proud of my work.

Horrified, Leon gasped, 'It's atrocious. You've ruined the hats.'

'Give me the un-picker,' I stated bluntly.

'You'll ruin the material.'

'No. Watch.' He glared at each movement as bit by bit I unpicked the stones.

Satisfied, he told me to look close and sewed a cluster of stones in the centre. Hours later, when he collected them they were passable.

'Can you machine?'

'Yes, and I zigzag edges.' The Colt Saloon was a landmark on the highway to Nimes. The large, white building stood out amongst a backdrop of green vines, with a gravel road leading to the entrance featuring an old fashioned nineteenth century carriage.

Entering the nightclub, there was an enormous orange poster advertising the cabaret/music-hall, with a caricature of a dancing girl in a bikini wearing high boots and a gun slung in her garter. Inside, red furnishings led to a bar and four orchestra places stood erect at the side of a reasonably sized stage. Rumour had it the owners were gangsters who'd retired and invested gold and their spoils into the club. The local clientele were from Nimes and Montpellier and continued to come as the international artists changed every four weeks.

We were lucky, changing one number every alternate month with few rehearsals. The presenter Milou Duchamp had the audience aching with laughter with his duck puppet and Can-can dancers Roger and Sheila completed the show of resident artists.

In four fast and exhausting days, we learnt routines on the stage with rehearsals. The Cancan, the highlight of the show, was ten minutes long and the spectacular dancing of Sheila and Roger made us work harder. Roger took a flying leap over the four of us as we knelt down, landing in a split. For solos, Vicki performed cross over splits on the ground. Val pirouetted as ballet dancers do, and I executed a double pirouette followed by a jump split. Cherry understudied Sheila, who held one leg high over her head – crash landing onto the ground in a split.

In one rehearsal Leon leapt onto the stage yelling, 'Watch me girls,' and performed a few fast intricate steps. 'Have you got it?' he tested us, hoping one of us could achieve the impossible.

We looked at him in despair. He repeated the steps a second time and Cherry triumphantly cried out, 'I've got it. I can do it.'

'OK girls, Cherry will teach you. I'll see you this afternoon.'

Leon made the costumes, chose the music and choreographed the numbers. He was a genius. Where did he learn these skills? I knew he'd belonged to a superb ballet company, but sewing is a craft and takes years to learn. It's an unwritten rule never to ask a choreographer where they trained or who they worked for. The desire to know was strong, and although I was almost exploding to find out, I was tight lipped.

It was torture when he fitted us for our Can-can bodices. He pulled our waists in tight.

'Oh no,' we wailed, 'we won't be able to dance.'

'Yes, you will,' he replied firmly. 'You'll look even better on stage.' He then pulled the material tighter. As we applied make-up in the dressing room on opening night, Leon appeared in the dressing room. Dangling a small phial of glitter in one hand, he declared, 'Apply a small amount to your eyelids and you'll look lovely.'

Putting an A4 black piece of art paper on my place in the dressing room, he cut out an eyelash with a small pair of scissors with swift strokes. 'You won't have to buy eyelashes again.' We didn't have to, although I often made them for the girls when they needed replacing.

'Dance well girls, you'll be brilliant,' he said, and went to watch our first performance.

We learnt a Chinese number using ribbons on sticks, and Clown, Indian and South American routines. My favourite was the miniature version of the ballet Coppelia.

'Please, please Leon, I haven't danced on my toes for years. I can't do it,' I'd implored him.

'No. You're an old man who looks down from a first floor balcony and climbs down the stairs to wind them up to dance.' The show was so successful we performed a free matinee for the children in the town. We settled into a cosy lifestyle. Val drove us to shop and occasionally after the show to a nearby pizzeria where we'd splash out on a meal and a bottle of Beaujolais. Val and Vicki cooked our main meal in the bungalow, while I make an apple pie and Cherry washed the dishes. Doormat became fatter. I bought a bicycle and enjoyed exploring the countryside, leaving the bike outside the bungalow at night.

One day when I went to use it I was shocked. Someone had stolen the tires, chain, mudguards and seat. It must've been the gypsies who lived on the outskirts of town.

'Make sure you always lock up,' I told the girls, hiding my disappointment.

The girls were tired of the constant whirling of the sewing machine when Leon gave me work. I didn't mind and understood their point of view, but it was becoming a problem. The following month Estelle Caresse starred in the show. Sexy and sensual, she was different. We realised by the false boobs, tiny bottom, outlandish make-up, swagger and her deep voice that she was a transvestite. The audience adored her.

Admiring our costumes, she inquired who made them. In Pidgin French I told her I had helped the choreographer with sewing.

'Carnival costume, pants and top with many frills,' she requested, and offered to pay me.

Seven hundred francs was the equivalent of two weeks' wages. Stunned and trying to keep a straight face, I agreed. I'd made hundreds of frills and pants at Joanie's. I knew I could do it, and had no intention of telling Leon.

She bought a lovely deep blue material decorated with splashes of red, white, yellow and green. Soft to the touch, it was the perfect fabric to make frills and an excellent choice for a carnival costume. I arranged to take her measurements the following evening in our dressing room.

'Pamela,' Val demanded with a wicked glint in her eyes. 'Find out if she's got one. See how big it is, or if it's cut off.'

'Oh yes,' Cherry giggled.

'Please try,' Vicky implored.

Looking at the three of them, I tried to be stern but they were young and inquisitive. 'Stop it you lot. I can't guarantee an answer. I'll do my best but if one of you starts giggling or does anything stupid, I'll um … '

They understood. Time to measure Estelle. I placed her in a position where the girls could see her. Three pairs of wide eyes watched as I measured the bust, arms, waist and outside leg. The crucial moment arrived. Legs slightly apart I took the tape up her inside leg. Up and up it went. Reaching the vital part my hand shook. I couldn't do it.

'What did you find out?' Val shrieked.

'Don't know. She must have tucked it away.'

The girls were appeased and it wasn't mentioned again.

'*Magnifique*', Estelle declared, twirling around to let us see the lovely frills. The girls were in awe and I was proud.

'I love the Can-can. Is it possible another costume?' Estelle inquired as she rustled the frills back and forth. I couldn't believe my luck. She wanted a black velvet circular skirt with strass (a line of small cut glass stones) sewn on the bottom edge to open in the middle, with white lace frills inside. Difficult.

I had to tell Leon as I didn't know where to get the strass from. Surprised, he inquired, 'What are you going to do with the money?'

'I haven't had time to think.'

'Why don't you buy a mobylette like mine?' It was the French version of a small moped, using petrol and travelling up to 50 kilometres an hour. I bought one the next day complete with side bags, thrilled to get my freedom to go back and forth where and when I wanted at a faster pace.

'Are you sure you can make the skirt?' Leon inquired. It was reassuring to know he would help, but I wanted to do this on my own, even if I sewed day and night.

Making the costume was difficult and I agonised over it. The white petticoat and black skirt didn't present a problem, but sewing them together at the waist and hem line took hours – as did the strass, which I hadn't worked with before. I earnt every cent.

Presenting it to Estelle, she was happy although I could see the odd tiny mistake. She promptly handed me the money and left the show the following week. What a pity!

'Why don't you buy a good sewing machine?' Leon asked, so I did and returned the old one to him.

There was only one thing lacking in this idyllic life. Doormat was the centre of attention and I yearned to have a dog. The problem was what to do when the six month contract ended.

Monty in Lunel

Head strong and ignoring my better judgement, I hopped onto the mobylette and raced to the pet shop in Nimes. Walking along the cages with puppies of different breeds and colours, there was one with patches of brown on its ears and body who immediately caught my attention. It ran up to the front of the cage to greet me, tail wagging non-stop, pestering me to look at him. As I stared into his big, brown eyes, I knew he was the one.

'What breed is he?' I inquired.

'A French Braque. He'll grow up to be too big for you.'

'He's so small.'

'Look at his paws, they're large.'

I couldn't tell the difference as I was already in love with the adorable pup. Placing him in the side bag where I'd put a small towel to make him comfortable I whizzed back to Lunel, with special puppy food in the other side bag. The journey didn't bother him.

The girls were surprised at the new arrival and Doormat was reluctant to come inside. He had to have a name. Yes, he was going to grow up to be strong and healthy and the name needed to reflect this. General Montgomery was a war hero. Perfect.

Monty became my constant companion. He'd only been with us for two days when I was almost blinded. I could hardly see or open my eyes. It was weird and the girls drove me to see the doctor.

'You've got pollen in your eyes through riding your mobylette without sunglasses on.' No dancing. 'Use these eye drops three times a day and stay in a dark room for four days and nights and you'll be cured.'

The girls were good bringing meals to the bedroom, and Monty refused to leave the room, playing havoc with the bed clothes. As predicted by the doctor, the eyes healed and I returned to the show, rested with energy to burn.

Mischievous Monty put his nose into everything. I tried to teach him to do wee wees outside but he was too young, and Doormat hissed, refusing to come in.

The last straw for the girls was when he pinched a pair of Val's lacy knickers and chewed a hole in the middle.

'Oh no,' wailed Val, 'They're the new ones I bought in England.'

'It's alright Val, I'll wash and mend them for you.'

After making an intricate lace pattern to cover the hole, she was satisfied. What else could go wrong?

It wasn't fair for the girls to listen to the buzzing noise from the sewing machine all day long, with naughty Monty chasing around and Doormat refusing to come in. It was time to move.

I found an ideal bedsitter with the usual amenities on the first floor above a barber's shop, close to the town centre. I could also park the mobylette safely downstairs in a large empty room. The jovial landlord was middle-aged with black hair and a pronounced moustache. He attended to his clientele in a white smock, darting everywhere with a beaming smile.

Monty and I relished our freedom but he grew fast. At first he'd travel in the side bag of the mobylette. We'd roam the countryside and he'd play in the fields by the canals, falling into them. Walking him on a lead around Lunel, people stopped to pat him and in return he'd give them give big licks. As his legs and strength grew, he ran alongside the mobylette, romping along the beach and splashing into the waves.

The landlord adored him. When I had rehearsals he looked after him and Monty became a favourite with the customers, who patted him as their hair was trimmed.

One day he escaped and I found him hanging by his lead from a big hook in the butcher's shop. As his teeth grew, he'd chew on anything. Big holes appeared in the bed mattress I slept on. As if that wasn't enough, I came home from the show one night to find the box of tissues and half a chair chewed up and strewn across the floor. What an adorable rascal! 'Pamela, do you want to stay here for another six months?' Leon asked when I took sewing to him. How stupid to forget the contract was for six months. 'Can you find out if the other girls wish to continue? I need to know.'

When I asked them Val was excited. She'd started a romance with the waiter Jean-Jacque, but the other two were hesitant. I confronted them, sure they'd agree. 'You're lucky to be given the chance to stay. Leon is pleased with you and loves your dancing, but he needs an answer now.'

'Will we go home in six months?' Cherry was hesitant.

'Of course,' I replied as Vicky murmured a weak acceptance, and I breathed a sigh of relief.

One day we were invited to a barbecue in a paddock with a few of the local lads. A huge lamb carcass was rotating on a large stick over an open wood fire. It wasn't what we'd expected.

'Killed a few days ago and hung for ten days to let the blood drip out,' one of the lads boasted as he threw beer down his throat.

'It's ready,' one lad screamed. They bolted like lightening, pushing and shoving each other to get to the best parts. Massive chunks of flesh and bones were ripped from the carcass and taken to eat at the bench. Behaving like cannibals with raucous laughter, their performance would have beaten King Henry VIII as they gnawed on bones. Forced to watch this disgusting display, we toyed with morsels of lamb and sipped wine. In October a new couple arrived to star in a psychedelic number. They'd worked for Leon before and had toured with him in the Middle East. Robert Kapikian was short, slim and muscular, with styled black, wavy hair and an olive skin. His gait was confident with an accent from distant lands. He was pleasant to talk to and often his dark brown eyes pinpointed you, appearing to search your soul, leaving one feeling hesitant and uncertain. He was a womaniser and a macho man who wanted to conquer the world.

His partner Gail Bracken was a highly intelligent Scottish lass with a curvaceous figure. Her shoulder length blonde hair, pale white skin and blue eyes were attractive. As a mediocre dancer, these qualities didn't matter. Her refined taste in clothes and clutching Robert's arm were enough to seal her success. In their late twenties they were a formidable team.

'That damned Gail,' Leon once uttered under his breath. I knew what he meant. In February the year's contract was coming to an end, and Leon approached me with an amazing offer.

'Pamela, I'm starting a touring ballet with eight girls in April. Robert will be the manager and will travel with you. Val, Vicky and Cherry are going home for a short holiday and returning here to rehearse. I'd like you to stay and sew for me before joining the new ballet.'

I agreed without hesitation. More time to spend with my beloved pooch before giving him to the landlord, who adored him.

Leon made the offer even easier to say yes to. 'I'll pay the rent of your flat and give you a little pocket money and your evening meal.'

'Yes, Leon. What about my belongings if I'm not returning to England?'

A huge smile erupted on his face. 'I'll take care of them and your mobylette until you return. You'll start at 10 am in the morning and we'll sew together.'

All went according to plan. Leon was a brilliant mentor, showing me how to cut and sew different materials for dancing costumes and make my own patterns. Two machines hummed in his apartment all day long, and his meals at night were no ordinary feed. Culinary delights I'd never tasted or heard of before cooked before my eyes. Steak cooked in garlic butter with a sizzling French brandy and cream sauce accompanied with fresh, crisp salad and vegies bought from the local market. Leon was a master of all trades.

Monty had his tea when I returned and we spent the evening playing together. The landlord looking after him in the daytime, but I missed our daily jaunts with Monty running alongside the mobylette to the beach or fields.

At dusk one day he was missing. People had said, 'Good breed of dog. Worth a lot of money.' Stolen? The town folk knew I'd be leaving soon and a new ballet was coming to the Colt Saloon…

Heading for the coffee bar I implored the people there, 'Have you seen Monty?'

'One of our clients came in and took him home. Told me the ballet had left and Monty belonged to him.'

Relieved I asked him, 'Do you have his address?'

Revving up the engine I roared into the night to a dark quiet street at the edge of town. The number was difficult to read. Pressing the doorbell hard, there was no answer so I yelled at the top of my lungs, 'MONTY.' My beloved pooch's face and paws appeared in a window at the top of the two story building as he clawed at the window pane, struggling to escape. Desperate minutes passed as a man opened the door.

'Where's my dog?' I yelled at him.

'It's alright. We were looking after him for you.'

I couldn't believe my eyes as his wife struggled to contain Monty on his lead, with a small glass of sherry in her hand as she walked down a steep flight of stairs. Bribery, but I accepted the apology and gulped down the small peace offering. No point in making a scene. Revving up the bike, we reached home at neck-breaking speed. Unusual, Vicky sent me a letter. Home life was good. She'd met Robert in London and now wanted to come to Lunel for a couple of days to talk to him as she was interested in him and had met him in London. Could she stay with me before rehearsals for a couple of days?

'Come if you wish, but the double mattress is chewed up,' I replied. 'Although I'll take you wherever you wish to go on my mobylette.'

She came and there was fun going shopping in Nimes and Vicky was able to understand the power of Gail over Robert. The other girls arrived in Lunel, and sewing was replaced with rigid rehearsals. The landlord was happy to take Monty, but a terrible thing happened. When I came home, he was gone again. The last time I saw Monty he was staring at me through the downstairs window, knowing I'd be gone most of the day when I took my bike out to go to rehearsals. He had a sad face, longing for a run along the beach.

Who took him is a mystery. The gypsies? Doormat had recently given birth to kittens in a cupboard, and they'd stolen them as well. Gone.

The landlord and I wept together. He took me in his car to the countryside searching everywhere, then into the town to ask the locals if they'd seen him.

Grieving, I gave my landlord Monty's papers as he told me not to worry about the chewed up bed.

What happened to my beloved Monty? I question it to this day. As rehearsals ended Leon spoke to me, with Robert at his side. 'Pamela, you'll be paid in American dollars. Would you like an extra $20 a week to sew and repair costumes?' My sewing skills were recognised.

'We're also wondering if you'd appear topless in a couple of numbers for an extra $20 a week?' he added. 'It won't be all the time. It'll depend where you work. You don't have to, but what do you think? Gail, Cherry and Vicky have agreed.' A clever tactic.

This news was unexpected and threw my mind into a turmoil. I was surprised Cherry and Vicky had agreed. The money was good, and we were overseas so my parents wouldn't know, but I was sceptical of the idea.

'What do you mean sometimes?'

'In the opening number you're wearing long cloaks and only open them when topless dancing is wanted.'

Reluctantly I agreed. Being far from home, the money was appealing.

Missing Monty, I stepped onto the train to Geneva, Switzerland in 1972 to start an epic dancing journey with a full troupe of eight dancers, known as The London Dancers. They were choreographed by Leon Grieg and under the management of Robert Kapikian.

Geneva, Switzerland

Geneva is a global city in Switzerland, filled with diplomats specialising in private banking and the financing of international trade. It's also the headquarters of the United Nations. French is the main language, although English is spoken everywhere. It lies at the tip of Lake Geneva, surrounded by three chains of mountains. Swans frolic in the calm waters of the lake as the Jet d'Eau (Jet of Water) soars high into the air.

I'd come from a sleepy village no-one knew of in the south of France to this amazing city. The hotel was comfortable and a short walk from the nightclub.

We soon settled into a pleasant routine after opening night. Maxims was the best nightclub in town and had recently been renovated in gold and red. We, the London dancers, were an instant success. Our huge feathers, jewels and dances set to vibrant music thrilled the audience, as an act of Russian Cossack dancers wowed them with specialised jumps and leaps. Robert added lighting effects on the costumes, with artistic touches of green, blue and other mosaic colours portraying a different style of leadership as Gail told him what was happening in the dressing room.

The first time my upper body was exposed was weird. Glancing at Cherry, Vicky, Gail and Sandy, they were untouchable goddesses, but it was comforting knowing Robert was there to protect us. Memories of enjoying the superb choreography and sewing together with Leon faded as Robert fully commanded our attention.

After a few days Robert called me aside. 'Pamela, can I talk to you?'

I'd been busy with an avalanche of sewing repairing, missing poppers and broken seams between numbers. Dancers are athletes and ripping a costume or muscle is commonplace. What was wrong?

'Pamela, you wear the wrong clothes. Your brown suede coat, mini dresses and gold Spanish bracelet must go. They're old fashioned and I want you to wear slacks.'

This hurt me. I adored them and the bracelet held wonderful memories of Majorca, but he meant business. I cried as I took them to the rubbish chute on the landing. It was a new beginning, yet I wasn't surprised to learn he'd said the same to everyone else. We all wore slacks now, with any style of top we liked. One night snuggled in bed and exhausted from the show, a gentle hand pulled the covers from my shoulders. Shock! Rushing out of bed, I couldn't see the intruder. The following day I told Robert, who advised, 'Lock your door.'

Another evening after the show, one of the waiters approached me as I was leaving. Handsome and charming, he inquired in a smattering of English, 'Coffee after show?' Why not get to know him? Coffee would quench my thirst after all the sweat and dancing.

We held hands and meandered down the main road until he led me into a side street. Odd. He'd hardly spoken. Wary, he seemed to sense my confusion and broke into a trot, leading me through small lanes away from the central lights as I demanded, 'Where's the coffee?' Grasping my hand tighter, he broke into a gallop. Unable to escape, confusion escalated as fear numbed my brain. My hand hurt from his tight grip as he ripped open a door to a large shed or garage. Wheels and tools lay by the far end of a wall as he pulled me into total darkness. Swinging my arm in a circle, I fell onto a concrete floor. Suffocating with fear, I was prey to a beast and no-one would hear my cries. Few memories exist.

Light from a street lamp crept under the door as I lay on the ground. How many times? The devil astride my torso began to demand, 'You give in. I count to ten'. No escape. What would he do when he'd finished – kill me? Fear subsided as the instinct for survival surfaced. Take a chance.

At the count of eight I croaked, 'You go prison. PRISON. Bad thing. Take me hotel, I say nothing.' My words were dynamite as he retreated in fear, changing from the monster to a slobbering child. Stripped of power and fearful of prison, he took me at a snail's pace back through the side streets to the hotel as I reinforced the message, 'I tell no-one. No prison.'

My confused brain was beginning to function, wondering if he'd raped before or would do so again. Silence was my best weapon, but I had to tell someone. I knocked on Cherry's door, praying she was awake and implored her to come to my room. She was concerned but skeptical of what she heard, as there were no visible signs of blood or bruising on my face.

'Try to sleep and put the ordeal behind you,' she suggested. 'It'll be alright.'

Relieved to have a friend to talk to and thankful for her advice, I put my shattered body to bed. Yes, I'd try to forget the experience. If Cherry didn't believe me, who would? The tabloids would have a field day with the story of a dancer from Maxims in Geneva being raped. In the seventies rape wasn't reported, and I'd be dragged into court without sympathy and accused of telling lies. I learnt a valuable lesson: never accept an invitation for coffee from a stranger after the show. But I'd survived. Late in the afternoon, during the Can-can I began to have stabbing pains in the stomach, increasing with each kick. No-one noticed. I kept quiet, hoping to recuperate after a good night's sleep – but it was annoying, as one of the girls had trodden on her white petticoat, ripping two yards of white frills from the skirt. Without a sewing machine, it was too big a job and would take half an hour to repair by hand.

Making my way back, the pain now was vicious. Doubled over, I stepped forward placing one foot in front of the other, gritting my teeth in determination to reach the hotel. In bed, the pain subsided.

At noon, awake without pain and feeling better, I noticed my stomach was swollen. I got dressed, hoping rest would help, and sat on the bed, reaching for the white petticoat to repair frills. A warm, sticky liquid trickled between my legs and stained the bedspread. Blood.

Geneva, Switzerland

Grabbing my handbag, I rushed from the room yelling, 'Taxi. Get a taxi. Urgent. Hospital.' People responded and a taxi arrived in minutes.

'There's a clinic close by,' the driver suggested.

'Take me to the nearest hospital,' I implored him and when we reached it I told him not to wait.

At reception, I explained the horrific pains and blood and was directed to take the lift to the fifth floor. 'Are you pregnant?' someone asked. It was the maternity section.

The pains had subsided, but the bloated stomach was uncomfortable. A kind doctor in a white smock greeted me in an office, and I felt sharp pains as he prodded my stomach.

'I know exactly what's wrong,' he declared, stating firmly, 'You must stay in hospital.'

'No, I must dance tonight.'

'If you value your life you will stay.'

I was horrified, realising how life threatening the situation was. I had no choice.

'Don't move,' the doctor said. 'A nurse will come with a bed. Get into it and stay still.'

I was frozen on the spot, unable to think. The nurse arrived and ordered me to change into a white gown. Tucking the sheets in around me firmly, the nurse whispered, 'Lie still,' then left.

Strange. I was an Egyptian mummy who talked. Glancing around the study, I noted shelves filled with medical books on one side, and a large business table with a leather chair in the centre where I'd greeted the doctor. In the middle of one of the book cases was a small clock, and gazing hard at it I saw the hands moving and tried to guess the time. Half past two. Silence.

Minutes and hours passed. Eternity beckoned as the hands of the clock moved forward. Was my life ticking away? Twenty eight was too young not to fulfil dreams.

Who'd take my place in the show or sew the costumes? Would I dance again?

My parents had no idea what had happened. Why worry them? Far away in England, they couldn't help.

Enough suffering. I'd obey the doctor's orders and breathe with minimal movement. If they knew what was wrong there was a chance of survival, but the lack of communication was frustrating.

At 4 pm Robert, Gail and Cherry burst into the room. How did they find me? The Egyptian mummy spoke. 'Don't know what's happened, pains last night.' Glaring at Cherry, I implored her to say nothing about the rape. 'I have to stay here if I value my life. What's happening?'

'I'll talk to the doctor and let you know,' Robert replied, with Gail on his arm as Cherry trailed behind them. They didn't return. Nothing.

I felt relieved that they knew where I was, but bored with looking at the hands of the clock. At least the bed felt comfortable.

In a state of confusion, I slipped in and out of sleep, unable to think, prepared for the slightest sound or movement as darkness descended. A light switched on. It was 9:30 pm. Activity as two doctors in blue smocks wheeled me out to another room. 'You're having an operation,' the big man stated as he started to shave my private parts. 'You must sign these papers.'

'What?' Shocked, I knew I had to contact someone. 'I've got to call my girlfriend to notify my parents.'

'We don't do that.'

'I'm not signing.' It was an emergency, so they handed me a phone. Cherry's worried voice answered. I'd caught her before she left for the show. 'I'm having an operation. If anything goes wrong, tell my parents I love them.' There was a gasp at the other end as I put down the phone.

I implored the surgeon, 'I'm a dancer. I can't work if there's a large cut across my stomach.'

Looking down at my terrified face, he replied, 'We'll open you up on your bikini line, if you'll sign the papers?' In intensive care after surgery, my dysfunctional brain was unable to comprehend thought or movement. Vague figures of people floated above. Were they photographs?

Life returned when I was transferred from intensive care with a drip attached to my arm to another ward full of bed ridden patients. Groaning and not knowing what was going to happen, depression set in.

Without warning, the patients shouted at me. 'Snap out of it. We were like you. You're alive and going to get better.' Their relentless coaxing pulled me out of the depths of despair.

They were right and I stopped feeling sorry for myself. It was a miracle and when other patients were wheeled in, I joined in the chorus to stop their distress.

A nurse pulled away the covers to check the wound. A sigh of relief came when I saw the large cut across my bikini line was clamped together with staples. The doctors had kept their promise.

'You're a lucky girl,' she stated, replacing the blankets. 'You nearly died.'

It was a gradual healing process, until one day the nurse said, 'Sit up and stretch your stomach muscles. It'll be painful, but if you don't do it you'll be bent over for the rest of your life.'

Meal times were torture of a different kind. Roast meals served with tea, juice or red wine were devoured by hungry patients, while I glanced at the drip in my arm, salivating, dreaming of gourmet meals and sipping white wine.

At last the nurse helped me out of bed and I was able to roam around the ward and corridor, attached to the weird contraption holding the drip. At the window, I stared at a simple park with green grass and a blue sky. A warm glow penetrated my heart as I gazed at nature, promising myself I'd never forget the moment if I could walk outside. The joy of living would always be there no matter what the future held, but would I be able to dance again? Eventually the nasty drip was taken away and I was given a warm cup of tea to soothe a parched throat, as frantic yearnings surfaced to leave the hospital. I'd been there for nine days. The doctors visited daily, except for the weekends.

'Nurse,' I implored her, 'I want to leave.'

'No. You can't leave.'

'Why not? I can walk.'

'You must see a doctor and sign release papers before you can go. It's Friday. Get into bed and I'll see what I can do for tomorrow.'

At 9 am the next morning, prancing up and down the ward, my antics delighted everyone. Freedom was at my fingertips. 'Get into bed and wait,' the flustered nurse yelled.

The doctor arrived at 10 am and to my delight ordered me to get out of bed. After a meticulous examination I was allowed to leave, with strict instructions to rest for six weeks and not to drink alcohol or eat spicy food. The doctor's form stated I'd suffered peritonitis, but he'd never know the truth. Walking out of the hospital was easy, but where was the green grass? Concrete buildings and dull roads confronted me. What next? A taxi came from nowhere and yes, I was back on the road to recovery.

Take me back to England I wanted to scream, but the driver stopped at the hotel like I'd instructed. It was impossible to believe, but there in the lobby was Leon with Robert.

Amazed to see me, Leon announced with a wicked grin, 'We were talking about you and deciding whether or not we could kidnap you from the hospital.'

'What?'

'Good,' Leon continued, taking charge of the situation. 'I've got business matters to attend to in Lunel tomorrow and we must leave this afternoon. Come with me.'

'No. I can't. I'm too ill. I must rest for six weeks on doctor's orders.'

'Yes, you can.'

'No.' I squeaked, 'I can't dance or anything.'

'It's alright. I'll put cushions in the back of the car to make you comfortable and look after you.' This was a surprise, as I'd been expecting to go to the hotel for a few days and return to England alone.

Staring at Leon's face as he waited for an answer, I knew I could trust him.

'Collect your things and I'll see you in reception at 4 pm,' he said with warmth and kindness. Leon held my fate in his hands as we drove up and down the mountains of the Swiss border into France, with me wedged between cushions in the back of the car. A vague memory of snow-capped mountains emerged until oblivion wiped away the extraordinary events of the day. Late in the evening I tumbled into another strange bed.

As my strength returned, Leon noticed the difference in me. One day he put a deckchair with cushions outside in the sun on the patio where I could rest and sew for him. It was a diamante necklace to sew on.

With the first stitch he winced, grabbing it off me. 'Don't you know how to sew diamante by now?' he growled. After a deep breath, he showed me how to begin and end, sewing the jewels. They had to be tucked in correctly or the cotton would fray. He was a perfectionist, and I was happy when Leon smiled at my work.

Helping him to prepare his usual gourmet meals was a new experience. Herbs, brandy and cream added to different meats complemented the flavour.

One night as we watched the small black and white TV together, he poured himself a drink. 'Have one with me.'

'No Leon. I'm not well enough to drink.'

'How about a Bloody Mary? It's tomato juice with a little vodka. I'll garnish it with a slice of celery. It won't hurt you.'

He returned with the cocktail and we settled down to enjoy the program. A third of the way through the Bloody Mary, an excruciating need to go to the bathroom exploded within me.

'Help,' I cried, 'I'm in trouble.' I rushed to the bathroom, smothering the tiles and locking the door.

'Open up,' Leon implored.

'No, it's horrid.'

Leon called one of the dancers from the top part of his apartment to help me, as I was too embarrassed to let him in. They handed me some towels to mop up the mess. In the morning, life continued as normal and the incident was forgotten. Leon was producing a new show at the Colt Saloon and within a few days I was well enough to help him. We were hurricanes on the sewing machines, glancing up at each other when a bobbin needed changing or piles of material fragments needed to be removed from the floor.

One night he took me to see his latest show. His creative, choreographic abilities were brilliant. In a new Can-can finale, with new multi-coloured velvet skirts, he'd used two of the resident artists to give the number a Parisian theme. Another highlight was a dance with four girls in crinoline gowns, who swayed in unison to classical music on swings hanging from the fly loft. It'd been almost five weeks since I'd left the hospital when one day Leon told me after lunch, 'I want you to machine four Can-can petticoats, but you must finish them this afternoon, as I'm driving you to the station to catch the 6 pm train to Geneva.'

'But Leon, I'm not allowed to dance.'

'You don't have to. We must have eight girls on stage. All you have to do is walk around in the opening number until you get better.' It seemed logical. 'Oh, you're flying to Porto in Portugal tomorrow morning, so you'd better work fast. You can't go until you finish the petticoats, as you're taking them with you.'

Jubilant to return to the ballet, I whizzed the lace around the petticoats and finished them at 5 pm. Exhausted, I took one last glance at my guitar and other luggage gathering dust in a corner of the bedroom. I wondered how long it would be before I returned.

At the station, a contented Leon waved goodbye as I boarded the train to Geneva with one suitcase and the precious petticoats.

Europe – Part One

Leaving the suitcase at the hotel, I took the petticoats to the nightclub and froze. The predator was serving drinks to customers at a front table while the show was in progress. Thank God he hadn't seen me.

Burying my head in the underskirts, I slipped backstage unnoticed. Robert was pleased I'd arrived on time and the girls hugged me. It was wonderful to be back after five weeks.

We set off at 7 am sharp to catch our plane, embarking on a journey to dance into the unknown under the new name of Ballet Mondial. Thrilled with the opportunity to be on stage again, my stomach wasn't complaining, but my lack of sleep was. I slept like a baby on the plane. The Alitalia flight to Lisbon was enjoyable and surrendering to the smooth humming of the engines I entered dreamland. Loud rumbling noises pierced my sub-conscious as the plane descended, extended its wheels and landed, jolting us back to reality. We were in Portugal, a land attached to Spain with a different language and culture.

Lisbon is the oldest known city in Western Europe. In my youth I'd learnt of their feats as maritime conquerors. What a pity I'd never see it.

Robert gathered us together in the domestic terminal to tell us there was a four hour wait for the flight to Porto in the North. Dismay. The airport was unimportant in the 70s and the coffee bar in the domestic terminal was our only retreat.

There were taxis outside. I looked at Robert. 'I want to take a taxi ride for an hour around Lisbon. Do you mind?'

His eyebrows lifted in amazement. Knowing he couldn't stop me, he replied, 'Make sure you're back in time for the flight.'

The taxi driver understood my Spanish and promised to return me within the hour, delighted I wanted to discover his city. We travelled up and down the hills, past the ancient university, plush green parks, tiny cobbled streets and long boulevards with historic statues. The highlight was viewing Belem in the harbour where Vasco de Gama set sail for India in 1497, creating a new trading path to the East.

'Hi Robert,' I laughed when I returned, as the brows on his face ascended. The next two hours dragged and the girls were lethargic, toying with their handbags. Nothing to do and nowhere to go.

We boarded the Portuguese plane, no doubt built twenty years earlier in the 1950s. The wings were heavy, the noise unbearable and the service mediocre. Several of the girls were scared but the pilot didn't want to die. Landing with a heavy thump we arrived at our destination.

Porto is a coastal tourist city in the northwest of Portugal and known for its port wine production. Arriving late, we headed straight to Povoa Casino to rehearse and perform at night. We were exhausted, and walking around in the opening number was all my poor stomach muscles could cope with. At one o'clock in the morning we crawled into our digs. During the month I hired a bicycle and rode around the city, strengthening my tummy muscles. The weather was warm and one day I came across a quaint old fishing village. On the beach men were dragging in nets from small boats onto golden sand – a flashback in time. They'd performed these tasks for centuries.

Mosquitoes are my enemy. They choose my royal blood every time. The pension had white washed walls and one day Cherry sprang into action, flinging her arms around my head. The battle was on. Too late – the blood-sucking beasty got me on the arm, but Cherry pursued it until she smashed it against the wall, leaving a big blob of blood the insect had devoured. They were the largest mozzies I'd ever encountered, almost an inch in length and insect repellent became a necessity.

We flew to Milan in Italy to commence a three month theatre tour. Coach trips were tiring and each week we danced in a different town except for Rome, Florence and Naples. The huge theatres were made of large stones and cold. Cheap spaghetti meals at the trattorias helped our finances and the famous Italian gelato was a firm favourite. An occasional coffee was costly but inexpensive if we sat at a bar. Tea was a life saver. I bought an electric plug to heat water in a mug. Using tea bags, powdered milk and sugar it was cheap. We were each limited to one suitcase, resulting in a minimum of only three or four slacks and tops to pack with our toiletries. Purchased artefacts were sent home, but regardless of the hardships we enjoyed the travel.

Milan was surprising. A Gothic cathedral covered in sheets of green plastic was being repaired while pigeons pestered tourists in the large square. Fast paced, well dressed people scurried to work in the office buildings, and arcaded shops displayed the latest fashions in the windows.

During long coach journeys we'd stop briefly for a bite to eat and a coffee and alas the inevitable happened. After a pit-stop, we'd been travelling for almost an hour when we realised a girl was missing. Brenda always lagged behind, lost in her own small world. She'd stood at the side of the road for two hours when we collected her and was in a state of complete despair. She soon quit the ballet.

Halfway through the contract I danced in all the numbers except for the Can-can, which appealed to me for its vibrant action and intoxicating music. Feeling strong and healthy, I yearned to overwhelm the audiences again with my specialised jump split. I'd astounded them in the past with a huge jump on the stage, landing facing them, crashing my right heal on impact to the floor and sending shock waves through the audience.

'No,' Robert stated, scared I'd hurt myself.

In the dressing room, I took a girl aside without Gail noticing. 'Can I take your place in the Can-can tonight? Just show me where you're placed. The steps are the same.'

Her amazement and delight at my suggestion was all I needed. She was relieved to have a break from the tortuous routine. Robert and Gail watched and said nothing as I continued to take each girl's place every night. Euphoria swept through me as at last I took my rightful place in the line. I was back.

Cherry was learning Italian and suffocating us with demands to know if her words were correct. The climax came when she announced she'd met a handsome Italian guy. We checked her make-up, hair and dress and sent her to meet him. Sobbing, she returned saying, 'He wasn't there.'

'What did you say to him?' we asked, concerned to see her so distressed. In her befuddled Italian she told him she'd meet him in nine months' time instead of nine o'clock. One day Robert told us we were having a ballet class in a hall the following afternoon. Unbelievable. Were the new dancers lacking in ability? I didn't think so. We were always travelling, rehearsing and dancing. The problem needed to be nipped in the bud before I contemplated returning to England. Easy.

Buying cheap white net and wire I hand sewed a make-shift tutu skirt. Borrowing Vicki's ballet shoes, tying the big satin bows in front I presented myself as the ballerina absolute. Robert was mortified. Without music, at each count from one to eight I thrust a foot forward, trod on my pink ribbons and curtseyed amid howls of laughter. I won. Roaming through off-beat lanes, grandiose plazas and unique buildings became an obsession I pursued throughout my career. I never got lost as the trick was to have a card or the address of the pension with me.

Denise, who'd recently joined the ballet, queried me about my daily jaunts and was eager to join me. We became buddies and shared a room together until she left several months later. In Genoa we came across a camera shop and bought Super 8 video cameras to record our travels. The films lasted three minutes and were sent to Kodak to develop, who posted them back to you. It was time consuming compared to today's technology, but I have some memorable old films of the ballet and countries we visited. Robert never danced with us, but was a good manager with excellent negotiating and marketing skills. When he announced we were going to Iran for a month I stared at him in disbelief. Ballets often worked in the Far East, but the Middle East? This was unusual. Iran, formerly known as Persia, was depicted in fairy tales as a place of bustling markets and carpets. Would I find a magic lamp?

In a modern Iranian plane, we flew over a landscape of parched, barren land until a mountain range came into sight and we descended into the capital of Tehran. Our room was in a dull, grey building on a main street on the tenth floor. The furniture was sparse but gazing through the window a lovely view of the snow-capped mountains in the distance compensated for the ordinary surroundings.

As the religion was Shieh, most of the women were clothed in long black hijabs covering them from head to toe with slits for their eyes. I was shocked. It was so unnatural and sinister, and quite frightening. The men wore normal European clothes and were impressive with dark skins, striking coal, black hair and heavy eyebrows. The royals were the Pahlavi family with the Shah as ruler over the vast country.

There were few shops and food was expensive. The odd café displayed rice with dill and Fava beans and lamb and chicken shish kebabs, but a cheap meal could be bought from a supermarket. We danced in a large cabaret club once a night which left us with idle hours in the daytime.

I felt uncomfortable at the prospect of walking alone in this strange city and, seeing a travel agency, realised it would be safer to go on a half day guided tour. A comfortable coach took me around the city to the main square, holy shrines and a stunning blue mosque with oriental architecture. Our last visit was to a mosaic workshop where we watched skillful workers insert minuscule pieces of coloured wood into intricate patterns onto little, wooden boxes. I bought one for Popsey. Bored, I was relieved there were only a few days left of the contract until Robert surprised us. 'We're invited to spend the day with the brother of the Shah at his mansion.'

We were amazed. Mixing with royalty was the last thing on our minds. What else could this man do?

Bombarding him with questions, he then silenced us. 'Relax, and be yourselves. Wear slacks and your favourite top. There's a small swimming pool if you want to chance it, but the water could be cold. Chauffeured limousines will be outside the hotel at 10 am.' Who could sleep?

At the city's edge a white mansion greeted our eyes, surrounded by lush well-kept green gardens, although April wasn't the season for flowers. We were greeted by the Shah's brother. Dressed in non-traditional clothes, he was surrounded by his ministers who resembled monks in long, white robes, but they spoke good English and made us welcome. We entered an enormous, carpeted room containing several lounges and coffee tables. At the side, glass doors opened up to the garden, while in the front a large cinema screen dominated the room. Several servants offered us drinks and nibbles but I was keen for a swim. Cherry had also brought her swim suit and joined me, looking fantastic in black bathers.

'You're sure the water's warm enough?' Robert inquired, and giving him an impish grin I stuck a finger into the water.

'Are we going in?' Cherry asked impatiently.

'It's cold. Let's dive in and swim to the other side. It's not far.'

We dived together into the freezing water and reached the other side with chattering teeth. After a vigorous rubbing with towels, we were dry and felt refreshed from the experience.

One of the ministers enjoyed talking to me and asked, 'Why don't you wear a skirt or dress?'

I was surprised and replied, 'I love wearing dresses, but Robert insists we wear slacks,' and he nodded his head in agreement.

For lunch, in a side room chefs had prepared rice and kebab dishes, with fruit for dessert. Returning to the lounge, our host asked what film we'd like to see and I spent the afternoon sitting in luxury sipping rum and coke watching the historical film *Ann of a Thousand Days*.

What a memorable day – but we were soon flying high above the clouds to our next destination, Vienna.

Europe – Part Two

As we approached Austria, the panoramic view of a mystical sea of clouds interspersed with crispy white, mountain peaks were a joy to behold. The Alps are the most extensive and highest mountain range in Europe and the beauty is breathtaking when viewed from above.

The capital of Vienna lies on the River Danube. The composers Mozart and Bach inaugurated many of their famous compositions at the Opera House, although Johann Strauss was born there and a statue of him is preserved for all to admire in a public garden. The city was a complete contrast to Tehran in culture, religion and dress code.

Denise and I were eager to explore this amazing city. It was full of museums, elaborate palaces and the Opera house, and its legacy of the Imperial grandeur of the Habsburg monarchy was overwhelming. There was so much to explore.

The German language sounded boisterous, but I wanted to learn a few phrases. At the back of my mind terrible stories of the Second World War surfaced, with harsh speeches delivered by Hitler, the most hated man in history, but this was a different era of peace and tranquility.

Transport was excellent with double length trams travelling throughout the city, but the price of food was exorbitant. Spicy sausages, smoked meats, dumplings and sauerkraut were heavy foods we weren't accustomed to. The apple strudel and chocolate cakes were delicious.

Situated close to the city centre and the hotel, the nightclub was small and cosy with plush red décor. Whenever we arrived the audience were always in a jovial mood as a trio of musicians serenaded the crowd with romantic melodies. We were never told, but it was easy to guess the sort of frolics or activities which were taking place. There were no rehearsals and for two months Denise and I would be able to explore the city.

The exorbitant food prices were a concern with no possibility of a wage increment from Robert. Remembering the lean Madrid times when I was in love and forced to cook for José with cheap eateries close by, I approached Denise with an idea. 'Would you mind if I bought a few cooking items? We could eat in the room, and buy the food we like?'

'Sounds good to me – as long as we eat in a restaurant once a week.'

We were on the same wave length. Without warning, our plans were thwarted when Robert came to our room carrying a heavy wooden article. 'Pamela, I need to talk to you. It's important.'

'Can Denise stay?'

'Of course. I've bought a sewing machine and need you to make costumes.'

My mind was in a whirlwind, buzzing with questions I wanted to ask him without risking offending him. I hadn't expected this. Leon had been wonderful in helping me when I was ill and as my mentor had taught me his tricks of the trade. They were partners, but did Leon know about this? Would I get paid extra? I didn't dare ask. Would I get any recognition in the future, named as the seamstress for the ballet?

As these thoughts crammed my brain, Robert asked, 'Can you copy the Cowboy and Indian costumes? They're looking shabby and need replacing.'

'I can. What about the stone decorations?'

'Can't you use the same ones?'

'Yes.'

Oh dear, more work. Making eight costumes would be an enormous task, but he continued, 'As we're here for a long time, I'll need other costumes made.' My heart sank. I'd have no time for myself, but remembering how Leon had helped me I agreed. 'I'll buy the materials tomorrow,' he stated and left.

Denise, who'd been silent in the background, came forward.

'Sorry Denise,' I sighed. 'You won't be able to cope with the noise of the machine all day long, with costumes and material strewn all over the place. Going out with you will be impossible.'

Tears were a second away when she put an arm on my shoulder. 'I understand,' she said. 'It won't bother me. I'll go out with the girls in the daytime.'

Feeling better, I disliked the amount of work ahead, yet it was a relief to know we'd see some of the city sights. We took off the heavy, wooden cover to discover a new Brother sewing machine, no doubt the cheapest on the market. I groaned. It was nothing like the ultra-modern Singer machine I'd bought and left in Lunel, but it would suffice. The zigzag and normal stitches were enough to work with.

Patterns, materials and half-finished costumes littered the room and the faster the costumes were completed, more material and designs flooded in. Forty costumes were made within two months. The girls groaned when I fitted them into corset-style costumes, leaving almost no room to breathe. Leon had taught me well, and I used his methods to create dancing costumes with speed and accuracy to enhance the figure and withstand the athletic movements required from dancers. It didn't matter that I wasn't paid. The ballet had a future, but where was our next destination?

Cherry had been upgraded with her brilliant dancing skills to Assistant Choreographer to help Robert produce new numbers. My desire was to get recognition to be known as the seamstress of the ballet. Nothing was said. All thoughts of discovering the culture of Vienna or learning a few German phrases had to be put aside, but Denise came to the rescue. She found interesting places we could go to on our day off, insisting I drop all sewing for a few hours.

At the revolving tower overlooking the Danube River we scoffed so many chocolate cream cakes we felt sick. On a half day tour to the lakes, we enjoyed a boat ride and visited old caves outside of the city. The Ferris wheel gave us a wonderful view of the city and landscape, and there was the hilarious visit to a beer hall. Although we didn't like the spicy sausages and sauerkraut, when a group of young men in Tyrolean costumes performed their national dance we exploded in laughter, trying to decide which guy had the best legs or tightest bottom. They kept patting them and we weren't noticed as everyone was hooting and whistling.

My favourite outing was to see the world famous Spanish riding school in the grounds of the Hofburg Palace. White stallions performed elegant, equine ballet paces in perfect precision. I recalled the horse number we'd performed in tight body suits for George Carden in Amsterdam. We could never have danced as eloquently as these graceful creatures. Robert announced our next engagement was to dance at the Casino in San Remo in Italy for four weeks, followed by a month in Athens. It was mid-summer and the thought of no sewing and lazing on the beach was a dream.

Travelling by coach, we passed through quaint Austrian villages which appeared isolated, almost lost among the deep, rolling, green hills with the majestic Alps in the background. The flight over Mont Blanc had been phenomenal and now we'd be travelling through a long tunnel completed in 1965, one of the latest marvels of human engineering. It was eerie, scary and claustrophobic as noise became amplified in the small space and traffic edged forward at a slow pace. Eleven kilometres doesn't seem a long way to travel, but knowing one of the highest mountains in the world was on top of us didn't allay our fears until we saw the light at the end of the tunnel.

At San Remo we were sunburnt fast lying on the beach in the sultry heat and I felt rejuvenated. There were no warning signs of anything dangerous lurking in the water. One day as I returned to the ocean for a refreshing swim, a starfish stung my arms and legs. Alone with no help around, I crawled up the sand, panting in excruciating pain. I waited for an hour on the deserted beach until the painful stings subsided. There were no side effects but I vowed never to swim alone in the ocean again. Who knows what poisonous fish or creatures lurk below the waves. A surprise visit by my parents thrilled me. Was it two years since I'd been home? Noting the lines on their faces and greying hairs, I realised how precious time was and was determined we'd enjoy our time together. They loved the show and we visited a perfume factory with Denise, ate crustaceans in a beachside café and spent a day in Monte Carlo.

At the casino it was different to how I'd imagined it. No longer a dancer there, I could visit the famous gambling hall as a tourist. It was impressive. The décor was frozen in time from the nineteenth century. On a dull, green background the high ceiling and walls were adorned with faded tapestries and the gambling tables were modern and busy.

Hidden at the back of the hall in a small room, we were shocked when the guide explained, 'This is where the gentry lost their wealth in the last century and came to commit suicide.' He opened a small drawer behind the desk, explaining, 'This is where the pistol was kept.' We shuddered, thinking of the poor lost souls and their families.

I was sad at the train station as we hugged and said our farewells. Mother's words, 'Never worry about us. Live your dream. Your bedroom will always be there for you,' were comforting, as I didn't know how long it'd be before I'd see them again.

Europe – Part Three

It was a short flight to Athens, the cradle of civilisation and the birthplace of democracy. The casino on top of Mont Parness revealed spectacular views of the city. Apart from the road winding up the mountain, a free chairlift operated throughout the day and night to entice gamblers, and we used it to go to the city. Beside the terrace of the casino was a tiny swimming pool where I enjoyed a refreshing dip. No-one else seemed to bother.

One day as I approached the pool I heard weird screeching noises. Hundreds of small, dark green frogs from the mountainside were vigorously procreating as though their lives depended on it. The following day the pool was drained.

Denise and I loved visiting the Acropolis, the ancient amphitheatre and the overgrown stadium where the first Olympics took place. We wandered through unknown roads and lanes, taking coffee in off-beat cafés amid dwellings painted white to deflect the heat from a scorching sun. The people were pleasant and calm and it was interesting and peaceful. One evening Robert took us to the Greek taverns. Plate smashing, an old Greek tradition, intrigued us. Music from Bouzouki instruments wafted in the warm air as we followed him and Gail into one of the taverns advertising a star singer. Low lights greeted us.

After a nourishing meal of stuffed vine leaves and a delicious Greek salad with wholesome meat, washed down with authentic white wine, we waited for the plate throwing. A shame – it'd been banned as a dangerous practice and as the artist finished his performance everyone threw carnations at him.

Disappointed, we weren't surprised when Robert led us onto the stage and shouted at the musicians, 'Play Zorba the Greek.' We laughed as legs went in different directions and carnations flooded the stage. Robert had looked after us and given us a wonderful night out.

After the show we'd sometimes go to the public area of the casino to relax and have a drink. Nothing in the world could have prepared us for the events which were to occur. Nature called and, excusing myself, a striking young man in an expensive suit approached me, speaking in a soft, American drawl. 'You're from the ballet.'

'Yes,' I replied, surprised at this unexpected encounter.

'Come and have a drink with me.'

'No. We've got rehearsals tomorrow,' I replied as an excuse, but he wasn't taking no for an answer.

'Meet me tomorrow afternoon and we can get to know each other.'

He was a gentleman. Looking into his mischievous eyes I could have said no, but a spark of chemistry had been ignited. Denise was pleased when I told her I'd met someone and made other plans.

Talking to Sam about America was interesting. Boston was his home town and he often visited Las Vegas. He'd arrived with a group of Americans for the Black Gammon World Championship and won. As I was telling him where the ballet had travelled, it seemed like all hell was let loose.

'Stay here,' Sam instructed, 'I'll find out what's happening.'

People were coming in from every corner, fear in their eyes. Something terrible and unexpected must have happened. Travelling as we did, we never heard the news or saw television. Robert must have relied on news from the agents to know if a country was safe to work in.

Athens had been in conflict for over a decade. The monarchy had been abolished and Papadopoulos reigned as President. This led to uprisings, unrest and fear for the Greek people with the absence of civil rights. The news was devastating. The airport and borders were closed and we wouldn't be dancing at night. Amidst the chaos I stood up to go back to my room.

'Don't go,' Sam pleaded, holding my hand. 'This is a coup. These other Americans don't understand. It'll be over in a couple of days.' His eyes grew brighter as he suggested, 'The group I'm with are in panic mode to go back to Athens to get a ship out. Come with me.'

'No, I can't. What about the ballet?

'Everything will shut down for a couple of days. Tonight I'll take you to the harbour to eat lobster and we'll stay at the Grand Hotel.'

The prospect of spending a couple of days with Sam was stimulating. We'd soon find out when the coup was over. As his imploring eyes looked into mine, trust was found. 'I must tell my friend Denise.'

'Be quick as the coach will leave soon.'

Amongst the yelling and incessant cries of, 'We're doomed. Oh my grandchildren, I won't see them or America,' my head found his shoulder during the bumpy ride down the mountain and I felt lucky to have met him. The hotel was luxurious with gold taps in the bathroom, and grey, satin sheets glistening on a king size bed.

It was twilight as we took a taxi and arrived at a tiny restaurant at the edge of the bay amongst small boats. Moonlight beamed over still water and the moored sails of boats in the distance as soft, musical notes from a guitar filtered the air was romantic. Jovial and laughing, oblivious to the outside world, we dined on fresh lobster and drank champagne.

In the hotel I was happy to have been plucked from danger by a rich young American, and in the morning he snuggled up, kissing my forehead as he said, 'I must see what's happening,' and left. On his return he told me, 'The women have calmed down, but we don't know when the airport and borders will open.'

After lunch Sam suggested a swim in the enormous blue pool. Sighing, I replied, 'I don't have a bikini. There was only time to grab underwear and a toothbrush before we left.' He darted out of the room, returning almost as fast as the flick of a card with a new multi-coloured flowered one.

'Put this on,' he grinned.

We lounged on our deckchairs sipping cocktails, enjoying the sun and taking refreshing dives into the water. Sauntering back to the room hand in hand, I knew we were comfortable with each other and prayed for more time to develop the relationship. Smart, handsome, well-travelled, kind and generous, he was a man I could grow to love and live with.

As I was about to take a shower, the telephone rang. Sam grabbed it. 'For you,' he said, frowning. Who on earth was it or knew where I was?

It was Robert's urgent voice. 'The ballet is working tonight, get back here now.'

'Yes,' I replied, shocked at the news. 'Sam, I've got to leave. The ballet is working tonight.' It was a hasty, rude decision made to a speechless Sam as I grabbed my things, uttering, 'I can't let the ballet down. I've got to go.' I'd panicked, and left without thanking him or giving us time to exchange contact details. I hurt his feelings. There was no going back.

How did Robert know where to find me? He would've asked Denise and phoned around to find out which hotel I was in. I arrived in time for the show and nothing was mentioned.

At the airport after a successful month at the casino, we were leaving for Milan when immigration officers stopped Robert, Gail and myself.

Staring at us, searching for signs of guilt, the officer asked, 'Have you got drachma money on you?'

I glanced at Robert. Perhaps this was interpreted as a sign of guilt. It was illegal to take Greek money out of the country. I didn't know this and Robert did. What had he done? Our salary only covered day to day expenses. Pointing to me, the officer demanded, 'Follow me.'

Glancing back at Robert, I saw the worried look on his face as they were allowed to leave. I followed the man to an office where a higher authority officer with limited English checked my personal belongings. Finding nothing illegal, he beckoned a woman officer to come forward and pointed at me to follow her and leave my possessions behind.

She took me outside to a white-washed stone building. There's no word in the dictionary to describe how scared I felt when she ordered, 'Take your clothes off.' I'd done nothing wrong and was being treated like a prisoner in a strange country. I hesitated.

'Strip,' she bellowed.

Trembling I complied, putting shaking hands over my ugly scar. Humiliated, in fear of the unknown or what else they could do, I screamed out in a hoarse voice, 'Don't touch me, I had an operation.'

An eternal minute dragged on before the tone of the woman's voice changed to a soft, 'Dress.' Composure gained with a few tears smearing my make-up, the woman lead me back to the office and nodded to the Gestapo man. He pointed at me to collect my possessions as the woman opened a door to freedom.

In a haze of uncertainty, I saw the girls in the distance and the bold figure of Robert waiting for me on the tarmac. I flung my arms around him after the terrifying ordeal, as a river of tears soaked my t-shirt.

'What did you do?' I screamed in his ear.

'I can't tell you but you saved the ballet. Dry your eyes. We've got to board the plane to Italy.'

Safe in the plane, it was a relief to leave all the trauma behind as I wondered what lay ahead. It'd been several days since the coup and my thoughts returned to Sam. I'd let a wonderful man slip through my fingers. He was probably in America. The lovely memories lingered.

***

In Milan thousands of pigeons continued to annoy tourists for tit bits, occasionally dropping their excrements on unaware people. The mighty cathedral was still plastered with sheets of green plastic for restoration and business people scurried back and forth. Life as a dancer settled into a reasonable routine, doing the same routines in the show. I spent pleasant days enjoying spaghetti meals, tea made with powdered milk and window shopping, wondering when it'd be possible to buy one of those wonderful creations.

One evening Robert rushed into the dressing room after the show with two Japanese business men. Snatching up our dressing gowns, we watched as Robert pointed to the costomes. Turning to the foreigners he looked as though he was praying to them. They prayed back. '*Ah so.*'

'New costumes,' Robert declared as they pawed and smelt the fabrics. I'd busted my guts to make them without payment and it hurt. It hurt badly. There'd been a golden opportunity for Robert to give me some sort of appreciation for my hard work. He didn't. Where was Leon? Would he have agreed to this?

The following day Robert bounced into the dressing room, 'Guess what girls? We're going to Japan for three months after Naples, and will rehearse in Rome for two weeks.'

It was thrilling news. We were going to the Far East. He continued, 'It's a tour of all the major cities and we'll be doing two half hour shows. Anyone who doesn't want to go must let me know.'

A rise in our wages wasn't discussed, but to travel to the Orient was an opportunity I couldn't miss.

I looked at Denise and her crestfallen face. She confided, 'I don't want to leave my boyfriend.' He was an Italian domestic flight steward she'd been dating for a year and I was going to lose my mate.

'Do you have to leave? It's a golden opportunity to see the Far East.'

'I don't want to leave him. We can write to each other.'

Robert bought blue lightweight suitcases to put the costumes in, telling us we'd have to carry them if we had to perform at several venues in an evening. Florence was an unexpected dream. Seven bridges spanning a glowing river in the sunset are unequalled in beauty in the Italian landscape. Stone buildings stood strong, proudly displaying medieval architecture. The main square exhibited artistic statues, including a copy of the world famous masterpiece David. Leather goods were cheap so we bought high heeled shoes and walked six inches taller. Robert organised photographs to be taken at the Piazza Michelangelo in the white opening, and Can-can costumes for the Japanese agents. They were exceptional, taken by a professional photographer. Robert allowed us to purchase copies.

Denise and I enjoyed walking up the hill to the Piazza to admire the layout of the city with the famous red dome of the cathedral rising up in the distance. We indulged in succulent pastries oozing with cream, accompanied by a hot cappuccino or chocolate for breakfast.

All was good except for one evening when loud chants outside our pension on the main street made us rush to look out of the second storey windows. Waving large red flags in a demanding way, hundreds of people angrily repeated unknown Italian words. Fascists on the march? Was there going to be a rebellion? They departed with the noise echoing in the distance as we returned to our beds, breathing a sigh of relief. In the morning the street was clear and life appeared normal. They never returned. It'd been a demonstration.

Rome, the city which ruled the known world from 753 BC until 476 AD, was steeped in ancient buildings and history. Romulus, the son of the god Mars, killed his twin brother and named the city after himself to create a great empire.

We visited the Colosseum, where in ancient times the best slaves fought powerful lions and tigers to the death as the Romans applauded, but a slave could be saved by a nod of a head from the ruling King. Descending below, Denise and I marveled at an intricate labyrinth of tunnels and learnt how they were able to transport the animals by lifts for the fight. Shuddering at this gory knowledge, we searched for better places to visit.

At the Vatican City and St Peters Cathedral, a huge open square led to enormous white columns, stretching as far as the eye could see. We were treading on holy ground, but there was no sign of the Pope.

'Go to the centre,' a tourist shouted. 'The columns will align as one if you stand there.'

It was a clever achievement of architecture from the past. We stared in awe at the brilliant paintings by Michelangelo on the ceiling of the Sistine Chapel and the magnificent portrayal of Adam touching God.

One lunch time I heard a commotion outside on the pavement of the pension and sprinted to the window to see what was happening. Leon was there in an open-air sports car, smiling and talking to some of the girls. He looked up and recognised me, waving and grinning as he drove away. It was obvious he'd come to talk to Robert. Years later I learnt from Cherry they'd had a huge argument. I believe this is when they went their separate ways and Robert took sole charge of the ballet, although the dancers were never notified of this.

Naples, the birthplace of pizzas, had a wall fortress along one side, overlooking a plain beach with Mount Vesuvius in the distance. After Florence and Rome it was ordinary. I longed to visit the famous Pompeii catacombs, but an outbreak of cholera put an end to those plans. With the sorrowful goodbye to my friend Denise, it was a lackluster month.

Hectic rehearsals in Rome commenced as new girls replaced those who'd left. Altering costumes to fit them was a breeze after the avalanche of sewing in Vienna.

Robert surprised me with how he'd organised the numbers into two compact half hour shows, using the expertise of Cherry's choreography. I'd been dancing the numbers for several years, but new girls required changes and further rehearsals to achieve perfection. Utterly boring. The day to leave dawned and, restless with excitement, we stepped onto an Alitalia flight taking us to Beirut to change planes for Tokyo. As the plane took off and circled Rome, I pinched myself to be sure it wasn't a dream. Yes, goodbye to Rome and Europe. The Orient and unknown lands I'd read about would be within our reach in a few hours.

Flying to Tokyo

After a seamless flight from Rome, we entered the International terminal in Beirut expecting to board an American Pan Am flight to Tokyo within the hour. The place was full of Middle Eastern travelers, strain and urgency on their faces as flights were cancelled.

We groaned when our flight was delayed for three hours. There was nothing to do and nowhere to go, as people continued to enter the crammed, large hall polluted with smells of heavy, stale tobacco and black coffee. I meandered through the crowd to a small newsagency. Alas they only sold Arabic literature. How I wished I had a book to read. The wait seemed interminable until our flight was called.

Chaos followed as hundreds of people pushed each other to form a long line at the departure gate. Robert and the girls joined them, but with the precious boarding pass in my hand I sat for half an hour until the line thinned. Why so many people and why did they look so desperate to board the plane? Had anything happened in Beirut? Was it another coup? But the airport was open and people were boarding our flight, so no need to panic.

Stepping onto the tarmac hot air hit my face. It was a relief to escape the stale atmosphere of the terminal. Before me was the largest aircraft in the world – a Boeing 747. Its massive wings held the weight of four, huge engines, and along the sleek body from head to tail two layers of lights glittered in the darkness from tiny windows. Above these, other lights shone from the cockpit. Excitement surged as I mingled with the last passengers up the outside iron staircase and walked into the big, white bird.

The layout of the plane was different to any I'd previously encountered, consisting of seven or eight seats in the middle, flanked on either side of the two aisles with three seats. As I moved forward in the dim light, a few Caucasians could be seen in a sea of dark faces, with no spare seats available. The plane was filled to capacity as the aisle continued on and on past several partitioned, curtained areas.

Reaching the back of the plane, the ballet group came into sight, huddled together in the middle rows. Robert was relieved to see me, but an Arab was sitting in my allotted seat.

'What am I to do?' I quizzed the air hostess. 'It's a long way to Tokyo without a seat.'

'Come with me and I'll find you a place.'

With a shrug of the shoulders to Robert and waving goodbye to the girls, I traipsed behind her to the front entrance, wondering where I was going. She exchanged a few words with a senior hostess and told me to follow her. We climbed up a spiral staircase to the upper level of the plane and entered a small space next to the cockpit.

'You can sit with me,' she laughed, as she pointed to a long seat capable of seating three people with a medium sized bench in front. After take-off the blonde with a stunning smile told me, 'I must look after the first class passengers. You'll be alright here if I leave you alone?'

'Yes,' I grinned. 'It's lovely up here and I can stretch out my legs.'

'What's your favourite drink?'

'Whiskey.' She returned later with a glass of Regal Whiskey on ice and a plate of assorted French cheeses, nuts, dates and biscuits. 'What's your name?' I ventured as she sat down.

'Yvette.'

'Sounds French.'

'Yes, my mother was born in Paris and moved to Los Angeles when she met my father. We're based there.'

Light hearted chatter continued as we discussed our different careers between her duties. Sometimes she'd disappear into the cockpit with delicacies for the air crew. This was heaven above the clouds and I'd no intention of leaving this haven if I could help it until we reached Tokyo. After a few hours the plane landed in another country. I didn't move until Yvette returned with more delicious delicacies and the news.

'We're lucky. A war broke out in Beirut. We were the last aircraft to leave the airport.' She heaved a sigh of relief. 'We had over 600 passengers on board as everyone was trying to escape. Many passengers have left and the plane isn't full. You can stay here if you like.'

Thanking her, I realised I'd made a partner in crime.

Whenever an aircrew member left the cockpit and walked past I ignored them, and quiet reigned apart from the constant humming of the engines. Tired from the day's events, my head, body and legs found ample space to rest. Slumber land was close when a light tap on my shoulder aroused me. I was staring up into the kind eyes of a middle-aged captain.

'Would you like to see sunrise from the cockpit? It's very beautiful.'

'Yes,' I breathed, thinking fast. 'Can I film it?'

'Of course,' he replied as I followed him into the cockpit.

A vacant seat, with another occupied by a first officer, facing a strange concoctions of flashing lights and buttons greeted me. Another pilot, sitting behind, was scribbling on something. There was no moon or stars. Was I staring into the black void of space? I wasn't afraid. It was exciting.

The captain introduced me to the pilot writing on a chart. 'This is the flight engineer. He repairs any electrical faults while we're airborne and notifies ground staff if problems exist.' He looked up, shook my hand and returned to his work. 'And this is my first officer,' the captain announced with pride.

The officer reached over from his seat to greet me, taking both hands from the joystick. Instant visions of the plane shooting up to another galaxy or diving into mountains or the sea were stopped as the captain sat down and I stood behind him.

He nodded to his first officer, before taking the joy stick in firm hands. 'We're flying at 40,000 feet, but you'll see a miracle as the sun rises.'

I aimed my camera, waiting.

'Film to the left as it will appear quickly,' the captain announced with pride. Slow at first, a pinpoint of light shone in the darkness and within mini-seconds burst forth, sending warm waves of life to the earth. As it rose higher, layers of thick, white clouds appeared beneath a dark, blue sky. It was intoxicating.

Thanking the captain, I crept back to my special seat. Yvette wasn't there, but food or drink was the last thing on my mind so I allowed my drooping eyelids to close. I stretched out, thinking how lucky I'd been.

It wasn't long before there was another flurry of activity. The brakes screeched with another soft landing, but I hadn't a clue where we were. Nor did I care.

Yvette appeared with a warm, red blanket and a pillow in her arms. 'Our shift has finished,' she explained. 'We work eight hour shifts and change crews. If anyone asks what you're doing up here, pretend to be sick.'

'Thanks,' I replied, flinging the blanket over me. 'Do I look sick enough?'

'Yes,' she grinned and I winked at her as she left. A steward from the new crew arrived. Seeing my nestled form under the blanket, he bluntly asked, 'Who are you?'

In a pathetic voice, and with what I assumed was a distressed look, I moaned, 'I've been sick. The air hostess put me here and I don't feel well.'

'Where are you going?'

'Tokyo,' I blurted out in tears. He nodded his head and left. It was an Oscar-winning performance.

Comfortable yet aware of any unusual movements, a noise on the stairs alerted me. A crop of bright, red curls was sneaking up the staircase. Oh no, it was Cherry.

'Are you all right?' she whispered.

'Go away,' I hissed, 'I'm pretending to be sick.' I stuck my head back into the blanket as she retreated.

Several hours passed until we landed again, and a stern voice woke me up. 'What are you doing here?' The crew had changed again and an older steward was not so gullible.

Struggling to sit up, I yawned and replied, 'What's happening?'

'You've got to move.'

'I've been sick,' I croaked. 'An air hostess put me here to rest.'

'You have to move. There's plenty of room in the front of the plane.'

'Can I have a window seat please?'

'All right.'

He helped me down the staircase as I feigned weakness and I settled into a window seat. The ballet must've been in cattle class. It wasn't as comfortable as upstairs, but with room by the window to rest my head I was content as the plane ascended into the sky. A few hours later there was an announcement. 'Return to your seats. Put them upright. Fasten your seatbelts. We'll be landing in Hong Kong in ten minutes.' Excitement surged.

We were on the other side of the world, a mere stepping stone from Japan and I'd get my first view of the Orient. Eyes glued to the window, I watched in awe as the plane descended out of the clouds to reveal a spectacular sight of hundreds of miniature, green islands in a glittering, velvet blue sea. Skyscrapers studded the horizon, surrounding a huge harbour dotted with tiny vessels.

Continuing the descent, wheels from the big belly released without warning and I gasped. The sea was rushing towards us. What was the pilot doing? He'd almost crashed into a mountain. As the plane lurched forward, seeming to take a dive, high rise, domestic buildings flew past, filled with washing hanging from every unit.

Although scary at first, the landing was smooth and we weren't sinking. The runway jetted out from the mainland into the sea. Waiting for passengers to depart or board the plane, I realised this city was unique. Wealth and poverty lived side by side in a glorious harbour setting. It'd be a wonderful place to explore.

The senior steward's face leaned across two passengers and glared at me as I continued to gaze at Hong Kong. He announced, 'Miss, your seat's reserved for another passenger. Take any seat in the centre and I'll bring you our special cocktail before we take off for Japan.'

I smiled and moved graciously to the centre seats. No one was sitting there.

'For you madam,' he announced with a flourish. 'Enjoy.'

Artistry. The frosted top of the glass and small portions of unusual fruits on top of the intoxicating liquid made my taste buds pulsate. I was fingering the colourful paper umbrella at the side and about to take a sip when out of nowhere Robert sat down beside me, looking worried. 'Pamela, are you alright? What happened to you?'

'There were no spare seats, so they took me upstairs. I ate first class food and filmed the dawn from the cockpit. When I was told to move, they gave me this drink to recover,' I gloated.

'I must get back to the others. See you in Tokyo,' he replied, with an envious look as I took my first sip. The deafening noise of wheels being lowered and screeching brakes bringing the big bird to a halt brought me to my senses. We'd landed in Tokyo after an epic journey flying for 24 hours. The local time was 6:30 am, eight hours ahead of Rome.

I caught up with the others at customs.

'What did you do?' a perplexed Cherry asked.

'Nothing. I went where they told me to go,' I replied, not wanting to make her jealous.

We were a weary group, jet lagged and praying for sleep. Entering the main hall it was perplexing, ultra-modern and a complete contrast to Beirut. The air was clean and large screens advertised flights as petite, well dressed people scurried around. Signs were written in incommunicable patterns. Arabic had a smooth running style of figures, while these symbols were bold and demanding to be read, giving a hint to the character of the people.

I'd read that the Japanese only opened their borders to foreigners in the late 19th century, wishing to contain their culture from the threat of foreign powers. China was huge and being so close must have had an effect on this small country of islands. Perhaps this is why Japan became defensive and strong, refusing to be overruled by their neighbours, yet influenced by them in some artistic way.

As we entered the main hall after clearing customs, two agents with a small, younger man were there to meet us.

'*Ah so*,' Robert bowed as they prayed back to him.

We waited for Robert as he spoke with them and afterwards he gave us a few foreign notes to be deducted from our pay as the younger man introduced himself. 'Me, Koji – san, (meaning small one) speak English. I interpret for you. With you for tour.

Come, go hotel. Sleep.'

They bundled us into taxies. We were overjoyed when they pulled into a minor hotel on the highway.

At the entrance Robert told us the awful news. 'We've got 24 hours to recuperate before our first engagement. Rest as much as you can.'

I'd been fortunate during the long flight but the girls were at the end of their tether and struggling with suitcases we entered our allotted rooms. The single beds were European but the fiasco of a toilet was yuck! Squat down to use it.

Cherry zonked out as soon as her head hit the pillow, but the urge to explore the unknown, the land of the rising sun, was killing me.

***

Taking a card from the hotel with the camera slung on my back, I walked into an early morning sprinkling of rain. People on the streets were business orientated. Ahead a woman was swaying her hips in a glamourous kimono, holding a large replica of the colourful, paper umbrella I'd admired from the cocktail, while grasping the arm of a well-dressed gentleman.

Cars were lining up and people were walking at a fast pace to a big building. It didn't make sense until I looked at my watch. Peak time. They were all going to work and it was the local metro, heralding the way to the heart of Tokyo. Following the throng, I waited in the queue at the office for train tickets to Ginza, the city centre.

'Ginza,' I shouted as I gave him a note. Grabbing the ticket and change I asked people, '*Ginza?*'

Polite, and no doubt amazed to see a European in their midst, they pointed the way to the correct platform which held five rows of Japanese commuters. As the doors of the train opened, a hurricane hit me from behind as the onslaught of them pushed me to the other side of the carriage.

'Ginza,' I yelled over the top of their heads and after a few stops a lady pointed, nodding her head. I thrust my way forward out of the carriage and made my way up the steel staircase to daylight.

Shimmering lights from huge screens screamed from every building. Six streets met at a centre point and I gazed in wonder as one of them held my attention. On a corner the Union Jack was flying from every window of a large, department store above a sign saying it was 'British Week'.

Once I'd finished filming, I ventured to another street to discover plastic food displayed in the windows of insignificant restaurants. It was strange to see raw cabbage with rice wrapped in strange bands of dark green and topped with what looked like raw fish – otherwise known as sushi. Although immaculate in presentation to lure in customers, I knew this food wouldn't suit my palate. Fatigue was becoming a problem as glaring lights led to an underground market. It was too much.

'Please,' I asked my body, 'one more look,' and an amazing shop appeared. A delight to the eye, it exhibited three feet tall crinoline dolls caged in glass, while others showed Japanese dolls in their historical splendour, eloquent and sophisticated. I was instantly captivated by their shiny, coal black wigs swept up into tiny knots, held in place with jewelled pins.

So much to learn, but I had to get back. The thirst for knowledge had been quenched, and exhaustion would spell disaster if I didn't sleep. Rush hour was over and it was easy to return, showing the card of the hotel.

I looked at my watch. It'd taken two hours. I left my shoes at the porch among an array of tiny-sized ones as I entered the hotel.

Touring Japan

'Wake up Pamela,' someone breathed in my ear. 'Please wake up.'

Bubbly, red curls made me see the light. Dear Cherry was there. We'd grown closer after Denise had left the ballet and often shared a room together. I turned over to doze, but a gentle tug of the bedclothes made me sit up.

'What is it?' I yawned.

'It's 6:30 and dinner is in half an hour downstairs. I'm going to chat with the girls. See you.'

Feeling giddy from jet lag and lack of sleep, I slipped into a long kimono dressing gown the hotel provided for guests. How lovely. European pensions never provided such luxuries and the towels were large and fluffy.

After showering and washing my undies and putting them on taps to dry (we all did it), I made my way downstairs.

Japanese diners sat cross legged on straw mats at low tables, while courteous well-dressed waiters directed me to a side section reserved for foreigners. Robert, the girls and Koji-san were sitting at a round table. Each setting had a rice bowl with chop sticks and fork at the side, while a vase of delicate, coloured flowers held centre place.

'Pamela, have you recuperated from the journey?' Robert asked as I joined them.

'No,' I replied stifling a yawn. 'I need more sleep. I'll feel better tomorrow.'

We were all exhausted. Steaming rice was placed on the table on a big plate, followed by smaller dishes of raw cabbage, chicken, a strange type of meat and various coloured dark sauces in miniature bowls. We tried to eat with chop sticks, which are supposed to represent an extension of the fingers, but the rice fell into bowls instead of mouths and I wondered how I'd survive eating this strange food. Hunger won as I toyed with a mouthful.

'We can have toast and tea in the morning,' Robert explained, looking at miserable faces and continued with the news. 'Get as much rest as you can tonight. Be ready with make-up on and dressed in Can-can costumes for 11 am tomorrow. A carnival is taking place in central Tokyo, and you'll be standing on a float swishing your skirts as the parade marches through the streets.' We stared at him in disbelief as he continued. 'The following day you'll dance the Can-can at a shopping centre, and in the evening the agents have invited us to dine at a posh restaurant to eat their famous Wagyu steak.'

Koji-san interrupted, 'Yes. Feed cows beer. Have massage. Listen music. Best Japanese meat.' We couldn't believe what we were hearing. Cows drinking beer and having massages? Lucky cows.

Robert continued, 'You'll enjoy it. The day after we take the train to Yokohama, a short train ride from Tokyo.'

Cherry interrupted, 'Will we dance in Tokyo?'

'Yes, later on. I haven't got the complete schedule yet, but we're touring throughout Japan by train, boat and plane staying a week in each place.'

Pleased with the news, we rushed back to our rooms to recuperate and prepare for the strenuous time ahead.

***

Brisk, cold air surrounded us as we stood in our allotted places on the float. The parade moved forward at a slow pace, lasting for two hours as thousands of people lined the streets. Others poked heads out of high rise windows to wave and cheer. Ahead of us, a Japanese drum band played as animal imitators dressed as Mickey Mouse, Donald Duck and giraffes on stilts mingled with the crowd.

Swishing our skirts helped to keep us warm, I still coughed and spluttered, trying to recuperate from the early morning escapade to Ginza. How on earth did Cherry manage to keep hopping on one leg at the front, while holding the other one high above her head when we stopped at cross roads? She didn't complain. Taking my camera Robert filmed the procession and it remains a special memory of our first appearance in Japan.

At the shopping centre we were upset to be told to dance on the centre floor. Concrete!

'Don't jump so high on your jump spits,' Robert pleaded. Crash went my right heel onto inflexible ground, causing a painful bruise.

The restaurant our agents took us to was superior in quality. We sat on benches in front of square hotplates as the premier chef prepared the food.

Loud screaming noises disappeared within seconds. What was it? A cook had taken a live lobster from a pan of cold water and placed it onto a sizzling hot plate. We shuddered at the cruelty and needless torture inflicted on the crustacean. Today they're placed in a fridge for several hours to numb their pain and senses before being cooked.

The chef presented the Wagyu steaks for our inspection. How could we eat such an enormous one? Pink flesh and the distinct marbling on the meat, caused by miniscule lines of fat running through them, made it all look appetising. Grilled to our liking, the steak was full of flavour, tender and juicy. Combined with the mystical story of special treatment given to Japanese cows, it was an amazing eating experience. We opened in Yokohama, a large port close to Tokyo. A major attraction was Chinatown, where there were coloured lanterns displayed outside the restaurants. What a relief to discover food I enjoyed – fried rice, wonton soup made with noodles and small dumplings. Another soup consisted of scalding hot water with lettuce leaves added and a raw egg thrown on top. Adding a dash of soya sauce, it was delicious. Main courses used every part of a chicken, including the claws, head, neck or entrails. Fresh herbal brown tea without milk or sugar was refreshing, but the hand-picked fruit churned with ice was delicious.

Continuing south we danced in Nagoya, another large city – but nothing of significance happened there. Osaka was a different story. It's the second largest city in Japan after Tokyo, with an expansive metropolis boasting five television stations. It's also famous as the prime centre for sumo wrestling.

'Tomorrow we're going to a television station to record two of our numbers to advertise the show,' Robert announced with pride. 'It's part of the contract, so we don't get paid.'

Television? We were thrilled, not expecting this. I'd danced in television shows in Holland, but for most of the girls it was a new experience.

Standing on the set with a blue backdrop and Robert dressed in an immaculate white suit, the compere spoke to him in stilted English and jabbered back in Japanese to the cameras. We performed our white opening number and a wonderful number Leon had choreographed based on the musical *Hair*. In dance form it depicted hippy America in the 60s. Dramatic and striking, the highlight was the finale. Gail leaped into the air in the role of a drug lord. We caught her high above our heads and paraded the stage with her corpse as she 'died,' her head hanging as her arms fell listless towards the ground. She played the part to perfection.

Many audiences adored the number and others didn't. The mention of drugs was taboo and a dance portraying the scene was frowned on in several countries. It wasn't in our repertoire for Japan and perhaps the Japanese would interpret it another way. Robert knew what he was doing. They loved it. Robert asked Koji-san to film the numbers with my camera and another memory was recorded. 'You like see sumo wrestling?' Koji-san was enjoying showing us his land and culture. On our day off we took taxies to a large, enclosed stadium. 'Come,' Koji-san shouted, 'I take you to back. You meet Sumo. How live. How eat.'

We followed him in anticipation. We'd never heard of this type of wrestling and were delighted to be taken backstage. Many Japanese would've loved to have been in our shoes. It's their national sport. Several large sumo wrestlers clothed in black cotton kimonos sat in a circle around a large cooking pot.

Their shiny black hair was swept up into a tiny knot on top of their heads. I'd seen wigs, an exact replica of their hair style, in the shop in Ginza. Some of them were eating small tangerines with a pile of the skins stacked at their sides.

Smiling, they pointed at the food as Koji-san explained, 'Much training. Twenty oranges a day. Cooking pot many vegetables. Herbs. Good for strong and fat.'

One of them, Mr Big Guy, stood up to speak to Koji-san and Robert, then they disappeared. It was unusual. For several minutes we were dummies, not knowing what to expect. Unannounced, Robert appeared naked apart from a loincloth, with the six and a half feet tall wrestler towering above him. We couldn't stop laughing. David was about to defeat Goliath. Still laughing, Robert showed his prowess, displaying small muscles in his arms and strutting around, ready for the kill. Mr Big Guy laughed, too.

Time for action. They crouched down on a makeshift circle filled with sand to face each other. It was game on as they threw a pinch of sand over their backs for good luck. Charge. Uncontrollable laughter continued as Robert was flung out of the ring in nanoseconds.

Mr Big Guy took us to a café to grab a bite to eat before the match. We were going to see a live performance. He kept looking down at me and was close by my side. Oh no! Was my long, black hair attracting him?

I smiled as he led us into the upper seats of the stadium and we bowed as was the custom to thank him for his hospitality. The stadium was filled to capacity. A grandiose procession commenced as sumo champions wearing belts with apron-like attachments full of bold, corporate designs walked into the ring to tremendous applause. Wrestling bouts started as the referee announced each contestant. Surreal, each bout lasted one minute. At half time Koji-san, noting our dour faces, suggested returning to the hotel. We agreed and a few of us thanked him, saying, '*Domo.*' In a town somewhere in the middle of Japan, Koji-san asked if we'd like to visit a shrine dedicated to the phallus. We jumped at the chance. They wouldn't have dedicated one to man's family jewels in Europe. Did this mean man ruled and women had no say in their society?

Leaving shoes outside, we entered the sacred undersized building and passed an indoor pond with goldfish a foot in length, swimming among rocks and green fernery. As we entered a room at the back, a skylight shed light onto a large, grey circle on the ground. The phalluses appeared to be made of steel as they glistened in the light. Big, small, fat or thin, they rose up strong. We stared in disbelief for a few seconds. Were they the departed ones or made by skilled craftsmen? Bowing our heads in homage, we left. We returned to Tokyo to perform in Ginza at a nightclub on the twentieth floor. The show was advertised on one of the huge television screens overlooking the streets. We were celebrities.

Passing through the club to reach the dressing room I was surprised to see Japanese women in elegant, long dresses or kimonos sitting with customers. They stayed a few minutes, sometimes ordering a drink, and when the men gave them a tip they moved to another table. At the end of the evening their purses were stuffed with notes.

Koji-san explained, 'Hostess is housewife. Make money. Talk. Make customer happy. No sleep. Go home to husband. Japanese tradition.'

One evening the Japanese compere of the show caught me off-guard and in stilted English asked, 'Me like you. Tomorrow go supermarket. Show you Japanese food. See Mother. Green tea ceremony. You come?'

Looking at his keen expression I hesitated for a second, weighing up the situation. Few European ballets toured Japan in the early 70s. He wanted to show me his way of life and get to know an English girl.

'Come?' he inquired and I nodded my acceptance.

As I liked to be early, I was waiting for him in the foyer of the hotel when he arrived in a taxi at nine o'clock on the dot. I knew how punctual the Japanese were, as our show never started late. My curly, red headed friend Cherry was fast asleep in dream land. She'd never know about this meeting.

In the taxi his masculine scent surrounded us as the sun peeped through the clouds promising us a glorious day. 'Me name Benjiro. You name?'

'Pamela. Me call you Benji. No. Me call you Benji- san.'

His eyes lit up and we mimicked communication until we arrived at the supermarket. Courteous, he opened the door and holding my hand rushed me into the store. Excited, he pointed to dreary lines of packaged seaweed and other foods I'd never seen or heard of. Lack of communication prevented me conveying to him my desire to purchase a traditional doll to send to Mother.

'Come. We see Mama-san. Green tea ceremony.'

Happy together in spite of our food preferences, he took me to where he lived. In a high rise building away from the centre of Tokyo, Mama-san was there to greet us.

'Benjiro,' she cried, hugging him as she looked curiously at my normal eyes and hand-made sheep skin coat. I bowed as she welcomed me into her home with elderly grace.

There was no doubt Benji-san looked after his mother as there was no sign of a father or other siblings in the apartment. Working in lavish nightclubs, his wage payed the expenses for his mother and the rent. In the mediocre-sized room the walls were a bare, dull yellow apart from the framed picture of a young man. On the large table places were set for four people. Benji-san and I communicated the best we could as Mama-san prepared the green tea. He explained in sign language his brother was dead. The custom was to set a place for a departed one. Their spirit would never be forgotten. Trying to be happy, I thought about the photos Europeans used for their remembrance of loved ones. No place in this megacity for a cemetery. It symbolised family unity in Japanese culture.

Mamma-san returned with a small pot of boiling broth and weird pastries.

'*Ah so*', I said, content I could at least speak one Japanese word.

She poured a pure, green liquid into three goblets and, raising hers in both hands, proclaimed something I couldn't understand. I repeated the movements to her approval. The pastries full of seaweed were nauseating. Gulping down the soothing green tea, with each mouthful I refrained from vomiting, trying hard to smile.

Benji-san rescued me. 'Pam-ee-la. You me happy.' He held a porcelain artefact in his hand of the white dog who sat on old gramophone players from the 1930s.

'Oh, how wonderful,' I exclaimed, holding the unexpected gift. Back at the hotel I packed the present with care and prepared for our last show in Tokyo, realising time had been against us to pursue a stronger relationship.

Kyoto is on the island of Honshu in the midst of high mountains and lush greenery. Situated in the middle of Japan, it was once the ancient, imperial capital, and is a sharp contrast to Tokyo, where there were no high rise buildings. The country is prone to strong earthquakes and traditional wooden houses on either side of small lanes collapse, causing less damage if large earth tremors occur. It's the birthplace of the original geisha and I enjoyed wandering down intricate, dusty pathways, hoping to see one. Perhaps they were at tea ceremonies as I failed to find them.

I was surprised one day when Robert asked us, 'Who wants to come with Gail and I to explore the ancient Samurai castle at Himedji? It's only a short taxi ride away.'

'Yes, Robert I'd love to come,' I replied, delighted at the chance to explore the countryside. Vicky and Cherry were interested and sharing a taxi would be cheap.

The magnificent castle was built in 1346. Perched on a hill beneath a green forest, it was a formidable fortress built of grey stone. Long, dark passageways inside made it easier to imagine the heavy battles taking place as samurai warriors defended their capital.

Another short taxi ride took us to the temple of the Golden Pavilion. We gazed in awe at the sight of the pure gold leaf on the superior architecture of the Pavilion, reflecting itself onto the still waters of a lake surrounded by natural foliage. Returning to the taxi, we were looking forward to returning to the hotel when the chauffeur kept jabbering in Japanese to Robert.

Shocked, Robert realised he didn't have the address. 'Gail do you have it?' he mumbled.

'No,' she replied.

With mounting agitation, he turned his head to look at us. 'Cherry? Vicky?' No reply. 'Pamela, you must have it,' he commanded as fear showed in his eyes.

'I'll have a look in my bag,' I replied, enjoying the moment and producing the hotel card to everyone's relief.

***

We travelled south on the celebrated bullet train which reaches speeds of over 300 kilometres an hour, and for a few fleeting moments saw Mt Fuji in all its glory. An active volcano, it was a pilgrimage site for centuries. The snow-capped peak soared high into the blue sky surrounded by long ribbons of cloud – a spectacular sight we were lucky to see, as it's often invisible.

We soon reached the city of Nagasaki on the coast of the southern island of Kyushu. Situated on a natural harbour, I was surprised to see how well it had been rebuilt after the devastating effects of the atomic bomb left it in catastrophic ruins. The city had acted as a bridge between Japan and mainland Asia for centuries. The Portuguese introduced bread in the 16th century and the British brought in beer.

I visited the Atomic War museum and was appalled to see pictures of the utter destruction of the city and the horror on maimed faces of civilian adults and children, the victims of this atrocity. Some of them were cooked alive and the agriculture became toxic, with the effects lasting several decades. I prayed there'd never be another World War.

Close by, a large pearl store displayed luxurious necklaces, bracelets and earrings in intricate designs and settings. I could only admire them. In the gift shop, a small frame caught my eye. It showed how the pearl is formed in four stages from birth to maturity. Excited, I purchased it as it was within my budget, which helped to relieve the sadness I'd felt at the war museum.

Travelling north we danced in smaller towns to great acclaim and applause. It was rare in the seventies to see European dancers perform and the nightclubs were packed to capacity.

***

It was Christmas and mid-winter as we arrived to take the ferry to Hakodate in the northern island of Hokkaido. Warm in the train, we stepped onto a crusted snow platform as a howling wind threatened to blow us to extinction. Reaching the end of the platform, we joined a long queue of huddled figures battling the freezing temperature. Local merchants were selling lunch boxes and we bought them to stifle our hunger pains. Dismayed, I stuffed rice with the dreaded seaweed in the sushi, down my throat.

Koji-san looked concerned. 'Stay here. I go. See what happen.' It seemed as though a century had passed before his tiny figure reappeared. 'Is good. People wait two days. Storm. Danger. Dance tonight. Ballet go first ferry. Come.'

Shocked at the news, yet relieved to be moving, we passed the kilometre long queue and boarded a catamaran completely enclosed except for glass windows at the sides. The boat rocked from side to side, heaving up and down against angry waves as they thrashed around, threatening to sink us. Gripping onto our arm rests, no one spoke. Fear of imminent doom showed on faces, but we landed safely after an hour of torture and the show went ahead as planned.

On Christmas Eve, Cherry and I found a Christian church on a hill. Bathed in snow it was magic, reminding us of our families. The service was simple, serene and holy, giving us joy and peace.

It was our last contract in Japan and we were expecting to return to Europe, but Robert surprised us.

'Girls, our tour has been successful. The agents are pleased and our contract has been extended for another three months.' He paused while we digested the news. Help. I was tired of the cold and touring, and looking forward to going home. 'We're going to Indonesia for a month, followed by Singapore and Hong Kong, before flying back to Europe.'

Thrilled to be heading to a warmer country, we threw our arms around each other, overjoyed with the news. We were returning to warmth and I was excited.

Asia

'What's happening?' Cherry cried as we landed, trying to look out of the airplane window.

'Condensation,' I replied. 'We've landed in hot weather after flying in freezing temperatures above the clouds.'

The uncomfortable long journey in cattle class had been uneventful and we were unprepared for the onslaught of roasting temperatures. Sweat trickled down our faces as we climbed down the staircase from the plane and stepped onto Indonesian soil. Ripping off coats and panting in a hot, sticky atmosphere, we rushed to enter the air conditioned terminal building.

We'd crossed the equator and landed in Jakarta, the largest city in Indonesia located on the world's most populous island of Java with five million people. The capital was packed with streets and chaotic traffic moving in every direction, a complete contrast to the immaculate precision in Japan.

It was the rainy season and a tropical, humid heat where without warning heavy rain poured from the skies, then stopped abruptly. A dirt track lead to our accommodation, a local hostel with air-conditioning.

International hotels where the elite resided rose up in the far distance as we were driven to the night club. Local restaurants served hot, spicy food full of chilies, rice and other exotic sauces I found unpalatable. Hidden among them was a gem – a small grocery store selling imported Australian cheese and dry, white bread and butter.

The night club was crowded every night, although the problem was more the size of the stage, which was half the size of a football pitch. Pre-show rehearsals took longer to stage and stronger lights dazzled our eyes. Extra effort was required to dance and, depleted of energy, we'd no desire to go out at night after the show. An urge to explore this strange country surfaced. Why not see what the city was like or find a market? Apart from the show, life was boring. Rickshaw bicycles that had been adapted to transport passengers rode past on the street at the end of the dirt track. No one spoke English, but perhaps they'd understand a few words.

'Cherry, how'd you like to come with me on one of those bicycle rickshaws to see if there's a market?'

Her eyes lit up. 'Yes. I was wondering when you'd ask me. You'll get us back in time for the show?'

'Yes. Grab your bag. We might find a few bargains or souvenirs.'

A *bekah* driver came who understood the word 'market'. We climbed into the back carriage and on the pushbike he rode away. I admired his strong leg muscles as he rode hard and fast to earn a few rupees for his impoverished family. We chuckled as he dodged puddles in potholes. As we waved to the locals, they smiled, probably thinking to themselves, 'Here comes another sucker.'

In the 70s we were the oddities. When we arrived, I handed the Indonesian a crisp note. Hesitant, he handed me dirty, soggy, mouldy rupees in change. I took the worst ones from underneath the pile and give him a tip.

The market buzzed with people of Indian, Malayan, Chinese and Indonesian origins. Stalls filled with fresh oriental fruits, vegetables, nuts and spices were owned by toothless, ragged locals. One fruit called a durian was almost three times the size of a grapefruit, while a small one called a rambutan was bright red with spine needles covering the surface. Flies hovered above raw meat.

We ventured further to discover an amazing array of stalls. Although the main religion was Muslim, no one wore black. People bustled back and forth as sales people tried to lure us in.

Prominent Indian stalls displayed bright satin cloths and cheap, jeweled bangles.

'Pamela, come and see what I've found,' Cherry shouted. Three Indonesians were picking up cheap bangles for her to see them glitter, sure of a sale. She purchased six and put them on one arm. What a happy Cherry.

'My turn next,' I insisted. 'Follow me.'

After a refreshing fruit juice we found an array of incredible shops. Eighteen carat gold bracelets and jewels with astronomical prices were displayed in the windows. The culture was so diverse in this country of mixed nationalities. What else did the Indonesians offer?

'I'm tired,' Cherry wailed, 'Let's go back please.'

'Alright.'

As we were returning to the main street we were shocked. Outside a shop, crude devil masks painted in black with long, red tongues poking out of stringy beards were hanging by a window. Was it part of their folklore or witchcraft? Fascinated, I entered.

An Indonesian man was squatting down, waiting for a sale. A tired Cherry was treading on my heels as he stood up on wobbly legs. I pointed to a wooden, devil mask – the perfect gift to send to Popsey. What a fit he'd have when he opened it. He'd chuckle and say, 'My crazy daughter is at it again, more travels and sending weird dolls.' Puppets in bright green and mauve shirts with ugly frog heads were strange, not to Mother's liking. She'd think they were witchcraft, but they'd be a safe purchase. Glad to be leaving a hot, sticky country and seated in a Singapore Airlines aircraft, we were happy when it rushed down the runway and took off for the short one hour flight. As the plane rose into the air, we were horrified to see a couple of army tanks on the road, heading at full speed to the airport. The captain never mentioned it, but we'd just missed an uprising by seconds and were safe. Later we were told it lasted a day and was caused by university students, revolting against corruption caused by a military power, struggle and competition from foreign investments.

When the unfasten seatbelt sign lit up we relaxed, and the hostesses began serving drinks. One of them approached me in the aisle seat. 'Where are you lovely girls going?'

'To Singapore to dance in a nightclub,' I replied with pride.

'How wonderful. Would you like a complimentary glass of champagne?'

Delighted I accepted, but Robert and Gail were frowning from the opposite seats, wondering what was happening.

Hesitant, I asked the hostess, 'The two people over there are with us. Can they have one, too?'

She returned a few moments later with a tray loaded with flutes of Brut Champagne for all of us to enjoy.

Heading north, we crossed the equator as a delightful view of a wonderful land surrounded by sea and palm trees among majestic white buildings came into view. The Republic of Singapore lies at the tip of the Malay Peninsular with a tropical rainforest climate. It's summer all year and often overcast with high humidity and rainfall. We were now accustomed to the heat and eager to enter the pristine clean, cool terminal.

'Oh my God,' I blurted out to Cherry, 'they must be strict here.' Large posters were everywhere, declaring the death penalty for importing illicit drugs.

'Won't apply to us,' she replied. 'We never touch the stuff.'

At immigration we were shocked when Robert was denied entry. Joining us, Gail explained, 'We have working visas. Robert must apply for a special one. He'll be detained a few hours until it's sorted out. No need to panic. The agents are waiting for us.'

At customs it was another story. All the bags were searched, including the costumes, but nothing suspicious was found and we were allowed to proceed to the exit.

Driven by taxies along wide roads lined with white, colonial buildings, we fell in love with the place. After the doom and gloom of Jakarta, this city of Singapore was a dream. We turned onto the main thoroughfare known as Orchard Road, teeming with buses and cars as crowds of well-dressed people darted in and out of large department stores and elegant, high class hotels.

We'd travelled five kilometres before the taxi passed a big night club on the corner and turned into a small road. Continuing up a hill, it turned into a secluded tree-lined street and stopped outside a dull, brown one storey building, very unattractive apart from the VIP name.

'I'm disappointed,' Cherry wailed. 'I was hoping we'd have good accommodation.'

'Remember the awful hostel we've just stayed at? This will be better,' I reassured her.

At reception Gail handed us keys to our rooms and we proceeded to a door at the side. Opening it we were speechless. It was dusk and lights were sparkling on a shimmering, blue swimming pool. A diving board was at the side and rooms on the ground floor were surrounding it. We burst into excited chatter at the prospect of a swim, but Gail stopped us.

'Wait. I didn't know about the pool,' she said. 'The good news is we don't have to work for two days. Make the most of it. Unpack and I'll see you there in half an hour. Afterwards we'll find a cheap restaurant.'

We flew to our rooms where another surprise awaited us – a carpeted floor, a modern shower and tea and coffee making facilities.

Cherry and I plunged into the warm water of the pool, followed a short time later by the others. We swam and sprayed each other, acting like sharks and dolphins or kids running along the diving board, jumping in and creating big splashes. Paradise. After a quick shower, it was a mere ten minute walk to Orchard Road to eat at a Chinese restaurant before returning to sleep in luxury.

Early in the afternoon I'd showered after a refreshing swim and was contemplating going for a walk with Cherry when there was a knock at the door. A troubled Robert and Gail stood there.

'Hello Robert, glad you're here. What's wrong?' I inquired.

Gail looked uneasy so I knew it was important.

'Pamela, do you remember the clown costumes? We've got a huge problem. I left them in Europe, thinking they weren't necessary. They need eight girls on stage for each number. I thought of using the *Hair* number but it refers to drugs. We can't work unless we have another number.' I sat back on my bed in shock, wondering what was coming next. 'Can you make eight clown costumes?'

I took a deep breath. This was a big ask. 'When do you need them?' I sighed, knowing what was coming next.

'In two and a half days' time for Saturday evening. If you can't do it, we can't work.'

'Let me think,' I replied, stunned at the enormity of the task ahead.

Robert continued, 'Management has arranged a room upstairs in the club where you can work any time.'

No patterns or photos were available, yet remembering the costume a plan emerged. Using my personal trouser pattern, and using Cherry to cut a pattern for the pinafore top, I could attach them together.

'I refuse to make the t-shirts. Where's the material?' I implored them. 'There's no time to lose.'

'We've got to buy it from the market,' Robert stated.

Grabbing scissors, pen and paper and a measuring tape, I made the white cuff and collar patterns using Gail to obtain measurements, and calculated the amount of material needed as we travelled to the market. Packed with haberdashery and material stalls, we found what we wanted within minutes as Robert purchased yellow t-shirts and settled on a mauve, thick jersey material. It would be hard to machine on, but strong to compensate for the energetic movements used in the dance. After buying assorted bits of material to use for patches, cottons, fasteners and machine needles, we grabbed a quick bite to eat and returned to the hotel.

The news had reached the girls and they were worried. Careful not to make an error, it took me longer to make the main pattern. By the time I'd cut everything out to my satisfaction it was 2 am, and exhausted I closed my eyes.

At 9 am I went to the room in the club and was surprised. The setup was perfect, with good light from a window and the machine set up on a table. Working at a steady pace, I made headway and had finished the main costumes on Saturday afternoon, leaving the cuffs and collars to do.

At 3 pm, Robert poked his head in. 'Pamela, we're rehearsing the clown number. You must come.'

'But I've danced it a thousand times,' I insisted. 'I won't finish the costumes in time.'

'Leave it. You've got to come.'

Precious time had been wasted. Rushing back I worked frantically. I was desperate to finish them, yet the machine needle refused to enter the stiff, white material and broke.

An hour before the show, musicians in the next room called through the doorway, 'Can we help?'

'Yes. Take these to the girls,' and they did as I completed them.

I grew increasingly frustrated with needles braking and, using the last one, the remaining collar was stitched in slow motion. It worked and I'd succeeded.

I raced to the dressing room with two minutes to change. We were putting on the costumes when Cherry squealed, 'My straps have been sewn on the wrong side.'

'I can't do anything now,' I moaned.

'We're clowns,' she laughed. 'I can still dance in it. It's funny.' The audience adored the number for its light hearted, comic choreography and the new clown costumes were perfect.

Exhausted, I didn't wake up until the following afternoon. At the end of the week Robert paid us separately. Proud of my achievement, I was hoping for a financial reward for the extra sewing. When I'd made the costumes in Vienna I'd been overwhelmed at how Leon had cared for me when I was ill and never expected to be paid. Now it was different as there'd been no news or contact with Leon for months and I suspected Robert had taken over the ballet. To my disbelief, he handed me the usual amount, noticing my disappointment.

'Robert,' I ventured, 'I made extra costumes for you. Do you think I should be paid a little extra?'

His response was unwavering as he explained, 'Yes, I do. You saved the ballet but I haven't got extra money at the moment. I'll give you something when we get to Hong Kong.'

Unhappy with the outcome, I had to wait. Travelling to unknown countries, however, was a joy. He was looking after us, but he was using me.

The following weeks before we left Singapore, we swam, shopped for fashionable clothing at cheap prices in department stores and indulged in avocado seafood cocktails.

A couple of times after the show we visited the open air night market at Boogie Street, a popular tourist haunt with a party atmosphere, although the stench from the toilets was excruciating. Transgender women in sexy, tight-fitting dresses, high heels and heavy make-up flirted with us, trying to sell us crude, sexy toys as we ate chilli crab. We tried water skiing – which was fun if you could stand up on them – and were also invited to go in speed boats to Sentosa, a tiny island without tourists, to swim and sunbathe on a bed of fine sand. We were sad to leave this safe haven of paradise. The plane dived on our way into Hong Kong, missing the mountain by inches. We knew what to expect a second time. It was a rollercoaster ride as the sea rushed towards us and the plane landed on the runway in Hong Kong. Again, we were in the dynamic centre of trading between the Orient and the West.

Kai Tac Airport is located on the mainland in Kowloon, where the main hub of society resided. It presented a different world to the playground of Singapore or the slums of Indonesia. Immigration and customs were a breeze and the Chinese agents bundled us into taxies, greeting us with huge smiles. Travelling towards the centre of Kowloon, we were greeted with dense high rise buildings teeming with life. Chinese banners advertising unknown goodies hung over shops. A passing glimpse was enough to understand that this was a dynamic trading place.

'Cherry, do you think they ever sleep here?' She was too busy looking at the people and shops to reply.

It was a short trip from the airport, with no sightings of the old rickshaws used for tourists. We entered the notorious Nathan Road in Tsim Sha Tsui, the epicentre for business and pleasure. What can one say? Red double decker buses were mingling with taxies and cars at a fast pace in a reasonable orderly fashion. On the pavements a few of the four million local inhabitants mingled with tourists and business owners, intent on their own activities.

The taxies pulled up outside Chungking Mansions, a large complex of five blocks reaching 17 storeys high. The first two floors were filled with tiny shops selling everything from saris to clothes, electronic goods, watches, cameras and pearls, interspersed with exchange rate offices and several cafés. It was a gathering place for ethnic minorities, petty thieves and prostitutes. Other floors contained the cheapest accommodation in Hong Kong with independently owned hostels and hotels.

The hostel on the eighth floor catered for artists and we were surprised to have English style meals of veggies, mashed potatoes and meat. A hearty Chinese man, Mr Chan, greeted us in perfect English. 'Dinner at 5 pm before your show.'

The agents invited us to a typical Chinese meal of shark fin soup and other unusual delicacies, followed by a visit to the New Territories border with Communist China. A mountain separated the two areas where soldiers shot anyone trying to enter China or escape to Hong Kong on sight. How many wretched souls had tried to escape the tyranny of Communism? Dangerous. We left.

Victoria Harbour is one of the most spectacular places in the world. On Hong Kong Island, modern high rise buildings surround the wharf and the mainland is overcrowded with skyscrapers touching the sky. The port is filled with cargo ships from many countries, and the Star Ferry dodges boats and sailing junks every ten minutes. Night time reveals a dazzling display of coloured lights flashed onto the water from skyscrapers. Arriving in Hong Kong, Robert stated, 'You have to dance three half hour shows involving quick costume changes and the Cancan at different nightclubs in one evening.'

No-one complained. After the first one in Nathan Road, we were transferred by taxi to the underpass leading to Hong Kong Island. Returning by ferry, taxies took us to the third venue. Exhausted, we never ventured out after the shows because we enjoyed the adulation from the public and didn't care. The strain of travel and dancing was evident as the thought of home penetrated our minds. How much longer? Robert commanded the ballet, and we knew we'd return to Europe – but when?

On pay day Robert startled me, counting out an extra 900 Hong Kong dollars, the equivalent of two English pounds per costume. 'Thanks for making the costumes,' he said, hoping it was sufficient payment.

Looking at the pittance for saving the ballet, I struggled to keep my composure. He'd used me.

Not sensing my anger, he continued in a low voice, 'Tell no-one. After here we return to the casino in Greece for a month and then to the new casino in Campione d'Italia.'

My heart missed a beat. Two and a half years was too long to be away from home, but at least returning to Europe I'd be one step closer.

His voice changed as he stated, 'The Can-can costumes are shoddy and need replacing.'

Inwardly I shuddered at the prospect of another heavy workload and struggled to keep a straight face.

'A small market on Hong Kong Island sells good quality materials,' he continued, 'and in the Ocean Grove complex they sell costume jewelry. I want pink, velvet skirts and black tops. We'll go together to buy the material and you can decorate the costumes any way you want.'

There was no time to think. He needed an immediate answer and money wasn't mentioned. He was presuming the extra $20 he paid me each week to repair the costumes during the show would cover it.

'I don't have the time or space to make them here,' I replied.

'You'll have time to make them in Athens. We only have one show a night.'

Reluctantly I agreed. Designing the decorations myself was appealing and I could always copy Leon's costumes. The array of materials to choose from was endless – Robert chose a bright pink for the skirts and a coal black for the bodices, while I chose small and large white glass stones to decorate the straps to continue down to the waist, with a cluster of stones in the middle of the bust line.

Robert spent a staggering amount of money and it took all three of us (Robert, myself and Gail) to carry the heavy load back to the hostel.

The rest of the time in Hong Kong passed quickly and we were soon on a British Airways flight to Athens.

Returning to Europe

Landing at Athens Airport I shuddered at the dark flashes of memory surfacing of my last time here, when I was ordered to strip as we were leaving. Other spasmodic memories floated through my mind – of Sam, who was long gone, and the delightful walks I'd enjoyed with Denise as we explored the highlights of the city. But this was now, with the pressing matter of making new Can-can costumes. The city and casino hadn't changed, although the small pool containing fresh water, without a frog in sight, was an invitation for a quick dip when I was tired or needed a break.

The dressing room was large, the perfect place to cut out the full length circular skirts – but was this the best solution? No. I decided to make the bodices first, which required lots of hand sewing – easy to do in my room. Then I would cut out the skirts towards the end of the month. Machining them in Italy was the best plan.

Leon had been a great mentor but the decisions this time were mine. Making a pattern from the bodice was difficult. I couldn't unpick one as we danced in them at night. Made in eight sections, it was time consuming and took longer than expected. Thoughts of returning home were uppermost in my mind. I would make the costumes to the best of my ability and leave the ballet with a good reputation. Zigzagging each section and careful to pin them in the correct place, it was time to fit them on the girls.

'No. Not so tight please. I can't breathe,' they moaned. Ignoring their pleas, I double stitched the seams ensuring they wouldn't burst open under the strain of energetic kicks. Decorated with the white crystal stones, it was a joy to see the finished design on the black velvet bodices.

'Brilliant,' Robert declared when I showed him the finished creation. 'But when are you going to do the skirts?'

'I'll cut them out here and machine them in Italy.'

'We've got to perform at a special gala at the end of the month in Campione d'Italia. If you could finish them in time I'd like to use them.'

This was not good news. I'd have to work like hell to do it.

'I can't promise but I'll try my best,' I replied. Spurred on, I worked like a rocket, cramming in every second available to sew or machine, with no room for errors.

Half way through the month we were told there was a new government law. Artists appearing at the casino also had to perform their numbers at the TV station without payment. No one complained but they did rush the recordings with no retakes, completing them in one day which was a small consolation. I was dreading the departure at the airport but Robert surprised us. We never knew if the agents or Robert arranged our travel. He was an astute negotiator and when he declared, 'We're taking a cruise ship for two days to get to Italy,' we were thrilled.

No strip searching at the airport. We left Athens on the small cruise ship, crowded with Greeks and Italians. We sunbathed by the pool, visited the miniature casino, ate in the buffet and at night watched the ocean waves glistening under the reflection of a full moon and sparkling stars. It was my first Mediterranean cruise and I loved every minute. Arriving in Italy, taxies were waiting to take us on the three hour journey north. It was a blistering hot day and as I entered the taxy mozzies began to attack me, attracted to my royal blood. The battle began. Armed with her magazine, Cherry bonked me on the head, screaming as the other two girls continued the rescue, throwing papers or whatever they could find at them. The enemy was outnumbered and flew out the window. Bitten twice, I soon recovered and we resumed our journey.

Surrounded by mountains on Lake Lugano, Campione d'Italia is a picturesque village of 2,000 inhabitants. Although it's in Italy, it is under Swiss administration. The casino was a dull, brown building with none of the décor of Monte Carlo, but set in a beautiful location with stunning views of the lake. Management were pleased with the show and there were no rehearsals.

Sight-seeing was out of the question as I raced against the clock to finish the skirts, petticoats and frilly panties. Machining for days, my back ached through the heavy workload, yet I continued and finished them on time. At the gala I felt an enormous sense of pride and joy at my achievement, as we stood on stage in front of a motorcade of new cars. The pink and black costumes looked stunning.

A few more days to go and I'd be heading home. It was time to tell Robert my plans. He didn't pay me for the costumes, which convinced me further not to continue with the ballet. But he surprised me again with the incredible news that we were going to dance at the casino in Kenya, Africa, for six months after the holiday in England. A new country. Did I want to go?

Unsure, I remained silent. Travel arrangements had to be made to go home. 'Robert, I left most of my luggage with Leon and I'm going to Lunel to collect them.' He raised a quizzical eyebrow, never mentioning Leon. I was right. Something had happened and they'd probably gone their separate ways. The girls returned to England and I took the train to Lunel. I couldn't let Leon know I was arriving and took a chance he'd be there. It was late in the afternoon when I arrived and knocked on his door.

'Can I stay for two days? I've come to collect my luggage.'

'Of course,' he replied, delighted to see me.

It felt as though I'd never left. He cooked a superb meal, and I told him of the amazing places we'd been to and the costumes I'd made. In Hong Kong I'd bought a cheap projector and, using the wall as a screen, he enjoyed seeing a few of the films I'd taken of the Far East as we sipped cocktails.

When I told him the next contract was in Africa he smiled. He'd travelled the world in his youth, yet refrained to talk about it or what company he was with. He also never mentioned Robert. What had happened was between them and no-one else, and I declined to ask him any questions, not wishing to spoil our relationship.

My luggage was as I'd left it and in the morning I told Leon I was going to visit my old landlord. Whizzing around on the mobylette was fun, retracing old haunts. Seeing my landlord's black moustache and cheeky smile was delightful. He insisted I join him for a pastiche (a local French drink) at the pub. I'd never been there and was surprised how the locals remembered the mobylette speeding around town with Monty, my adorable dog, running and prancing beside it. Sadly he'd never been found. Was it the gypsies? Did he get killed on the highway? He'd been left inside the downstairs room for the landlord to collect him, to amuse his clients as he cut their hair. It remained a mystery.

I was hoping Leon would invite me to see his latest show at the Colt Saloon and when he asked me I was happy. It was a chance to see the latest creations from this talented choreographer. As to be expected, the show was excellent. The girls were highly trained dancers, the choreography superb and the lavish new costumes made by Leon were spectacular. I told him so. He was proud and smiled.

The thought of returning to work for Leon was on my mind. There was the problem of continuing to dance with Robert or not. Would I betray Robert if I switched sides there and then?

During the interval I felt a strong urge to say something to see what his response would be, and blurted out, 'I'd love to come back and work here.'

He stared at me and opened his mouth to say something, but nothing came forth. We knew it would mean several months without work before I could join a new group of his girls. Contracts were involved. I let it go, knowing I had to move forward. My priority was to go home after three years.

In the morning Leon shocked me, 'I'm taking you to lunch in a town built with luxurious buildings for the future. It's the only one in France, and a fish restaurant by the beach serves unusual crustaceans you'll enjoy.' He never invited dancers out and I felt honoured.

White tiered buildings on the waterfront had glass windows reaching from the ceiling to the floor, similar to today's lavish houses. Plodding along in sandals, shorts and a high necked jumper to combat the wind, Leon led me to a restaurant close to the sea and ordered our meals, which were served in minutes.

Perplexed at the weird assortment of long, round and small shell fish on the plate, I tried to copy Leon as he cracked a long one open, pulled out the flesh and devoured it. I tasted one, tugging the flesh and making a mess everywhere.

'Like it?'

'Scrumptious,' I said, grabbing more.

We sat relaxing in the sun, eating strange fish and enjoying small talk. It came to an end too soon and with his approval I captured a few fleeting moments of him on film. Perhaps they're the last known pictures of him. Who knows? Time to leave. The mobylette had been shipped to England and an impossible task lay ahead. The sewing machine, guitar, wig box, camera, projector, suitcases and handbag had to be carried by me. As the train stopped at the small station in Lunel for a brief minute, Leon helped me load each item from the platform to the carriage. The whistle blew.

'You'll never get it all back to England,' he stated as the train pulled out.

I laughed, shouting against the noise, 'Yes I will.'

Dragging the luggage into a compartment, I piled it into a corner and sat down as other travellers stared in disbelief. Paris was four hours away. My heart sank. Would I ever dance for such a world class choreographer again? No chance of this in the near future. I focused my thoughts on the mammoth task ahead. Getting the luggage home and hugging my beloved parents was all I wanted.

The train chugged and whistled its way through country towns, arriving in Paris in the early afternoon. Dragging the luggage onto the platform, I waited until most of the people had left. If opportunists decided to strike I'd be helpless to catch them. Carrying half the items, I walked twenty paces forward and placed them on the ground then back tracked to retrieve the remaining ones. I needn't have worried. People were too busy to notice luggage left alone for a few seconds. The strategy worked and I reached the bus stop outside the station with everything safe, and was transferred to Gare de Nord without a hitch.

The train to Calais was early, and I put my belongings on the upper racks in an empty compartment and popped out to buy a newspaper. How silly not to realise this was France, and English papers weren't available. I bought a French one and settled down to read the headlines to improve my French. The train was filling up fast, yet people bypassed my compartment. How strange.

I was beginning to worry. How would I manage when we arrived at the border with the long trek to customs? Would they believe one person could accumulate so much luggage? It would be difficult to get on the ferry and again in Dover to board the train to London.

A young guy poked his head into the carriage. 'How many seats are taken?' he asked.

'They're free.'

He seemed surprised, hardly able to believe his luck. 'Oh you speak English. I thought you were French reading the newspaper. Who does the luggage belong to?'

'It's mine,' I explained as he looked at me in disbelief. 'I've been away from home for three years. Come in.'

'I'm with five friends. I'll go and get them.' He returned with his excited friends within minutes, who settled down for an unexpectedly comfortable journey. They'd been back packing in Europe during the holidays and thought my dilemma was funny. They also insisted on carrying my luggage for me at the border. I breathed a sigh of relief.

Raucous fun, jokes and laughter continued all the way to Calais as we exchanged tales of our travels. On arrival the guys grabbed the heavy stuff while two of the girls argued as to who should carry the guitar, leaving the small projector for me to carry. In single file we breezed through customs and enjoyed a few drinks on the smooth crossing to England. With light hearted banter, they continued helping until we reached Victoria Station in London.

Placing the luggage neatly at the taxi rank, they chorused, 'Sorry we can't help you more.'

'No, I'm fine. You've been fantastic. Go. Tell your friends.'

They'd scarpered before I'd finished speaking, rushing to catch their trains to various parts of England. It was dark as the taxi took me to St Pancras Station and I bought a ticket for Kettering and headed for the platform, using the same strategy to move the luggage. Few people were about and I noticed a large, heavy twelve feet tall iron cage, no doubt used for transporting mail. It was easy to manoeuvre on wheels with the luggage aboard, and I discarded it half way up the platform, putting it in the shadows by the back wall.

The fast train took a mere hour to arrive at Kettering. Exhaustion had kicked in as another dragging and relay session was needed to go under the small tunnel to the exit. At eleven o'clock, my prayer was answered when I saw a taxi outside the station.

I was thrilled as we turned into Broadway and the taxi stopped outside our house. There was no light on or signs of any movement. I knocked and knocked. No one was home and I had no way of knowing when they'd return.

Shivering in the freezing night air, I spotted a light from a front window across the road. I piled the luggage behind the small, brick wall in front of our house and knocked on their door. An elderly gentleman opened it and when I explained the situation they welcomed me inside for a cup of tea. They knew my parents and time slipped past as we chatted.

At midnight, I left to find the luggage gone. They'd returned.

'Where were you, me duck?' Mother cried, overjoyed to see me, her voice and dialect music to my ears. Knowing it was mine and amazed at the quantity, they'd taken everything inside.

The following few days were lovely. Exhausted from travel and the backache from sewing, a doting Mother attended to every whim or whimper and I soon recovered in this relaxed lifestyle.

Mother was a worry puss and gave me a house key. 'Don't lose it me duck, you'll always be able to get in if we're not here.' When I told her I didn't want to go to Africa, she was astounded. 'Why not?'

'I'm tired of sewing for nothing and performing the same routines.'

'But Africa is wonderful. Think of the animals you'll see, the lions and tigers.'

'It's scary with witch doctors and half naked cannibals running around in jungles,' I retaliated. It made no difference. She was relentless, imploring, drumming it into my ears how good Africa would be. I'd never get the chance to go there again. Weighing up the situation, my choice was either a career sewing for Joanie, which was unappealing, or waiting a few months to re-join Leon.

Perhaps she was right. Reluctantly I agreed to go.

Robert phoned asking for visa photos and I sent them. Staying with Joanie a few days to help her and catch up on news strengthened my realisation that a sewing career was not for me.

Cherry and I visited each other for a few days. She was living on the island of Guernsey, and her mother had grown a large grape vine. Mother was thrilled with the fresh fruit and produced an award-winning wine with them. A deeper understanding of our different environments, heritage and families bonded my friendship with Cherry. Time to pack with the minimum amount of luggage, one suitcase, coat, camera and handbag. Robert phoned to say we were rehearsing in Italy for ten days and two new girls were joining us. We were meeting at Liverpool Station in London to catch the two o'clock train to Stanstead Airport for a flight to Milan. Wonderful news not to travel by ferry and train. Saying farewell to my parents was always difficult.

'It's only a six month contract,' I told them.

'I've heard that before,' Mother retaliated.

'If I ever get the chance, I'll repay you,' I replied as we hugged. Then the taxi arrived. I'd left early to take unexpected delays crossing London into account.

Humming to myself in the cab from St Pancras Station, the unexpected happened as I was thinking of witchdoctors and tigers. There was an accident and the traffic was motionless. How was it possible? I hadn't wanted to go and through no fault of mine I'd miss the train. Panic set in.

'I've got to get the two o'clock train,' I yelled at the driver. 'Can you go another way? I'll pay you extra.'

'It's alright Missy, I'll get you there.' He took amazing risks, darting in and out of the traffic, and arrived as the clock on the tower was about to strike on the hour. Money in hand, I tossed it to him with a big tip and ran as fast as I could into the station.

Grabbing a nearby trolley, I hurled the suitcase and camera into it and steered them onto the platform as the whistle blew. The Station Master had his hand raised with a green flag. Damn it, the girls and Robert were hanging out the train windows half way down the platform. I had a super burst of energy as the screaming and yelling of the girls reached me and the trolley went faster and faster.

Cherry's helping hand was there as the others struggled to get the suitcase on board. In a mega second, the train began to move.

Touch and go. Africa was in sight.

Kenya, Africa

In Italy, rehearsals were tedious. The new girls learnt the routines fast but I was bored, repeating steps I knew backwards over and over again. After ten days the polished routines met Robert's approval and we arrived to warm weather in Nairobi after a perfect flight with British Airways. It was the ideal climate to live in for the next six months, being too close to the equator to experience a real summer or winter.

On the outskirts of the city, shanty towns displayed abject poverty. Tin shacks had been erected on swampy ground and the locals meandered around with vacant faces. They'd come to the lucky city in their thousands to find work and were living a life of hopelessness. Mosquitos, the most dangerous predator in Africa, would be prevalent. I was glad we'd had our painful injections before we left England.

Our accommodation was excellent and close to the casino. Bungalows were dotted around a main building in what appeared to be a small park, while a line of close knit cottages on the right appeared to disappear into wilderness. Avocado trees littered the scene as birds chirruped among the trees against a full blue sky, with no lions or witch doctors lurking in the distance. How wonderful to spend the next six months here and have my own bungalow.

Meals included afternoon high tea served in the main building by polite African waiters. It couldn't get better as we experienced the charm and charisma of the old colonial days.

As to be expected, the show was successful. We performed three numbers while a trumpeter, who later married one of the girls, and an English singer called Anthea performed between numbers. In the Can-can, Cherry's acrobatic solo and my high jump split wowed the audience.

Our days were free. We were invited to the wildlife hospital on the outskirts of Nairobi in the National Park. Most of the injured animals were in large enclosures and free to roam until they were healed. In a huge, wired cage a gigantic black gorilla hissed, clapping his hands while smoking a cigarette. Seeing us approach, he grabbed a rope and began to swing back and forth, pounding the cage at the audience and clapping his hands again. Of course we applauded. A man lit another cigarette and gave it to him. Performing tricks and smoking like a trooper, he was disgusted when we moved away and started howling in a grotesque rage, screaming for attention.

Independence from the British left a few friendly colonials still living nearby, who occupied several of the cottages. After lunch I was leaving when a young girl with long, blonde hair was wandering around, looking distraught. She seemed out of place.

Intrigued, I approached her. 'Hello, what's the matter?'

'Are you with the new ballet?'

'Yes, I am. Can I help you?'

She appeared to be relieved to talk to someone. 'You can't do anything,' she replied with a tear in her eye. 'I was with the ballet for six months and fell in love with an Indian. When the ballet left, I stayed here to be with him. He loves me but his family will disown him if he continues to see me.'

What shocking news – but I was interested to know more. 'Did the ballet treat you well?'

'Wonderful. I loved the free board and food, and saved some money.'

'Did they pay you a good wage?'

'Yes.' When she told me it was twice the amount we received, I was stunned and found it difficult to act normal.

'Thanks for listening,' she replied, and walked away after I'd wished her good luck. I never saw her again, and presumed she must have returned to England.

Robert was ripping money off us two fold. There was nothing I could do. To confront him or confide in Cherry would only lead to disaster for the ballet. Lips sealed. Surely fate would intervene in some way? On Friday night a crowded audience applauded furiously as we returned to the stage for our final bow. After the show we dressed in normal clothes and make-up and walked to the back of the auditorium, where a couple of tables were prepared for us to relax away from pestering patrons. In the half-light, a tiny, middle-aged Kenyan from another table shuffled towards me. Always alert, Robert was ready to pounce at any sign of danger.

'Missy,' the Kenyan said in a quiet voice, 'Handbag no good.' I looked at it slung on the arm of my chair. Yes, tatty thing, I'd have to buy a new one. 'I take you tomorrow morning. You handbag you want.'

'What?' The girls and Robert strained their heads to listen. This was unheard of. Was it a hoax? The Kenyan continued pointing to the table he'd come from as someone in the semi darkness waved in response to him. 'He boss. He shop. You handbag.'

Robert leaned over, whispering, 'What are you going to do, Pamela?'

'Shush,' I replied, agitated. 'I'm going. It's in the daytime.' I turned my attention to the Kenyan. 'I'll come.'

'Tomorrow. Ten. I here.'

He arrived in an ancient blue car and opened the back door for me to enter. Unaccustomed to the polite etiquette, I felt safe and relaxed, enjoying the journey as we trundled along the highway to the city centre.

'I chauffeur for Boss,' he explained. 'Good man. Family man.'

'What's his name?' I inquired.

'Mr Pradah.' So, the mysterious man was Indian.

We arrived at a shop displaying top quality African products made from local animal skins, and I was directed by the sales assistant to the handbag section. There were so many in all shapes and sizes that it was impossible to choose one. Then a medium, oblong shaped vanity case made from impala fur caught my interest. It was big enough to hold the kitchen sink. No money passed hands. I emptied the contents from the old bag into my new acquisition and, shrieking with delight, threw the tatty bag into the garbage bin.

Caressing the layer of brown and white fur, I wondered how the lovely animal had died. Had it been killed for its fur? Animal activism against the fur trade came later.

The girls thought it was amazing, yet I wondered why I'd been chosen. I remembered dancing at the Windmill Theatre when other girls had been given expensive gifts by stage door Johnnies. This man must've been smitten by my stage performance. A couple of days later after the show, a large table had been set for the ballet at the back of the auditorium and mystery man sat at the top. Mr Pradah introduced himself and ordered drinks. A packet of cigarettes had been carefully placed before each girl, and a carton for myself. Mr Pradah was jovial and middle-aged. I was stunned when the waiters bowed to him as he gave each one an American dollar from his top shirt pocket. He was pleased I liked the handbag, and told me he owned a sugar plantation and the handbag shop and would come again. Lucky at last. I was his favourite. True to his word and a gentleman in admiration of my dancing, he always brought me a gift.

Several light aircraft flew over Nairobi and I jokingly told him I'd love to learn to fly like a bird high in the sky above the tree tops.

Expecting him to laugh or say no, he instead replied, 'I have friends and can arrange a lesson for you, but you must pay for them and never mention my name. I'll give you the money.' It all happened within two weeks of our arrival and I was ecstatic.

On the appointed day, I caught the local bus to Safari Air Services and was greeted by Dave, the chief flying instructor. There were several motionless, light aircraft on the tarmac, their wings gleaming in the sunlight as he directed me to a Cessna 172.

'Before you begin lessons I must see your reactions in the air,' he said.

The four seater plane took off and as we climbed higher he gave me the controls.

'All the fun of the fair,' I shrieked, pulling the stick back and forth, lapping up every second.

I tried to go higher. 'No,' Dave yelled, taking back over the controls. 'You were taking us into a stall. The plane will shudder and nosedive and fall to the ground.'

I'd otherwise passed with flying colours and a course of two lessons a week was organised for the following months.

'You must buy the book *How to Become a Pilot* and study it,' said Dave.

The first lesson after that was terrible – no flying, but instead learning how to put wooden blocks by the wheels, view various parts of the plane and what they did, and how to put petrol in the tank.

Mr Pradah was delighted with my progress, and continued to come to the casino to see the show. He'd invite us afterwards for a drink, chat with me and pay for the lessons. Gifts included a gold watch, several summer tops, and a lovely necklace with authentic African stones on a thin nine carat gold chain which I treasure to this day.

What a lovely life – studying and flying in the daytime, and dancing at night. I was mastering how to fly the plane until one day after a lesson Dave delivered shocking news.

'Come at 10 am on Monday. You'll miss the rising currents of hot air and turbulence at midday. You're taking your first solo flight.'

Help. I read the chapter on solo flights several times. Not possible. I was tossing and turning all night. I dreamt the plane stalled and problems occurred lowering the flaps. I crashed in front of a den of lions, with witch doctors waiting to boil my bones for magical cures for the insane after the lions had ripped me apart.

I was shaking from head to toe after three take offs and landings.

Dave looked at me. 'You're not going solo today.' He knew I was a blithering mess. 'Come back on Thursday.'

Happy to fly with Dave to guide me, I took control of the aircraft. Typical fun and laughter continued until he demanded I stop after three circuits. Jumping out of the plane, he commanded, 'One circuit and land here.'

No time to think. It was a perfect take off, but on the long straight preparing for landing, I froze. An empty seat was beside me. Alone, I had to get the plane down or crash. I lowered the flaps on time as the earth rushed up to greet me, and with a hearty thump I careered off the runway, stopping on the grass verge.

Afterwards it became second nature to fly solo and I learnt how to pirouette in the sky. Climbing to 6,000 feet using the right rudder, the plane took a deep spiraling dive turning three times upside down before returning to a normal height. It was fascinating learning to make flight plans, checking the weather, using the radio and navigating by map and compass. The 'bump' was the new dance craze and sometimes we'd go to a discotheque to bumpity bump bum to bum with the locals. Great fun.

Robert was buying expensive wooden artefacts and ivory and shipping them to England. He could afford to. One evening he suggested to me, 'Why don't you ask your Sugar Daddy to pay for your parents to come and see you?'

'No Robert. I'm not a gold digger.'

'Why not? He can afford it.'

Reluctantly I asked Mr Pradah, who replied, 'Yes, I'll pay for a ticket, but you must organise it yourself,'

I was ecstatic. Phoning home, a bewildered Popsey told me he must discuss it with Mother and I prayed he'd choose to come. He'd love the environment, wild animals and the old colonial lifestyle, but they decided between them Mother should come. I paid for the hotel myself. It was a great reunion, but Mother's loneliness and concern at leaving Popsey at home was sad. She enjoyed the show and accompanying me to a flying lesson, but I couldn't be with her night and day.

One day Mr Pradah's chauffeur drove us to the Maasai Lodge tourist attraction on the outskirts of Nairobi. The small, round huts reminded us of those in the *Tarzan* movies. We heard how cows are considered as a signature of wealth and are exchanged for a teenage virgin bride.

Directed to a vast auditorium, similar to a circus on solid earth, acrobatic dancers in white tutus showed their muscles and strength. A fake witch doctor ran around the audience while natives in grass skirts beat African bongos. One ran up to Mother, shaking a handful of bones in her face. Rigid, she didn't bat an eyelid. After lunch she appeared more relaxed, watching wild monkeys cavorting among delicate, green leaves by a stream.

On our way back I spotted a group of natives not far from the road. Could they be the genuine Maasai, a semi-nomadic warrior tribe found throughout Kenya? Red sheets of cloth dyed from local roots covered their bodies and they displayed strings of coloured beads on their necks and arms. Their tribal beauty was enhanced with ear piercing stretching the lobes with metal bands – a spectacular sight.

The chauffeur stopped the car. As I lowered the window to take a quick film, one of the natives leapt forward, running like lightening towards us.

'Get down, Mother,' I screamed as I shut the window. The glorious warrior had picked up a large stone to throw at us. 'Go. Let's go,' I yelled at the chauffeur.

The car trundled forward at a slow pace as the warrior dropped the stone and retreated. Danger had passed. Poor Mother thought she was going to end up in the cooking pot. Later I was told the Maasai tribe believe if you film them without their permission you are looking into their souls.

It was time for Mother to leave and Mr Pradah presented her with a black and white rug made from the skin of the colobus monkeys. She was overwhelmed and adored the gift.

At the airport I reassured her, 'Mother it won't be long. I'll be home in three months.'

'I'll believe it when I see you,' she sighed. 'Your next lesson will be for an hour and a half,' Dave grinned at me, pleased with my progress. 'Read up on cross country flying. You'll be flying over the Great Rift Valley to land on a dirt track at a small village called Malu, then continue to a landing track at Lake Nakuru. I'll guide you all the way.'

Wonderful news. The Great Rift Valley is a crack caused by two tectonic plates moving apart under the earth. Creating a lowland valley, it has a barren terrain stretching for thousands of kilometres between mountains, with a few dormant volcanoes waiting to explode.

Confident, I arrived early to sort out flight plans, the weather and check the plane for faults and petrol before take-off. It was a new adventurous day. Mountains soared above the barren valley and I landed safely on the track in Mala. A lone African stood at the side, watching us holding a stick for balance with one leg tucked high under the other. Poverty to the extreme.

Dave, noting my wonder of the scene, authorised immediate instructions. 'Take off now. Radio communication. Good. Watch your compass.'

At Lake Nauru we landed close to the edge of the water and the wonder of nature revealed itself as a huge flock of flamingos rose up fluttering their wings, to show a dazzling display of bright pink feathers.

'No time to stay. Take us home,' Dave laughed. 'Come early next week. You're repeating the cross country flight solo.'

Full of confidence, I took my camera to record this momentous achievement and film as I flew over the vast expanse of uninhabited land. The plane fell into a sharp dive. Dropping the camera, I pulled the stick forward and back as I'd been taught to avoid disaster, missed my compass reading by two degrees and landed at Malu a few seconds late. I'd learnt an important lesson – to never, ever divert attention from the controls. Mr Pradah embarked on a world trip, forgetting to give me money for my flying lessons. What a relief when my savings covered the cost of the extra flying hours needed to complete the course.

In 1964 President Kenyatta was instrumental in the smooth transition of power from the British. To my delight, Anthea the singer invited me to join her friends at the celebrations marking the eleventh year of Independence at Uhuru Park. Planes screeched overhead and bands played as soldiers in smart black and red uniforms formed a line of honour to salute Kenyatta on his arrival. Afterwards, a long procession of tribes representing all areas of Kenya performed traditional dances. Natives wielding shields and spears leapt up and down screaming war cries, while grass skirted groups with plumed head dresses and war paint danced in a frenzy and witch doctors rattled bones, chanting magical spells as bongo drums filled the air. It was mesmerising and spectacular.

Flying over the mountains to the other side of Kenya was amazing. I was invited by one of the pilots in the Aero Club to stay overnight at the Keekorok Lodge in the Maasai Mara grasslands. The view in the morning of wild elephants sauntering at a gentle pace to the secluded water hole against the rising sun was magic.

Another marvel to witness was the supersonic Concorde jet thunder overhead to glide to a perfect landing at Nairobi Airport. Dave presented me with an East African Pilots License and asked, 'Why don't you take a flight as a qualified pilot?'

He climbed into the back of the Cessna 172 with the Air Controller and laughed. 'You've got our lives in your hands. Take us wherever you want to go.' Confident, I flew over the Rift Valley for the last time. Robert announced we were returning to Singapore after a stop-over in Bombay, India. We didn't want to leave this wonderful country, full of friendly people and wild animals. It was with sad, heavy hearts that we departed.

As usual, Mother had been right. When would I go home?

Back to the Far East

Sticky heat combined with putrid rubbish smells surrounded us at Calcutta Airport in India. Exhausted from the long flight, it was late when we were transferred to an old blue bus without windows. Miniature fans placed on top of the seats screeched their presence, blowing a relief from the claustrophobic air. In the eerie darkness we passed kilometre after kilometre of people sleeping on pavements with their feet touching the kerb – lost souls beyond despair or poverty.

The bus trundled onto another highway leading away from the city and stopped at an old colonial palace. We breathed a sigh of relief when courteous staff led us to our rooms. A noisy overhead fan had little effect against the stifling heat as I tossed and turned, struggling to snatch what sleep I could.

In the morning we were greeted with classical music played on a grand piano by an Indian Maestro. The huge, elaborate dining room was a new experience, with eloquent Indians and other characters sitting together at large, round tables enjoying spicy food. Plunging into the soothing, cool waters of the indoor pool afterwards was ecstasy, surrounded by ancient Indian sculptured figures. I experienced seeing the lowest level of poverty and realised how lucky we were to live in educated countries. I was glad to leave and return to Singapore. In the short stop-over of a couple of days, my adventurous spirit took hold and I hailed a taxi for an hour. The pavements in the city bustled with movement as sacred cows mingled with crowds against a backdrop of dilapidated ghettoes. The beach revealed white robed figures bathing their feet in some sort of religious ceremony, while young kids ran amok and splashed each other.

In Singapore we stayed at the same hotel, enjoying the pristine cleanliness and often visited Boogie Street after the show.

One day a charming, friendly girl in the ballet called Joan approached me. 'Pamela, did you know Robert asked me to make four costumes?'

Stunned at the news, I was speechless for a few seconds, trying to analyse the situation. It wasn't her fault. Why was Robert doing this? I'd sewed every costume meticulously for years and only received a meagre twenty dollars a week for repairing the costumes. Why this sudden change of tactics?

Gutted and betrayed, my heart sank – but she'd been brave to tell me and I had to be careful how I replied. 'Yes Joan, thanks for telling me.'

I rushed to find Robert and confronted him. 'What's wrong? Why are you asking Joan to make the costumes?'

'You've done so much work. Have a holiday from sewing.'

'No Robert. It's not good enough. If you go ahead. I'll never make another costume for you.'

He was silent as I left. Maybe he thought in the future I'd back down, but my decision was firm. I'd leave the ballet at the first available opportunity, tell no-one and continue as normal, hiding my hurt feelings.

Joan made the costumes and they looked good. In them we looked like ladies from the silent films, holding feathered boas in long dresses with a lengthy slit at the side of the skirt. Cherry choreographed a delightful routine and Robert used strobe lighting for special effects. The audience liked it. After a quick flight to Kuala Lumpur in Malaysia we almost fainted in the stifling heat, but air conditioning was provided in every building. Staying at the luxurious Federal Hotel, we performed in the Chinese banqueting hall. Surrounded by tall ferns and green foliage, the Olympic size swimming pool was a joy to swim in, but smothering myself in insect repellent was vital to stop angry mosquito bites. Without rehearsals or sewing, there was plenty of time for other pursuits.

One afternoon while swimming and laughing round the pool with a teenager and his father, they suggested, 'Come with us tomorrow. We're going to the Genting Highlands in a hired car to catch butterflies in the jungle.'

At the crack of dawn we set out, passing small villages, rubber plantations, tin mines and orchid farms. Arriving at a look-out on top of a mountain, the view of a tea plantation was magnificent, stretching as far as the eye could see. After lunch at a Tudor style hotel, we were driven to the edge of the jungle. Trying to catch the delightful creatures with small nets on the end of long sticks was fun. Darting around to evade capture, their mauve, yellow and green wings shimmered in the sunlight. The unlucky ones were put into jam jars on a bed of green leaves, and we were careful not to touch them. Returning to the hotel at dusk, I realised how lucky I'd been to have experienced another amazing adventure. A longing to fly again surfaced and I found the local Aero Club. 'No, you can't fly here until you pass our air law exam.' Within a week I was airborne again, enjoying the views of the city below, and on one trip took Cherry with me.

'Fantastic,' she exclaimed as we landed.

It was sad to realise I couldn't continue with this expensive hobby. Civil Aviation Law requires a pilot to fly once every six months to retain a license. Who knows which country I'd be in when I left the ballet? Flying prospects were grim.

The world heavyweight boxing championship between Joe Bugner and Mohammed Ali was being held on 30th June at the huge Merdeka Stadium.

The day before the match, Robert announced with his usual entrepreneurial flair, 'Girls, you're having your photo taken with Joe Bugner.'

We went to the pavilion wearing different coloured t-shirts with 'Joe Is Our Champ' emblazoned on the front. At the back of the hall Ali was sparring, preparing for the fight.

Delighted with our support, Joe posed with us for publicity shots and the pictures appeared in the English newspapers. Tall, tough and young, he was a formidable opponent for Ali with every chance of winning. During the fight, the streets of Kuala Lumpur were almost deserted with the stadium packed to capacity. Fighting in broad daylight, Ali expected a quick victory in the heat. Televised in many nations, the eyes of the world watched as Joe dodged the champ's dancing steps and thwarted the damaging fist blows. After a grueling 15 rounds, a disappointed Ali won on points. After the excitement of the boxing match in Malaysia, we flew to the island of Taiwan. It's close to mainland China and millions of people fled there after the communist victory in 1949. China refuses to accept a second Republic of China, so the threat of a military attack is always present. Cantonese is spoken but they considered themselves Taiwanese. The capital of Taipei is a modern metropolis, teeming with people and shops selling jade and 18 carat gold rings, with department stores displaying knitted garments in wonderful styles and colours.

We'd hoped to enjoy a cooler sub-tropical climate, but in August the humidity and heat was unbearable. Luckily the hotel and Chinese nightclub had air conditioning.

After a week we travelled in an old coach via the main highway (a glorified dirt road) to the old capital Tainan. Peaceful compared to Taipei, the small roads were lined with broken pavements full of pot holes, and we had to judge where we walked. A clean hotel with air conditioning and jugs containing ice and water were left in our rooms each day and made life bearable. We performed in a theatre close to the hotel, but the moment you stepped outside into clammy humidity, mosquitoes would attack with a quick bite, adding to our discomfort.

During the afternoon rehearsal there was no air conditioning. It was almost as stifling inside the theatre as in the street.

'We can't dance like this,' we cried, but Robert reassured us he'd arrange something.

At night as we entered the theatre, hundreds of bicycles were stacked in the side streets and people were pushing and jostling each other to get to the box office. During the opening number it was a nightmare. Massive ice cubes had been placed in front of two large fans at the back of the stage to blow cool air onto us. Three thousand men were crammed together in the medium sized auditorium. We must've been the first European ballet to perform there as each night they seemed to be packed even tighter. Perhaps it was our professionalism or the good response from the audience, but we danced to the best of our ability, knowing the torture would only last a week. The Can-can drained us of energy and after the last performance, the soaking wet bodices from the constant sweat had turned the rhinestones green. How lucky we'd used the old Can-can costumes.

'Don't worry girls,' Gail sighed, 'I'll get the costumes dry cleaned. We'll use the new ones for Kaohsiung.'

Vicky unexpectedly called me aside. This was unusual. We'd worked together since Lunel in France. She'd met Arthos in Switzerland and their relationship was serious.

'What's wrong?' I quizzed.

'I can't stand it,' she revealed, almost sobbing. 'I want to leave the ballet now. I hate the heat and dancing in damp costumes. I can't continue.'

'No,' I sighed, knowing we all wanted to leave this hell hole. 'Next week we are in Kaohsiung. Conditions will be better there. We're going to Hong Kong for a month and Robert has promised we'll go back to England for a holiday. If you leave now, the ballet is finished. We must have eight girls on stage.'

I'd hoped to change her mind. Shocked at my reply, she was silent for a few moments before blurting out, 'Alright. I'll stay, but will you make my wedding dress?'

Relieved and realising she was missing Arthos, I reassured her, 'Yes, when we get back to England.' A calamity had been averted. One day Gail caught me unawares and whispered, 'You speak Spanish.' Looking directly into my eyes, she revealed, 'Our next contract is in Spain.'

'Oh,' I replied, struggling to hide my inner feelings as she moved away, convinced I was happy. On the contrary it was terrible news. Memories of José and the stress of leaving Madrid the city of my dreams surfaced. No. I'd escaped Spain and never wanted to return. A new beginning was what I wanted. Dance for Leon again or for someone else? Sealed lips. Let no-one know my intentions. Boundless opportunities were waiting in London to be explored. Before we left Kaohsiung, Robert came to see me. 'Pamela, you know the opening costumes with the four cloaks?'

'Yes,' I replied on my guard, not knowing what was coming next.

'They're rather tatty. Can you copy them?'

'No,' I replied, frustrated and unable to control hurt feelings. 'Joan, can do them.'

His next words dumbfounded me as he leaned closer to try to take advantage of any weakness I possessed. 'Pamela, you saved the ballet in Singapore.'

'Yes,' I responded in a softer tone. I accepted the recognition I'd craved for, but was amazed he thought he could praise me and think I was putty to be moulded at his command. An inner rebellion surfaced. 'No,' I snapped, 'I'm not doing them.'

'Pamela, in the future I'll have two ballets and I want you to take charge of one of them.'

I retreated to my room. It was perplexing. My befuddled brain couldn't function until it dawned on me what Robert planned to do. In Hong Kong we'd buy materials at the market and I'd have to sew four cloaks in a cramped space with a dilapidated, over-used sewing machine with a deadline of finishing them before flying to England. This was an achievable job that I didn't want to do. It would have been difficult to copy Leon's art and design work to produce four white, full length cloaks made of imitation leather with fur on long sleeves, and the huge box hats coated in fur. Robert never mentioned it again. Returning to Hong Kong was a joy after Taiwan. Nothing had changed with the constant stream of cosmopolitan travellers pouring in and out of the city. The agents had booked us into a pension on the highest level of Chungking Mansions, as the one for artists had no vacancies. It offered the barest of essentials and was pretty grim, with basic rooms and showers and no food available to purchase.

I discovered a back door leading to the roof top. 'Come and see the sights,' I told Cherry. We danced and frolicked against a wonderful view of the city lights and the harbour.

Performing three shows a night was strenuous and tiring so we never ventured out afterwards. One night we'd just settled into our rooms when loud yelling and screams shattered the peace.

Frightened, someone pounded on my door. Robert pleaded, 'Don't come out. Stay inside.' Relieved when the calm returned, we came out of our rooms as he explained, 'It was a police raid. The owners of the pension rent out half of the rooms to prostitutes and they were trying to catch them in the act.' It made me wonder if the police were in collaboration with the pension owners. It couldn't happen, but it did. A ferocious noise engulfed the entire city, shutting it down for 24 hours. A dangerous hurricane at level five had struck the harbour and everyone was ordered to stay inside. Who could have imagined such a vibrant city without life? The hurricane did. I watched from a window as a blistering wind blew away everything in its path. A newspaper was blown from one side of the road to the other, then lifted again so high I could reach out to touch it. The hurricane subsided as easily as it had started and Hong Kong sprang back to life as normal. Remembering the thrill of flying over the Rift Valley in Kenya and the uncultivated landscape of Kuala Lumpur, my urge to fly again surfaced. Kai Tak International Airport was close to the city but I shuddered, recalling the terrifying descent as the jumbo jet we'd travelled on appeared to crash into the mountain and dive into the sea. Would such a large airport allow light aircraft to be present? Did they have an Aero Club and would my African license qualify me to fly there? Undaunted, it was worth a try before returning home. Much could be achieved in a month.

Nathan Road was filled with many double decker busses and I discovered number 19 would take me there. The club was not in the main airport but in a secluded side street. Entering, I noticed a well-stocked bar with a small floor in front and several tidy tables and chairs at the back. It was mid-day and the place was almost deserted.

I approached the Chinese barman. 'I've got a light aircraft license and want to fly here.'

Helpfully he replied, 'Go through the door over there onto the tarmac and into the first building you see on your left. They'll help you.'

Outside, it was thrilling to see several light aircraft and a couple of Cessna 172s. The view of the main runways was wonderful and the loud noise of a constant stream of jumbo jets taking off and landing was deafening.

After examining my license and log book, I was booked to fly with an instructor for the following day in the afternoon. This time the place was busy with Cathay Pacific Captains and pilots, looking resplendent in their smart black and white uniforms as they arrived after international flights for a refreshing drink to socialise and hear the latest gossip. My instructor was an ex-captain and I loved the excitement of going onto the runway in line with the jumbo jets. We both realised I needed more coaching.

One day we flew into the distance. Several outlying green islands were mesmerising bathed in sunlight against a background of the glittering, deep blue ocean, far away from the claustrophobic skyscraper buildings. Another time he guided me towards an inland mountain range.

'This is the boundary,' he declared. 'On the other side is communist China. If you fly over it they'll shoot you down.'

I grinned and declared, 'I want to live.' It was almost the end of the month and our departure to England was imminent. My inner thoughts were mixed as I realised I'd probably never return to Hong Kong. When could I fly again?

Robert didn't know I was intending to leave the ballet. The idea of sewing again for Joanie while looking for a job was uninspiring, as was the thought of returning to Kettering for several months under my dear Mother's constant advice.

My flying skills had improved and the problem was resolved in an unexpected way. The instructor didn't know I had to leave and when we landed told me, 'There's a flying competition at the club at the end of next week. I think you should try for it.'

'I'd love to. I'll let you know.' His quizzical look spoke volumes. He'd taught me to fly in an intense, business environment. Was his tutoring for nothing?' How could I do it?

Our flight to England was booked to fly out on British Airways two days after our dancing contract finished, and the competition was to be held three days later, so time was critical. I rushed back to see Robert. Gail was as attentive as ever, listening to every word and noting every gesture.

'Robert,' I implored him, 'I want to ask you a favour.' Alert and staring into my eyes, he was perplexed as I spoke. 'There's a flying competition and I want to try to win. Could you change my ticket and let me fly back ten days later?'

I suspect his mind was stretched to the limit at this sudden news and was trying to read my thoughts. *Yes*, he surmised, *she can't live in Hong Kong on her own. She's proved she can fly. Let her do it and after a holiday she'll be good to dance, sew costumes and help us with her knowledge of Spanish.*

Decision made his eyes softened as he replied, 'OK. We'll go to Hong Kong Island in the morning. I'll introduce you to the agent and you can pay the extra cost to change the ticket.'

It was a pleasant ride on the ferry to Hong Kong Island, and going to see the agent reminded me of when I'd walked off the street to find one years ago in London. Sitting in a huge leather chair behind a desk, he was plump, middle-aged and had kind eyes. There were photos of artists on the wall behind him.

'Happy?' Robert asked, as I handed the extra few dollars to the agent.

'Yes,' I replied.

'And we'll see you in Spain?'

'Of course,' I lied.

The agent smiled and stated, 'If you have any problems come back and see me.' I was impressed by his caring nature.

Travelling with them to the airport to say goodbye was difficult, and as I gave Cherry one last hug I knew I was going to miss her. She had no idea I'd probably never see her again. As I left I put on a brave face and told them, 'I'll watch the plane fly out from the Aero Club.'

It was mid-afternoon when I walked into the busy club. I knew a couple of the pilots and when I told them what was happening they decided to join me on the tarmac. The plane was leaving on time and as it took off a feeling of euphoria swept over me. I screamed and leapt into the air. Free at last.

Surviving in Hong Kong

'Let's go inside,' the pilots suggested. 'We'll buy you a drink to celebrate your freedom.'

It was different this time. There was no rushing back to prepare for the hard grind of three shows a night and I could do as I pleased. Jokes and laughter flowed. They were proud that I was staying to enter the flying competition.

'What are you going to do in England?' someone interrupted.

'I'd love to stay in Hong Kong,' I sighed, thinking it was an impossible dream. 'The ballet has left and there's no work here.'

'You could waitress at the Go Down,' the cheeky captain replied.

'What's a Go Down?'

'The Chinese stored barrels of goods and liquor there years ago.' Grinning, he asked the barman for a pen and paper and wrote down an address. 'Go there if you want work. Today it's a restaurant and they always need waitresses.'

Alone in the pension, decisions needed to be made fast. In the morning I transferred to the artists' pension and phoned the Go Down. Vacancies for waitresses were available, but uppermost in my mind was the flying competition.

On the day I woke up feeling good. How great if I won the silver cup, but reality kicked in. Alone, none of the girls would be there to cheer me on.

At midday the Aero Club was filled to capacity and a large bull's eye had been chalked on the runway directly in front of the club. As I lined up for take-off my instructor declared, 'You're on your own. Tell me if you want to change anything.'

Safety was a priority and my confidence escalated when I saw another pilot in a light aircraft in the distance. They'd taken longer to make the right hand turn. If I made the turn at my usual reference point, there was the chance of a collision.

'I'm going to delay a little longer before the turn or I'll be too close to the aircraft ahead,' I told my instructor. He didn't reply and I presumed I'd made the right decision.

Coming in to land amidst thunderous applause, I missed the target by inches and was placed third.

'Time to pass the air law exam,' my instructor stated to my delight.

The seed to stay had been sown and blossomed the more I thought about it. Waitressing could be a fill-in job until other opportunities arose. The problem was changing my flight home for a second time. Surprised to see me again, the agent rebooked it with ease to return within a year. 'Thanks,' I replied as he gave me the ticket and his card.

'I'm here if you need me,' he replied in a knowledgeable voice. The Go Down restaurant was in a huge, glorified cellar with a small lounge bar. Away from the beaten track of tourists, it catered for influential people and the locals. Garlic and other intoxicating aromas greeted you on arrival, luring one in to enjoy high class cuisine. It was always full, with a casual and sometimes boisterous atmosphere. My shift commenced at 6 pm, lasting five hours for six days a week. Sore feet were never a deterrent as the wage covered living expenses and the cost of a couple of flights a week. Dancing no longer mattered. A new beginning and studies for the impending law exam were vital. One had to know the restricted areas and all the territories, including the outlying islands, and flying at different altitudes.

One evening in the restaurant the supervisor instructed me to work in the bar. I'd never pulled a pint of beer in my life. Flustered and horrified, I watched the beer rise fast and splutter and bubble over the glass, saturating the bar bench and myself. Perhaps the customer complained. No more bar duty.

I'd been working there for almost five weeks when one night the supervisor told me, 'You can serve on the ten tables at the entrance.' Faith in me at last, or was this the reverse?

Customers flowed in and the venue filled up quickly. Weird. Half of my tables were empty. An insignificant figure entered, shielding her face with a hood from her coat. Two hefty bodyguards towered above her as I recognised her. She was Eartha Kitt, the world famous American singing sensation and one of my idols from the 60s.

The trembling voice and passion in her songs was unique. I directed them to one of my tables as a manager rushed over to speak to me. 'We'll take over.'

'No,' I retorted, 'they're on my tables. I'll serve them.' He watched as I took the orders for two straight whiskeys and a bowl of hot soup, treating them like normal customers. Polite, discrete and showing no emotion, I served soup to the star, knowing she wished seclusion from the public eye.

In the morning the phone rang. 'We don't need you anymore.' No surprise. Ah well, casual jobs come and go. My savings were untouched and I had the precious ticket to England. The following week was the air law exam. What the heck, after another flight I stayed at the club for a couple of drinks. Telling the pilots I'd lost the job and was concentrating to pass the air law exam, one of them took me aside.

'Photocopy the map of all the Hong Kong territories twenty times and learn them thoroughly,' he whispered. 'Show the examiners you know the area.' Brilliant advice.

As I was about to leave I quipped, 'I lost the job, but if I pass the air law exam, watch out you pilots.'

'No-one passes the air law exam the first time,' a voice replied.

Dressed in an immaculate, grey suit, a man thrust his card into my hand. He was clearly enjoying the challenge, disbelieving that a mere whisker of a girl could do the impossible. 'I'm the CEO of several hotels. If you pass first time, phone me and I'll give you a job.' Waitress in a high class hotel? At least it would be work.

Days passed, with the determination to succeed pressuring me to forget the loneliness and missing the girls and my dear friend Cherry. It was too early to write to her. They'd be somewhere in Spain by now, doing the same routines and meeting young Spaniards willing to woo them off their feet, while I'd be sewing costumes for Robert for peanuts.

Many people sat the exam and half of the questions were a blob in my mind. Failure loomed. Head bent scribbling to remember facts, I recalled the pilot's advice. Time was running out as the pen slid across the pages. Perhaps knowing the map of the territories and recalling the important details there was a chance to succeed. The exam was tough and complicated and thoughts of a future life in Hong Kong, known as Honkers to the locals, were fading fast.

The waiting game for the results was torture. Listless with nothing to do, I meandered around the shops in Nathan Road or stayed in my room.

After a few days the important call came. Anticipating failure, I picked up the phone. A composed voice announced, 'You passed with 70 marks.'

Thrilled, I realised I'd scraped through and achieved the impossible. Unable to contain my excitement, I rushed to the Aero Club to tell my instructor.

'You don't need me anymore,' he replied, delighted with the news. 'Go and book yourself a solo flight.' Confident in my ability, I lined up in front of a jumbo jet and thrust the throttle forward as I turned onto the runway and soared high into the sky above the ocean and the skyscrapers.

Jubilant with my accomplishment, it was time to phone the CEO. 'Well done,' he replied. 'I have a position for you as supervisor at the Bavarian Bistro on the lower floor of the Holiday Inn Hotel in Nathan Road. Be there at 8:30 am on Monday. They'll be expecting you.'

It was amazing that he'd remembered me and kept his promise – yet I was perplexed. How could I, with no training and a few fleeting weeks' experience as a casual waitress, become a supervisor in such a big hotel? It was daunting and another challenge. Bright and alert, I walked the short distance to the famous hotel and took the escalator down to the bistro on the lower floor.

The tall German manager dressed in a neat, white jacket greeted me and frowned as he noticed my nervousness. Did he realise I had no training? The décor of the bistro reminded one of a restaurant in the Bavarian Alps. Tones of a soft brown covered the walls, though there were no windows. Polished wooden chairs and tables seating two to four people were scattered around the room, interspersed with four columns which held long mirrors. It catered for eighty people. At the back on the side there was an unobtrusive bar and next to it the serving area. On the right side was a chocolatier and a complete delicatessen displaying various cuts of meat, Behind, in open grills cooks prepared gourmet German sausages and sauerkraut.

The manager took me to a tiny room at the back, telling me to change into a uniform. It was a delightful Bavarian costume, brown with a flared miniskirt and white petticoats. The puffy, white mini-sleeves were cute and the little white apron surrounded by delicate frills completed the picture – a costume designed for the stage.

He showed me a large pot beginning to simmer with a white paste inside.

'This is my specialty,' he explained as he stirred it with a large spoon. 'Mashed potato has to be the right consistency, not too much milk or butter and not runny or thick.' It was obvious he took great pride in his work. Giving me a set of keys he explained, 'You must be here every morning to open up in case I'm late, and the bar must only be opened when a customer requests an alcoholic drink. You work from 8:30 am until 7 pm with an hour for lunch. We're open from 9 am until 6 pm and the last hour is spent cleaning and preparing for the morning. Sunday is your day off.'

Nodding my head in agreement, I wondered how I would survive. Long hours working all day with few breaks could become unbearable. I'd have to be attentive and watch how everyone worked.

Soon the Chinese staff and cooks arrived and were ready to start the moment the doors opened. I was no match for these tireless workers as they gave satisfaction to a constant stream of customers throughout the day.

A week later the manager asked for my passport. 'You're getting Hong Kong residency.' Elated, I realised I could stay in Hong Kong for as long as I wanted. Had I underestimated my abilities? I was too tired to visit the Aero Club after long hours working constantly on aching feet. Exhaustion kicked in. Sundays were spent recuperating and catching up on personal chores. The wage was good, though, and I was beginning to feel a sense of security.

'Well,' I told myself in an unusual idle moment as I looked at one of the full length mirrors, 'You're thirty one years old and a waitress, dressed in a delightful Bavarian costume. This time last year you were in Africa having fun. Where will you be next year?'

An unexpected urge to dance surged through my heart. How wonderful it would be to pirouette among the tables and crash onto the floor in a gigantic jump split? They'd forget to eat their spicy sausages. Looking around no-one had noticed what I'd done, and I served the people as usual.

'Hi,' a Canadian voice called to get my attention. Turning around, there was Bruce whom I'd met on several occasions at the Aero club sitting at a table by the entrance, looking immaculate in his captain's uniform. Warm, chubby and friendly, I'd spoken to him on several occasions at the club. He was a devoted husband with three children and had taken a keen interest in my flying progress.

I smiled as I recalled the memory of when he took me to a flight simulator to try my hand flying a jumbo jet. He'd yelled, 'Don't crash into the ocean, nose up and more speed.' Trying hard, I'd avoided the ocean and mountain and landed on top of a group of sky scrapers. A fantastic memory.

'Hello,' I replied. 'I can't talk now, it's busy. You'll get me the sack.'

'I came to see you,' he grinned and in a swift movement held up a couple of keys, dangling them in my face.

'What are they for?' I whispered, wondering what he had planned.

'I'm on the way to the airport and flying overseas for ten days. Here are the keys to my apartment and the address. Put them into the letter box before I return.'

The minutes couldn't fly fast enough and by dusk I'd transferred from the pension to a luxurious dwelling with a spectacular view of the ocean. Sinking into a luxurious bed at night helped my aching limbs to recover. Bliss. However, rising half an hour earlier to catch the Star Ferry to Kowloon and combatting blustering winds was draining, and my health deteriorated. Glorious nights spent sleeping in luxury passed too quickly and reluctantly I put the key into the letter box.

The constant crossing on the ferry twice daily and the overload of work had taken its toll. Back at Chungking Mansions I sneezed. Ill with a high temperature, I knew I'd caught a cold and would be unable to function properly.

It was noon and the Bistro was filled to capacity. Noting my pretty uniform, an elegant lady insisted I serve her. 'I want six spicy sausages.'

'Yes ma'am.'

'Get me ten slices of that good ham, too,' she demanded, expecting to be served fast.

'Yes ma'am.'

'No. Thicker,' she insisted, 'much thicker.'

Struggling not to sneeze and meet her commands, I made a mistake with the settings on the machine, almost slicing off part of my little finger. Blood spurted out, dripping onto the lovely costume. The cooks heard me shrieking from behind the counter and instantly packed the poor thing into a bag of flour. They were used to chopping off their fingers or other bits, and when they thought the blood had congealed they stuffed the poor thing into a condom so I could continue to work. Another lady came in asking for specific chocolates to be packed in a box. The finger was aching and stretching to reach for more chocolates I couldn't keep the box steady. They scattered everywhere onto the polished floor.

The manager was angry and after a few moments told me I was wanted in the office on the first floor. Doom. I knew what was going to happen, yet I felt light headed. It didn't matter anymore. The thought of no more exhausting work was a relief.

In the office three managers in immaculate black suits greeted me. 'Pamela we've brought you here for a reason.'

'I know,' I replied flippantly. 'You're going to sack me.'

'We don't do that,' the leader of the pack replied.

'Well, what are you asking?'

'We're asking you to leave.'

'But it's the same thing,' I replied, and was glad to escape.

***

Back in the pension I wondered what to do next. There was an easy answer – take a few more flying trips with the money I had left, and return to England to begin a new life. I'd been away for eighteen months and the thought of home was wonderful. I'd miss Honkers and the constant buzz of activity, but there was no other choice.

I decided to walk down Nathan Road for a breath of fresh air, not knowing it would completely change my life. It was mid-afternoon and the pavement was packed to capacity with people scurrying everywhere when a voice yelled, 'Pamela.' Who could it be? No one knew me except for the Aero Club members.

'Pamela,' the voice shouted again. Turning around, I was stunned to see Louis with a South American girl on his arm. He was a tall, slim Argentinian dancer I'd lived with at the pension in Madrid five years ago when I was with my lover José.

Coming to my senses, I asked, 'Do you have time for a coffee?'

He appeared as amazed as I was at this chance meeting. How much Spanish could I remember? Louis spoke limited English but I needn't have worried. As we talked and understood each other, the Spanish flowed. Nina was his partner. He'd produced and choreographed his own ballet and toured Europe. Afterwards he'd choreographed a duo act with Nina and they were working in nightclubs in Hong Kong for three more days. Then it was my turn to recall events. I laughed as I told him I'd sold sausages, almost sliced off a finger and spilt chocolates onto the floor at the Holiday Inn Hotel, while he chuckled, too. He stared at me in disbelief as I revealed my plans for the inevitable departure to England in a few days' time. Exploding with enthusiasm and in a loud Spanish voice, he declared, 'You're a brilliant dancer. You can't go. I won't let you. My mind is made up. You must get your own show. I'm not letting you out of my sight. Where are you staying?'

'Chungking Mansions.'

'Good. We're staying there a few days, too, before going to Japan. Let's go.'

'But?'

There was no time for 'buts' as he steered me out of the place and continued to talk non-stop as Nina nodded her head in agreement. They were drawing me back into a world I knew and understood, not wasting a second. Nina showed me her costumes, describing how they were made while Louis inundated me with information on the type of show required.

'You need fifteen minutes on stage. Music is important. Dynamic music to enter, soft and alluring in the middle and a dramatic ending.'

'Yes,' I whispered, not knowing how I could achieve it. They were leaving so soon, yet it didn't matter how much I argued; both of them were persistent.

Watching their show from the wings, I was mesmerised as a dazzling Louis commanded the stage in a brown and gold Apache costume, and with macho strides lifted Nina in her jewelled costume into breathtaking lifts, caressing her in lighter moods in the music. It was stunning. Entranced, ideas formed as I watched.

When they left, leaving no contact details, I felt a great loss. Such a short time had seemed like months and my head was a whirlwind of ideas. Hong Kong was the ideal place to buy materials but I had no sewing machine, and how long could I last without work? Did they expect me to try in England? Dejection set in. It would be impossible to do, and I made up my mind to continue with my previous plan and at least enjoy the thrill of flying again before returning home.

How can a second miracle occur within a few days? It did.

'What's wrong with you?' a man said as he sat down beside me at the Aero Club bar. I must have looked lethargic.

'Nothing,' I replied, but he insisted on knowing, so I told him what had happened and how I'd love to create my own show, knowing it was impossible. I'd already decided on the costume – a black velvet skirt with bundles of white lace petticoats, a delicate white laced top, knee length silver boots and a blonde wig. I drew him a diagram, and he was impressed.

'I can help.'

'How?' I replied. 'I'll need music, photos, a sewing machine and a place to live.'

'I'm John, one of the airport managers. My colleague has a room you can stay in while you make your costume, but you must provide your own food and I'll take photos and record the music.'

'Why do you want to help a complete stranger?'

'We believe in helping a person we believe in. Go and buy

your materials. Here's my card. Phone me tomorrow at five o'clock and I'll have everything ready for you.'

I felt as though I'd been struck by a thunderbolt. It was a chance in a million and I decided to trust him. Rushing to the market where we'd bought the Can-Can materials, I found everything and staggered into Chungking Mansions, exhausted. True to his word, the following day John had a sewing machine set up in his colleague's apartment, with a bedroom for me to sleep in.

For four weeks I sewed day and night, hardly venturing out except to grab food. The hard work was worth it. The costume looked stunning once finished. John loved it and took the photos. They weren't professional but were good enough.

Rushing around to find appropriate music was difficult. Searching through several record shops, I found what I thought were good melodies and John recorded the required fifteen minutes of music onto a cassette.

I returned to the pension, content with everything finished. What a shock to be living in mediocre conditions again. It didn't matter and I was almost broke. It was time to speak to the agent. If he couldn't give me work, I'd take the costume back to England to try my luck there. Clutching the precious photos, I crossed Nathan Road when once again I heard Louis shouting my name. He came across to me.

'I'm taking these to the agent to try to get work,' I told him, excited.

'What?' Louis replied, as he looked in amazement at the photos. 'You did it. Good luck. We'll see you back at the pension.'

The agent peered at the photos, commenting on the intricate artistry of the jewels on the necklace. 'You made the costume yourself?' he asked, no doubt wondering how I'd managed to do it. I nodded. 'Do you have a fifteen minute number?'

'Yes I do,' I replied, holding my breath and praying he'd give me a chance.

'You can start on Monday, doing three shows a night for three weeks,' he replied, noting my relieved look. When he told me the salary it was hard not to show my surprise. It was phenomenal, almost four times what Robert had paid me.

Back at the pension Louis and Nina were as excited as I was, but on the first night they declined to come. I wasn't nervous but hopeful the audience would enjoy the performance. The agent didn't phone and I presumed all was well.

Nina and Louis were busy in the daytime, chasing around shops and agents and without my knowledge watched me perform on the fourth night.

'Not bad,' Louis declared. 'Come to our room tomorrow. I've got music for you.'

It was brilliant with a thunderous, full orchestral beginning, lilting soft music in the middle and a good ending. 'You need a better opening,' he stated and demonstrated what I should do. 'Swish your skirt to the sides, perform pirouettes around the stage, followed by quick turns into a split. The rest you can choreograph yourself.'

Using the new music and performing the opening as Louis had suggested had an enormous impact on the audience, who loved it and applauded wildly. I was at last a success and felt indebted to Louis and Nina, who were happy I had made it.

Louis surprised me again. 'I've organised an agent to see you. He's looking for artists for a hotel in Japan.' He knew work was limited in Hong Kong and was helping me every way he could. His altruism knew no boundaries.

The time came for them to leave for Tokyo and I was alone again. This time it was different and I knew I'd overcome any obstacles crossing my path.

'See you in Japan,' they chorused – and somehow I knew that I would.

Touring Solo

The agent was impressed with the show's success, and called to tell me so. 'I saw your show and can offer you a contract for a hotel in Japan for three months.'

'Yes,' I replied, trying to keep my voice steady. I'd been nervous, waiting for his call. 'We require two twenty minute shows.'

'When does the contract start?'

'At the end of the month. Come to my office in three weeks to sign the contract. Your show is good.'

My head was spinning with ideas as I accepted. It wasn't impossible. I'd saved the ballet in Singapore and had to grab this opportunity. It was a huge challenge to create a number within a month, but paid weekly by the agent there was money to buy the equipment and materials. John? He'd already turned my dream into reality. I'd do the rest myself.

The first problem was how to lengthen the black and white number by five minutes. To tack a tune onto the beginning or ending of the brilliant music Louis had given me would be catastrophic. There was a solution – sing a song, but I hadn't sung in years. I adored the song 'Raindrops Keep Falling on My Head' and surely the Japanese would forgive me speaking the odd high note. They'd adore the costume and the song was perfect for the number.

Scouring through music shops for a couple of days and knowing where to shop was a blessing in disguise. I hit the jackpot and found the perfect melody.

Buying the recording machine was easier with many shops and hundreds of brands to choose from. I settled for one which recorded from one cassette to another and from records. I had borrowed a sewing machine from John and was glad to be able to purchase one for myself and chose an Elna machine. 'It's not fancy but does the trick,' the jolly salesman explained. 'They're easy to carry around, and I've sold many to sailors who use them to mend their sails.'

A large, straw hat, covered with remnants from the black velvet skirt and smothered with a line of white ostrich feathers, was perfect. To complete the look I sewed several lines of white lace around a black umbrella. Humming the words of the song as I shopped I was ecstatic. But time was slipping away.

The second number had to be completely different, bold and quick to make. Once the design of the costume and concept was there, finding music for it would be easy. Creative visions were surfacing. Thinking back to the ballets and companies I'd worked with, an idea surfaced – be a gothic, likeable demon on stage. Slender grey trousers made of jersey would look good with a silver thread decorated with sequins on the wide bottoms. A black chiffon cloak lined with feathers and a coronet with protruding cock feathers should give a stunning effect, bunched together with a jeweled eye mask. There'd be time to make a third number in Japan, a softer, contrasting one with blue, chiffon material for the dress, complemented by a large feathered hat and long gloves. The gothic costume had been machined, just needing sequins to be added. The recordings were finished and materials and music bought for the blue number. The future looked good. On the last show of the night, a lightning pain soared through my right rib while executing a double pirouette. I staggered off the stage as staff helped me to return to Chungking Mansions, feeling nauseous with a fever developing. Artists in the pension gathered around to help.

A Russian acrobat told me, 'You not put dressing gown on. You sweat, get cold. I walk on your back. You be better.' They turned me over onto my stomach and he did it. My body became rigid, with the pain unbearable.

'Hospital, quick,' someone suggested, and they carried my limp body down the lift to a taxi.

Night attendants helped me into a dull lit building and a large room filled with wailing patients who lay on thin raffia mats on a hard floor. Lowering me onto a vacant one, they left.

In the eerie darkness, the moans and groans continued unabated. I was thirsty, but there was no sign of water or food. How bad could this living nightmare get? I prayed frantically for a warm bed and pillow.

Dawn was approaching and light crept through the windows as I detected feeling returning to my limbs. Twiddling my toes felt good and the pain in my ribs had subsided. A burning desire to get out of this hell hole and rest in a bed was overwhelming.

I held my hand high to grab the attention of a nurse. A white skirt headed in my direction as I croaked, 'When is the doctor coming?'

'Ten o'clock,' she replied and left. The wailing grew louder as patients stirred.

No. I couldn't wait for three hours. I stood up on wobbly feet. Turning to the left, a sharp pain attacked my ribcage, although stooping a little I could manage to walk. I slowly traipsed my way around the bodies on the mats and headed to the exit. To my amazement, no-one asked where I was going or stopped me, and I made it safely back by taxi to the pension.

'I was worried about you. You don't look well,' my landlord Mr Chan remarked when I arrived.

'I couldn't stay at the hospital. It's a terrible place. I'm gasping for hot tea, toast and my bed,' I replied, comforted in knowing he'd look after me – which he did, bringing food and drinks for three days as I recovered.

Desperate to be cured, I ventured out to see what I could find. A Chinese pharmacy looked interesting. There were rows of large jars in the window filled with different coloured liquids, which drew my attention. Weren't their medicines supposed to cure any ailment? I'd heard of bile from bears, tiger balls and snake livers being used in their concoctions. Worth a try. Language was a barrier so I resorted to using body movements and pointing to my rib. The pharmacist nodded his head and gave me a potion – an insipid mustard coloured jar with bits in it. The smell was unbearable as I smothered it over the wound. It proved hopeless and a waste of time.

I had to know what was wrong and realised only a qualified doctor could help. Close by in an international hotel, the receptionist directed me to a suite on the twentieth floor. He was European and trustworthy – what a relief.

'Chinese medicine had no effect,' I explained. 'I have a contract to dance in Japan in ten days' time. I don't know what's wrong. If it's serious I'll return to England.'

'X-rays will show the extent of the damage,' he replied gently. 'Come back on Monday and I'll give you the results.'

Two days later as I sat waiting in the surgery, trembling in anticipation of the unknown, I knew it was go home or dance. The doctor entered with a broad smile, lifting my hopes for good news.

'Go to Japan,' he declared. 'It's a torn muscle. Keep warm and wrap a towel around you. It helps the healing process and you'll soon be back to normal.' Overjoyed I'd survived the trauma, now the future looked positive.

Wearing a thick jumper to conceal the towel, I walked into the agent's office smiling and signed the contract, hoping he wouldn't notice the bulkiness around my waist. Delighted at how I'd lengthened the show, he'd arranged a professional photographer to take shots of the completed costume. They were taken two days later. John had tried his best but these photos were flawless and captivating.

The doctor was right. Each day the pain receded and when it was time to pack I was fit.

Another problem occurred. Money was running out and I only possessed one suitcase. The agents would pay the excess baggage, but how was I to pack the costumes? Chasing around luggage shops I found the perfect solution – a cheap, synthetic garment bag would hold them and the spare materials. Departure day arrived and I was excited to be returning to Japan with my own show. Flying with Cathay Pacific, I wondered if I'd know the captain. Check in of luggage was smooth and I bought a few toiletries at duty free. Looking at my purse, a ten dollar note was left. Undeterred, I knew I could get an advance as I was confident the Japanese would adore my show.

As I walked to the gangway of the plane, an air hostess stopped me. *What's this?* I thought. *Can anything else go wrong?*

'Come this way,' she said. 'You've been upgraded to first class.' After I'd finished tasting delicious delicacies, the air hostess indicated that the captain wished to talk to me. I suspect he'd heard of me from the other pilots.

A beaming smile greeted me as he steered the plane to our destination. 'Where are you going?' he inquired.

'Beppu on the Southern Island of Kyushu, to dance in a hotel for three months.'

'Oh,' he smiled as he steered the plane. 'We fly all over the world to cities, but not to towns. Good luck.' Arriving in Kyushu, a cavalcade of luxury cars escorted me to the hotel. I was a celebrity.

On the east coast and directly opposite to Nagasaki, Beppu is surrounded by mountains and famous for its hot springs. The majestic hotel on the sea front catered for Japanese tourists who'd arrive in droves at the weekends. Facilities included an outdoor swimming pool, a hot pool for therapeutic bathing, tennis courts and several restaurants.

A Philippine ballet performed in the theatre on the third floor. Delightful to watch, they danced with candles, fire, garlands and poles as a female singer sang with a nightingale voice. The cosy nightclub on the lower level, where I performed, had a small stage and my room was comfortable with a European bed, a TV and a kitchenette.

Mr Makino, owner of the hotel, was a strong, tall character with kind eyes who spoke a smattering of English. Realising how lonely it was for a foreigner who was unable to speak Japanese, he'd often meet me for a coffee at the café in the mornings. He'd ask how I was and how the blue costume was progressing. Occasionally he'd mention the Americans with a sad, faraway look in his eyes. He couldn't forget the suffering caused by the atomic bomb in Nagasaki.

Before opening night, the Japanese agent came from Tokyo to see a rehearsal and insisted I speak a few Japanese words as an introduction to the audience. To overcome the problem, I wrote the phonetics on a piece of paper to read from and threw it unnoticed into the wings until I'd learnt the words.

The audience loved the show and I was glad to be my own boss, without the hardship of wondering where the next penny was coming from. Performing twice nightly and the occasional gala in the banqueting hall for visiting dignitaries, my bones and muscles ached from the constant high kicks and splits. Bathing in the therapeutic pond afterwards helped to relieve the pain.

I was thrilled when my contract was extended for another three months. Life was good, except for a huge problem I hadn't anticipated. It was forbidden to leave the hotel unless taken by a chauffeured car to town. This may seem glamorous but it wasn't. My freedom was suppressed and I was living in a glorious open air prison. Respite came from the few kind conversations with Mr Makino, the American TV program *Sesame Street* and letters from home.

Unexpectedly there was a phone call from Louis. 'We'll be in Tokyo for a week and not working. Can you come?'

What wonderful news and Mr Makino agreed. 'Yes, see friends three days. You hard work. Holiday good. Chauffeur take you airport.'

What a joyous time, conversing with them in Spanish and meandering through the shops and supermarkets. They were so happy to see me. Nina had bought a miniature poodle who followed us everywhere.

'How do you get him through customs?' I inquired.

'I give him a tiny sleeping tablet and carry him in a basket with a shawl on top.'

It was a bright interlude and over too soon. It's a pity we didn't exchange home addresses as I never saw them again, and I often wondered if the dog was discovered by customs – but they were lenient in the 70s. Strange as it might seem, I felt sad to leave Beppu. Mr Makino, a caring person, arranged a disco night with the Philippine ballet. He presented me with a golden pen and the agent offered me a contract in another hotel after six months.

Hong Kong is the crown city in the world for duty free shopping. How wild can one get with a healthy bank account when freedom returns? A celebrity needs good clothes and I bought the best tailor-made blouses, an elegant Grecian styled dress and a dark blue leather coat sporting a fluffy fur collar.

Visiting the Aero Club felt awkward as I no longer flew, preferring to stay in the pension with the other artists. John, my saviour, was delighted when I phoned, and an amazing evening was spent with him and his partner discussing the news and my adventures.

The urge to return to the Holiday Inn Bistro where I'd been sacked was irresistible. Dressed to kill and flaunting expensive clothes, the manager was shocked and stunned when I told him I'd worked in Japan. Word spread to other agents that I was an available established artist and I flew to Taiwan on a month's contract. In autumn the weather was cool and the incessant, annoying mosquitoes had hibernated. The nightclub in Taipei was unusual. There was a bar in the middle, surrounded by the audience and rotating at a gentle pace, with three extensions protruding out towards round, metre-wide satellite stages. Performing in such a tiny area seemed impossible, but I was ready for the challenge. Stepping onto one of them singing 'What the World Needs Now Is Love, Sweet Love', I captivated the audience in a pretty blue costume, using soft movements for the dance.

Working in Tainan at the theatre in cooler weather was pleasant, although I shuddered remembering how the ballet had suffered dancing the Can-can in wet costumes, unable to breathe in stifling heat. Performing twice nightly, the show also included Chinese and international artists. A large placard of my act was erected outside the theatre and stolen within a couple of days.

One evening after the show, a shrewd-eyed, short, fat Taiwanese agent swaggered up to introduce himself, dressed in an immaculate brown suit.

'Me agent. Mr Lin. You show good. Book you Taipei. BIG theatre restaurant. BIG nightclubs. Sing Chinese song. Book you two months.'

Hesitant at first, I realised it meant I could stay in the Far East without having to return home through lack of work.

'How long to learn song?' I asked as my mind bubbled over with catastrophic thoughts of failure and the audience booing me.

'One week. Song is Mei-hua. National Taiwan flower,' he replied with a huge grin as he handed me a cassette.

I played the cassette non-stop as I learnt the sounds and phonetics of words I didn't understand in parrot fashion.

The walls of the hotel must've been impenetrable as no-one complained.

The Taiwanese audience adored seeing an English girl sing in Chinese, but I was perplexed. In the theatre restaurant the diners were too busy pecking at rice with their chopsticks to applaud. This was their custom and I wondered why they bothered to pay to see the show if all they were interested in was eating. Working with the Chinese singers, acrobats and fire eaters, it became clear I needed live music and I paid musicians to transpose cassette music to orchestral scores. After a successful two months, I returned to Hong Kong to work in the nightclubs for another three weeks before returning to Japan. Working to different audiences and recalling the aching loneliness in Beppu, it was time to create a new number while I had the chance. Spanish would be different, with vibrant, flowing music, a bright red costume and a long train filled with frills and sequins. I could also practise playing the castanets I'd always kept in my luggage.

Jason, an American entrepreneur who often commuted between Hong Kong and Singapore, produced acts for artists. His ideas were brilliant. 'Use a large, green ostrich fan with black tips. I'll have the music on tape and cassette completed when you return.' We were both thrilled and brimming with ideas. Jason questioned me, though, 'Do you think you're perhaps getting too old to dance? How old are you?'

'Almost thirty three. My contract is for six months and I'll continue while I'm able to dance.'

'Good. I'll see you on your return to take professional photos in the new costume.'

I chased around the markets and shops, excited to be making another brilliant costume for the future. Misasa is a charming country town on the western coast of the main island of Honshu. Nestled between mountains and lush green valleys, it's famous for its hot springs. Eagles soared high into the sky searching for prey. Perched on high electric wires and alert, they'd swoop down to kill a lethargic victim.

I couldn't eat the elaborate fish food and fasted for three days until management gave me a small room over the road from the hotel where I could cook food I enjoyed. A manager accompanied me over to the room each day at 5 o'clock for an hour, but after a month I was allowed to go there alone.

Boredom set in and a kind manager explained he owned a small bar a short walk from the hotel. What joy, miming to the locals or teaching them the odd word in English while drowning a couple of Sartori whiskies with nibbles after the show. It was innocent fun and occasionally I borrowed the manager's daughter's bicycle to ride amongst the green, picturesque valleys.

Alas, I committed a catastrophic mistake. When the Japanese agent's representative came to pay me, I invited him to the bar. He willingly accepted and appeared to be enjoying himself. Early the next morning, it was a different scenario as he stormed into my room screaming, 'Miss Pamela how dare you. Your show is good and management are pleased but you must NEVER, EVER go to the bar again. If you do we'll terminate your contract, sack the manager and never use an artist from your Hong Kong agent again.'

When he left I threw my head into a pillow and wept. For three months I'd have to survive in this open air prison. I looked longingly out of the tiny window at the wonderful valleys I'd enjoyed cycling through, and realised on reflection that it wasn't all bad news. My show and the money were important. It wasn't the local people but the Japanese system which was harsh.

I sewed thousands of sequins onto the Spanish train and completed a spectacular costume ready for Hong Kong. I never saw the manager again, and on the last day the agent offered me a contract for the following year to a different hotel, which I accepted. The money was too good.

The music Jason had prepared and the photos taken of the Spanish costume were brilliant. 'I can get you a contract in Singapore,' Jason suggested.

'Wonderful', I replied, 'but there's a small problem. I was too lonely in Japan and I'm going to return to England for a short holiday. Will it pose a problem?'

'No, but you'll have to pay for your own flight to Singapore.' We exchanged the necessary contact details and at last I flew to England on the unused ticket from the ballet to spend a few precious weeks in homely comfort with my parents. Lethargic and bored after the wonderful homecoming, however, and suffering from the freezing winter weather, I was soon itching to leave.

The weeks turned into a couple of months and still no news. When oh when would they contact me? At last a telegram arrived, stating I was to be in Singapore on the 1st of March. I yelped with delight, telling Mother, 'Don't know when I'll be back, but I love you both.'

'Don't worry me duck,' she replied. 'Follow your dream, but please don't go back to Japan. Your letters told me how lonely you were. Your home is always here.'

I bought a cheap one way ticket flying with Aeroflot.

When the day came to leave London, at Heathrow Airport Mother insisted, 'Give me your camera. They might think you're a spy in Moscow.'

Reluctant, I handed it over. She didn't understand that aero planes had to have stopovers to refuel and I knew she'd send it when I was settled somewhere. Stepping into blazing sunshine in Singapore, a rush of adrenalin overwhelmed me as I was escorted by the Singapore agent to a small apartment on the outskirts of the city. He explained, 'We'll give you $7 a day for food until a contract for Indonesia is confirmed.'

I'd expected to work immediately but nothing could dampen my enthusiasm. During the idle two weeks I rehearsed my act and caught taxis to the Hyatt Hotel in the city, where the manager allowed me to use the outside pool whenever I wanted. Later he proved to be very helpful.

Flying to Jakarta for a month I performed four shows a night at various venues. Afterwards I was met at Singapore Airport by the agent, who gave me a ticket to fly directly to Penang. The audiences were mainly Chinese and Indian, and singing Chinese songs was my salvation.

An avid reader, books were my solace during long tedious journeys as I toured Malaysia performing in small and large towns. Grabbing a novel from a book stall, I'd read it and leave it behind for an unknown person to enjoy.

While starring for two weeks at the Golden Theatre Restaurant in Singapore, I became friendly with John and Annie, an American duo who'd come from Australia. It was a happy time, visiting local attractions in the day time.

I was due to return to Japan in a few days. Unexpectedly a telegram arrived. Staring in disbelief, I read, 'We've cancelled your contract,' without any explanation.

I turned to Annie, 'This is terrible news. I have no other contracts and don't know what to do. I'm finished.'

Annie soothed me and her words gave me a glimmer of hope in the darkness of despair. 'You've got a great act. We've come from a revue in Melbourne, run by an old entrepreneur. It's only an eight week contract but it may lead to other things. He'll love your show. Send him photos and plague him with phone calls.'

I did what she'd suggested and the manager of the Hyatt Hotel allowed me to pay for calls to Australia. Learning of the terrible news, the Singapore agents helped by getting me spasmodic contracts, but the work was running out.

'You've worked everywhere. There are no more contracts,' they sighed. 'We're sorry. You'll have to return to England.'

'You've helped,' I told them, 'but I'm not giving up yet.'

Annie was right. When I was able to contact the entrepreneur, I could sense he liked my photos.

'I'll send you a letter with details,' he replied in a professional manner. 'If you agree I'll arrange your working visa.'

Giddy with excitement and relief, I put down the phone. No need to go home.

When his letter arrived, I ripped the envelope open in a frenzy, keen to learn what he was offering. The weekly wage was lower and board and lodging weren't included. The contract was to commence on 21st September for eight weeks, with a one way ticket from Singapore to Melbourne provided.

My knowledge of Australia was limited. I'd heard that the people lived on the edge of large deserts and kangaroos jumped down the main streets. It couldn't be as expensive as Japan and how delightful to cuddle a koala bear. No work for a month was a problem, but my bank balance was healthy.

I accepted the offer and was fortunate to secure a couple of weeks' work to cover living expenses. A new country beckoned with guaranteed work for a short time, which could lead to other avenues. I relaxed on the long journey as the plane headed south.

Burlesque in Melbourne

Flying over Sydney through the clouds, the world famous harbour appeared. In the morning sunlight, miniature boats appeared motionless on the sparkling blue ocean.

What was this? We were flying over bright red rooftops which reminded me of England. Attached to the odd one were patches of blue – no doubt swimming pools in backyards, giving a promise of a moderate climate.

Arriving in Melbourne in 1978, after the long flight I was eager to meet the entrepreneur. Standing in a long queue at immigration I felt a tap on my shoulder. Surprised, I turned around to face an officer.

'Are you Pamela Brown?' he inquired.

'No, but my name is Pamela.'

'You must be the one. Follow me.'

In a daze I followed him past the crowds to a side door leading to the arrival hall, where he left me in front of an elderly man, puffing away at a cigar. The impresario!

'Pamela Brown,' he exclaimed as a broad grin lit up his wrinkled face.

From my photos where I was wearing a wig, he'd been expecting a blonde and had compared me to an old Hollywood film star. He had to have influence with government connections for me to bypass immigration, and I felt honoured.

Taking my luggage, he explained, 'I was on a world tour looking for artists and wanted to see your show, but you were never in one place long enough.'

I smiled. 'Yes, it was hectic after the Japanese cancelled my contract without any explanation.'

'I'll take you to see the showroom and afterwards you can relax for a couple of days.'

We trundled along in an old car, passing several main highways towards the city centre as I marvelled at the green parks, lovely buildings and wide streets. No sightings of kangaroos but I felt an immediate warmth towards this lovely city.

Arriving at the hotel where the show was held, a creepy feeling crept up my spine as I saw the names Sensational Misty, Gypsy from the Far East, Magical Ziggy Stardust, Carole the Dancing Darling and The Golden Girls splashed across a billboard. On the right was a large photo of a voluptuous, sexy lady, and on the left a photo of the entire cast showing girls in leotards, feathered hats and silver shoes. What sort of show was this?

Fearing the worst I froze on the spot, but seeing my glum face the entrepreneur ushered me inside to the show room. What a lovely surprise. There was an enchanting stage with bright red curtains. Still perplexed, I thought to myself that he hadn't seen my show. Maybe it wasn't what he wanted or where I wanted to work. On impulse I decided to show him.

'I want to rehearse now,' I demanded, fearful of a rebuke.

'I'll get the technician,' he replied in haste as I rummaged through my suitcase for a cassette.

The curtains parted, the house lights dimmed and bright flashing lights lit up the stage as the music Louis had given me roared into life. The complete setting reminded me of the Windmill Stage in London and I felt content. Knowing the entrepreneur was watching every movement, I semi-rehearsed the number as a silent figure joined him in the shadows and left as the rehearsal ended. His eyes portrayed nothing.

Unsure if he liked what he'd seen, I told him, 'I'll need a rehearsal for my Spanish number.'

'Rehearse when you like, but be ready to perform on Monday,' he said. 'Come. I'll show you where you're staying.' He took me to a side street and up some stairs to an apartment with a balcony. Instantly I recognised the tall, dark woman who opened the door – Sammy. It was her photo which was displayed outside the show room.

'Sammy is leaving tomorrow morning,' the entrepreneur stated with authority. 'You can stay here until your contract finishes.' Then he left abruptly.

'Like a cuppa tea?' Sammy asked in a strong American drawl. Friendly and chatty she continued, 'I'm flying back to Hollywood. Oh, how I wish I could stay here or come back. I met a man who wined and dined me and gave me a diamond ring.'

She talked non-stop as I admired the spacious living room, enjoying the thought of no more dingy hotel rooms. My eyes were drooping through lack of sleep and the arduous journey as she led me to a small bedroom, saying, 'Don't forget to pay the cleaning lady $30 a week.' A good idea.

Everything was going to be fine and I fell into a deep sleep.

***

The telephone rang. It was late in the afternoon. The impresario stated, 'I'll meet you at 7 pm at the hotel and we'll watch the show together.'

Sitting at the back at a secluded table I watched men arriving with the odd escorted woman being ushered into crammed seats. Glasses clicked as the auditorium became crowded. Smoke wafted into the air from cigarettes, mingling with the smell of chicken to be served in the interval.

The noise became boisterous until the lights dimmed and the show began. The curtains parted and four dancing girls, in glittering green leotards with orange feathered hats, pranced around the stage as the audience clapped wildly. The young compere, dressed in a grey suit, entered to tell a few jokes, which became fast paced and coarse as the show continued. Several mediocre girly acts followed.

The impresario was watching to see my reactions, but I showed no emotion until Gina came onto the stage. There was a gasp from the audience. A live python was curled around her neck and arms, and she enticed the audience to touch it as it slithered around her body. An extravagant transvestite with gawky legs and a tight bottom strutted onto the stage, dripping in diamonds and feathers and made me laugh. Christina, the contortionist, thrust her body over her head and picked up a handkerchief with her feet. I was expecting another dumb act when to the music of 'Teachers Pet' a girl in a school uniform bounced onto the stage with a backflip. She poked her tongue out and made funny faces as she performed intricate dance steps.

'What a great dancer,' I exclaimed.

'She's my wife,' the entrepreneur pronounced, beaming with pride.

The audience loved her, but when she produced a small bottle of whiskey from her pocket and proceeded to pour it down her throat, the audience were rollicking in the aisles with laughter as the entrepreneur wailed, 'Oh no, not again.'

A boisterous Can-can with lots of yells and screams was the perfect finale. The show was a mixture of good and bad acts and I enjoyed it. I knew my act would be well received and it was, and to my surprise I received a standing ovation for the Spanish number.

The one dressing room for all artists was overcrowded and I found myself sitting next to the New Zealand transvestite. Young and lovely, her pastel face was surrounded by flowing blonde curls. When she changed into her jeweled gown, it was hard to control myself as she made no attempt to hide her large dingle dangle.

Keeping to myself, I hardly spoke to the others for days, until one night I was approached in the wings by a strange girl – the dancer from the show. Her reddish hair was swept back into a pony tail. Wearing a bright green jumper and skirt, she looked stunning as she stood against the black curtain.

'Can you help me?' she whimpered. 'I've just swallowed forty vitamin tablets. Will they harm me?' She started to laugh. It was a ruse to break the ice.

From that moment Becky and I became buddies, and I relaxed and joined in the banter and comradery in the dressing room. She was the naughty school girl and the entrepreneur's wife, who filled in if someone didn't turn up for the show. Later she revealed she'd watched my first rehearsal and told her husband, 'She's a wonderful dancer. We must keep her.'

Becky's husband had been a performer and later produced shows on the Gold Coast before coming to Melbourne. I was happy and loving life. My contract was extended to six months, and I helped Becky with costumes and rehearsals. It was wonderful to visit the zoos, feeding kangaroos and cuddling a koala bear, panning for gold at Ballarat and travelling on the rattling old tram to St Kilda on sunny days to enjoy the beach. When they extended my contract for a further six months, I knew I had to create a new number. Clowns are fun and the store Lincraft had an amazing array of materials to choose from. I designed a harlequin costume with white frills on the neck and cuffs. Tying a hula-hoop inside the costume, it was gigantic and funny. A face mask and miniature top hat completed the outfit. Pulling the line of velcro open in the centre, I was able to step out of the costume in seconds and dazzle the audience in a sparkling sequined gown.

'A good number,' Becky and her husband said, 'but you need tricks.'

They gave me the music 'Be a Clown' and a bugle to blast on – another excellent number.

***

Time passed quickly. Had I already been in Australia for almost a year? The impresario approached me.

'Pamela, do you want to continue to work for us?'

'Yes, I love it here.'

'Unfortunately you have to leave the country as your work permit will expire,' he said. 'But you can return after two months. I have connections and can get you work in Las Vegas.'

Unprepared, it was a shock to be told I had to leave and the thought of America was unappealing.

'No. I'll return to Hong Kong and Taiwan. I know I can get work there.'

'Good. I'll arrange your work permit for your return.'

Heavy hearted, I booked a return flight for 4th December, packed my belongings and left the apartment I'd called home. After two years Hong Kong hadn't changed, with an endless rush of people packing the streets, chaotic traffic and new skyscrapers being built. Chungking Mansions remained the same and the pension was dull and uninviting. The glory of working there had diminished, and Australia was already pulling at my heart strings.

I decided to create a South American number for my return. The colours of Brazil and Australia are yellow and green, and I found chiffon materials at the market to make flowing frills, then bought hundreds of gold sequins to cover the bodice. The vibrant music of the Americas was easy to find and there was time in Taiwan to make the costume.

Working with the clown and Spanish numbers for the usual three weeks in the nightclubs was successful, but I was surprised when the agent called to tell me, 'It's law. The Government insists that any artist working in the colony must perform a free television show.'

They wanted two songs for the *Saturday Night Variety Show*. I chose 'Raindrops' and 'What Love Needs Now'. The costumes would look good on the screen and perhaps help to make up for the mediocre singing. I was petrified when told I had to sing each word correctly as Chinese subtitles would be displayed at the bottom of the screen.

The rehearsal was perfect, but during the live performance I suffered an unexpected attack of nerves and stage fright. It had happened once before in Amsterdam. Trying to shake off the nerves between numbers, I banged my head on the wall in despair, which brought me to my senses and I was able to perform. There were no mistakes and nothing was said, but the artists in the pension told me I'd looked nervous.

I completed the new costume and was delighted with the end result. Becky would love it.

It was in the final week at the Tainan theatre when several naked Chinese girls ran across the stage in front of me as I sang. Disgusted, I continued singing, determined never to work there again.

***

The plane couldn't fly fast enough – I was so keen to walk on Australian soil again. Two familiar figures were waiting in the crowded arrival hall. Becky hugged me as her husband took my luggage.

'We're going to Adelaide to stay with my aunt for a few days,' she announced, beaming with happiness to have me back. 'You need a holiday. You're going to be working very hard.'

Grinning, I replied, 'I'm tired after the ten hour journey.'

'You can sleep in the back of the car.'

That was difficult as I was fascinated with the wide open plains I'd never seen before, but we spent a wonderful few days together, relaxing without a worry in the world and becoming close mates.

On our return to Melbourne, I found another two bedroom apartment in the same block as before and commenced work. Except for there being a few new artists there, I felt as though I'd never left. True to her word, Becky kept me busy, helping with the costumes and rehearsals. I loved it – having peace of mind for twelve months, with no more country swapping or fears of being without work. The South American number was well received but couldn't surpass the triumph of the Spanish number. Life was idyllic. One evening Gina asked, 'Can I visit you on Sunday afternoon with a friend?'

This was unusual and I knew there had to be an underlying reason. Perplexed and delighted I replied, 'Please do. I'll have tea and cake ready.'

I couldn't believe my eyes when they arrived with a snow white Maltese cross pup called Buttons.

'Would you like to look after him for a couple of days?' Gina inquired, already knowing the answer.

For three days the pup hardly ate but soon succumbed to my charms. As the days passed, I taunted Gina, 'If you don't come and take the dog back he'll be mine.' She said nothing and smiled.

Potty trained and performing tricks, he became my constant companion and we frolicked together or played ball, taking long, leisurely walks in the park. Could life get any better? Listening to the news one night while playing with Buttons, I was stunned to hear, 'The Government is offering an amnesty to anyone who arrived in Australia before 1980 to apply for permanent residency.' It involved visits to the doctor for health tests, police checks and answering many personal questions. When my residency certificate arrived, the entrepreneur told me, 'You can stay as long as you want.'

I'd been working constantly for eighteen months when, without warning, my life was thrown upside down. The impresario became seriously ill and Becky was at his side to look after him. A young manager was appointed to run the show, but he lacked managerial experience and tended to flirt with the young girls.

He came to me stating, 'You are finishing at the end of the week,' without any explanation. Astounded, I was in a quandary. I should have known this could happen. Show business can be so fickle at times.

Hearing of my dilemma, other artists I knew told me I could join a show going to Japan. I didn't want to go back there or leave Australia, and Buttons was anxious, sensing my despair. Recalling the endless years of travel and cheap hotel rooms, I was content to call Australia home. I was no spring chicken, and having residency I could apply to social services while searching for normal work.

Decision made, I swept the bundle of joy into my arms. Looking into his big, brown eyes, I held him close and whispered, 'Don't worry my darling, I'm going to look after you for the rest of your life.'

Yes, it was time to hang up my shoes.

The Aftermath

After my dancing career

Working full time as a public servant, it became difficult to perform in charity shows. My final performance as a Spanish dancer and clown, though, occurred in the gardens at the 1981 Melbourne Moomba Festival. While celebrating my 60th birthday, I took a flying leap into a jump split and couldn't walk for three days.

After studying at RMIT I became a secretary until I retired and my beloved companion Buttons passed away at the ripe old age of sixteen.

I met my Aussie husband in Melbourne and have been married for many years, living contentedly with our loveable pooch, Tazzie the devil.

Joan Luxton

When I'd retired from dancing and returned to England for a short holiday, I'd hoped to say hello to Joanie. Although she never wrote to me or I to her, it never mattered if I returned from a short or very long contract – she would always welcome me with open arms, and was eager to hear about my adventures.

Without her help, I could never have attended auditions, as Kettering was a long way from London. She also became a very good friend.

So I was horrified to arrive and, from a short distance walking along Kensington Park Road, notice swirling stains of smoke were visible in the outside walls downstairs. Instantly I realised what had happened – the flat had burnt down (though fortunately the house was still OK).

Crumpling into a sobbing heap on the suitcase, time stood still as precious memories flooded through me. Heartbroken and wanting to know the truth for sure, I rang the doorbell. A middle-aged Arab opened the door.

'Hello, I'm inquiring about a Joan Luxton.'

'She's dead. Died in the fire. Everything was burnt.'

'Do you know where she's buried?'

'We know nothing. This is our house now.' He slammed the door closed.

At the local coffee bar they were compassionate, realising I was someone who'd known Joanie. They told me everything had gone up in flames, thousands of costumes and all of her belongings. The cats died in the fire, too. Alone at night, Joanie would have nodded off to sleep and left a candle alight on the table by the curtains, which would have caught fire, destroying all signs of life. Smoke inhalation would have rendered her unconscious. It was comforting to know that she didn't suffer.

No family existed, and Joanie's remains were buried in a pauper's grave. I went to the graveyard and placed a bunch of flowers where I thought she'd be, said a prayer and left with a heavy heart. Today, the ground floor is a two bedroom ultra-modernised unit worth three million pounds.

Peggy Hale

Peggy Hale ran her school for 31 years and was well respected in the town. She trained several local teachers, but it's a great pity she never produced a professional dancer.

Aunty Bett

Aunty Bett, the mother of Denise Pitt-Draffen, opened her first school in 1947 and later bought Lilac House to start the academy. She was the backbone of the business, inspiring and giving advice to pupils, and delighting in their successes.

Denise Pitt-Draffen

Denise Pitt-Draffen was a Tiller girl at the Coliseum Theatre in London, and later became an adjudicator for the prestigious All England Dancing Competitions. A co-founder of The Northampton Festival of Dance, she was active in the dancing world until she passed away, aged 92 in 2015.

Jo Cook

Jo Cook's life is fascinating. She trained at the Pitt-Draffen Academy and worked at the Pigalle Club in London. Her group The Gojos appeared for three years on the popular television show *Top of the Pops* in the late sixties. Later she choreographed several teams to tour English theatres and a concert in New York.

George Carden

George Carden left for England and became the principal dancer at the Windmill Theatre during World War Two. Later he was contacted by Val Parnell to produce shows at the London Palladium, where he reigned as king for thirteen years. He retired to Australia and continued to produce a few shows until he died of cancer in 1981.

Miss Doriss

Miss Doriss passed away in 2014, but her legacy at the Moulin Rouge remains today.

Leon Grieg

In his youth, Leon Grieg performed with the Royal Festival Ballet in London and overseas. After Lunel in France he went to Italy, where he was the resident choreographer at the Pipers nightclub on the outskirts of Rome. In 1981 The Leon Grieg Dancers toured the Far East and he lived on the isle of Elba, where Napoleon was imprisoned. Close by at Palermo in Southern Italy, the Mafia was active. Leon was tragically murdered by them in 1991/2. His costume maker was in Rome and his house keeper was ill.

After the murder, a screaming woman came from the village and burnt most of his dancing albums and books. His scattered remains were taken to the morgue and kept there for ten years, as there was no known next of kin to contact. I was devastated when I found out. He was a great choreographer and friend, who happened to be in the wrong place at the wrong time.

Robert Kapikian and Gail

As I pursued my career in Hong Kong, Ballet Mondial (which Robert Kapikian had taken over from Leon) became resident at a nightclub in Southern Spain. Years later the ballet folded and Robert and Gail remained in the country. Robert bought a high class restaurant which failed, and Gail became a successful estate agent, renting out apartments in the area to residents and tourists. Robert died of a sudden heart attack in 2004 and Gail passed away of cancer in 2013.

Becky

Becky left Melbourne to return to her home town Adelaide. We continued to see each other once a year until her demise from cancer in 2014.

Cherry

While writing this story, I was able to find Cherry and visit her in Guernsey. She left Ballet Mondial in 1977 and joined a magician act touring Spain, but she became ill and returned home. Studying accountancy, she became a bookkeeper and is now retired and happily married.

Acknowledgments

Writing a book is similar to running a marathon race. At the beginning is excitement and tension as you write the first words. There are hiccups and stumbling blocks and the end seems impossible. These were overcome through the help and support from family, friends and others.

Posthumously, I thank Joan Luxton for giving me the opportunity to stay in London for auditions and Leon Grieg for passing on his sewing skills and caring for me when I was ill.

Thanks to Blaise van Hecke, Kev Howlett and Les Zigomanis for their encouragement and Busybird editor Meg Hellyer who smoothed out the rough edges to make the book presentable.

Special thanks to Lynne Siejka from Watsonia Library who facilitated many workshops with the Odyssey Writers Group. She also gave me the opportunity to attend the 'Reflections' memoir writing course, run by Lindell Caffrey from Writers Victoria, to hone my writing skills.

Most of all I'd like to acknowledge the patience and support of my husband – who on several occasions during long writing sessions would yell, 'Where's my tea?'